The End of the Corporations

The End of the Corporations

An explanation from left to capitalist world economic crisis

The End of the Corporations

The End of the Corporations

"To those who for centuries haave been fighting, are fighting and will fight against oppression and exploitation.
To Mariana, my love, my mate"

The End of the Corporations

The End of the Corporations

An explanation from left to capitalist world economic crisis

Contents

Introduction 7
CHAPTER I - Bailouts ....,,,, ... 11
CHAPTER II 37
CHAPTER III -1929 & 2007 73
CHAPTER IV - Globalisation 116
CHAPTER V - Forms 152
CHAPTER VI - Accumulation 194

Translation: Elizabeth Jezierski

National Directorate of Copyright (Argentina) - Made the deposit on28/3/2011- File number 915814

The End of the Corporations

Introduction

> *"The chances of accumulation of the system have peak. We can be sure that in 30 years we no longer will live under the capitalist world system. But what system will we live in then? It could be much better or much worse. All possibilities are open"*

Immanuel Wallerstein 31/1/09

The economic crisis affecting the world economy since 2007 is the most important in the history of capitalism. Its most spectacular expression are the bailouts, a massive injection of funds in excess of U$S 30 trillion, and which continues to grow. This operation was carried out by the capitalist governments in order to save multinational corporations from bankruptcy, is of a colossal scale: a proportion that would rebuild Haiti 40 times, banish world hunger, stop the destruction of the environment or housing grant all inhabitants of the planet.

This occurs because the heart attack is in the core of the world capitalist system, the multinational corporations, large companies and banks in the U.S, Europe and Japan. For decades, the heart of the world capitalist system have been the modern and large multinational corporations & banks and investment funds, whose interests are more and more deeply and intimately intertwined. After the collapse, they were revived by the massive intervention of the G7 states and the underdeveloped countries.

This crisis is the product of a long process of capitalist decadence, which began in the early twentieth century- after World War Two established U.S. supremacy in the global economy and in the emergence and development of multinationals. From then to today, the capitalist world economy went through two phases or accumulation schemes of unequal and combined development, in order to counteract its decline and its historical crisis. The first began in the '40s, followed in the '50s, '60s and sold in the '70s, which was known as the Keynesian model or "welfare state".

The second scheme, the so-called globalization, neoliberalism or "New Economics", began in the '80s & '90s, and it started to exhaust itself in the first decade of the 21st century. Both regimes of accumulation contributed to the sharpening, in different ways, of the historical contradictions of capitalism and had exhausted themselves. The current crisis that started in 2007, shows the depletion of the globalization regime and multinational corporations which, had it not been for the massive intervention of central banks and the backing of the G7 states, would have disappeared.

Multinational corporations are the highest expression of the valorization of capital and private property, and concentrate high percentages of GDP and world trade. Its massive bankruptcy revealed what appears to be hidden, which is an obstacle to the development of productive forces, a parasitic outgrowth that is highly destructive, whose defense of earnings and profits are a serious danger to man, nature and draws humanity to barbarism.

Multinationals continue to exist, despite having collapsed, because they emerged with the support of the most formidable imperialist state in the history of mankind, the U.S. The G7 countries will support them with massive funding, with its overwhelming technological dominance and the military might of their armies. They will disappear if the states that support them disappear. And while never before this crisis has the vulnerability of the transnational character as an economical entity been shown, it is a reflection of the increasingly vulnerable political situation in which governments and states are supporting them, mainly the U.S.

The current crisis shows that multinationals are not viable and need to be expropriated and nationalized, which would allow a massive development of the productive forces. The objective situation of the capitalist system required these measures in a manner such that at the peak of the crisis, General Motors, the emblem of the domain of multinational corporations and U.S. hegemony, had to be rescued with state funds so it could continue to exist.

But to expropriate multinationals is a measure that should be part of a program that can only be carried out by governments with a class interest that is diametrically opposed to the current capitalist governments in the G7 and the under- developed countries. These governments are acting in defense of the interests of big businesses and directors of multinationals. Never before has the economy and politics been so closely intertwined. This is precisely why the explanation for the crisis cannot be reduced merely to the economic sphere.

Let us leave such explanations to journalists, economists and vulgar Marxism, which attempt to explain such development and economic crises separately and in isolation from the class struggle and political processes, as if economic processes were developed in a laboratory, or as if they could be a cold process, insulated from political and social phenomena.

In this book we will go deep inside and analyze the longest decadency that capitalism has seen, without which it is impossible to understand the current crisis. Neither can it be understood without linking it with the revolutionary processes that have occurred since the last century that have challenged capitalism and moved the world. Marx's concept of political economy is precisely that of the economy deeply intertwined with political events and the class struggle.

If in the birth of Marxism, political, social and cultural events begin to be explained by the economy, in the decline of capitalism, this relationship is reversed, and the policy goes on to explain the economy.

Nahuel Moreno put it like this with the Investment Law of Causality: *"... In relation to the major historical periods and normal development of societies, Marxism has argued that the red thread that explains all phenomena are economic processes But in an age of revolutionary crisis, this general law has a particular refractive effect that reversed causal relationships, transforming the most subjective factor, the revolutionary leadership, as the root of all other phenomena, including economic ... In short, the two determinants of all contemporary phenomena, the first and ultimate causes, which determine with their different combinations all phenomena, are the rise of the revolutionary struggles of the working class and people on one side, and the crisis of revolutionary leadership on the other"* **(1)**

Indeed, this helps in understanding the current crisis in the period of the economic decline of capitalism. This period spanned different phases, stages, times and even rebirths such as the post-war "boom". By overcome the two world wars, senile capitalism acquired the character which we know.

In turn, we need to analyze the concatenation and intimate link of each of these moments or phases with the respective political events. The fall of the Berlin Wall and the current crisis of capitalism, when a heart attack is produced in the heart of the world capitalist system, are the most important events of this new world stage. Furthermore, they are a foundation to the advent of social and political events that are most important in history.

(1) Nahuel Moreno. Actualización al Programa de Transición (1980)

The End of Corporations

An explanation from left to capitalist world economic crisis

CHAPTER I
Bailouts

The End of the Corporations

The End of the Corporations

CHAPTER I: Bailouts

"Just a minute ago, carried away by his rationalistic chimera and his intoxication by prosperity, the citizen proclaimed money as void illusion .There was no more money but goods. The yell that now echoes from one end of the world to the other is, "there are no more goods but money!" And just as the doe craves for fresh water, his soul roars for money, the only wealth."

Karl Marx. Capital, Volume I

The crisis broke out on 9th of August, (1) when the French bank BNP Paribas announced that their fund had run out of money. This announcement was preceded by serious events such as when the Mortgage New Century was withdrawn from the Exchange because of lack of solvency and an alleged accounting offense, bankruptcy of the Bear Steams hedge funds, of the German IKB and of National City Home Equity.

On that day the generalised bankruptcy soared throughout the entire capitalist system and triggered a chain progress of bankruptcies of multinationals and investment banks. Even if many warned against existing misbalance in economy, no economist, no ruler or civil servant wrote about it nor foresaw the course or the magnitude of the crisis that went rampant as from that moment.

The crisis was the outcome of the fall of the irrecoverable sub-prime loans that began beating banks and investment funds mercilessly and then it spread on to all the papers, debts and assets and derivatives of the world. The entire world financial system collapsed at different pace and varying unevenness.

This compelled central banks and the Federal Reserve (Fed) and the European Central Bank (ECB), the bank of Japan and the Bank of England, which, as if they were following Walter Baguehot's advise, (2) began with bailouts. Since the beginning of the crisis, the intervention of the Central Banks became chronic and the bailouts a permanent maneuver. Immediately, interbank credit, one of the most important capitalist institutions, went bankrupt.

American President asserted, *"the foundation of American economy are still solid"* but the bank did not pay attention to him and did not lend any more money to each other did so reluctantly, at very high rates of interest due to mutual distrust. Bank of England saved Northern Rock, whose clients withdrew 3 billion euros in one weekend, the Swiss bank UBS announced loss for $ 3.4 billion, Merrill Lynch for $ 7.9 The British bank, Barclays lost assets for 1.9 billion euros and the Citygroup for $3.1 billion.

The Swiss insurer, Swiss RE, announce loss for 733 million euros. The British bank, Royal Bank of Scotland (RBS) quoted bad debts for 1.7 billion euros. In Spain their own estate bubble collapsed. The banks of Island and Ireland sank. The second investment bank in the USA, Morgan Stanley, reported losses for $ 9 billion and the sale of 10% of its hare to Chinese government. The rate of interest, expression of the rate of profit, collapsed at the beginning of the crisis and still remains at almost zero.

The bankruptcy of interbank credit, of credit in general and of the collapse of the rates of interest affected the process of circulation of capitals, as vital for capitalism to function as blood circulation is for human organism. By means of bailouts, central banks tried to reanimate the process of circulation of capitals, but the damage was immense and required enormous operations to stop them from growing.

Year 2007 closed with serious unrest of the process of amplified reproduction and circulation of capitals, and this cleared the path for the infarcts that took place in the capitalist system in 2008. This was the year when the heart of capitalism collapsed, because between March and September, banks of investment began to collapse. Bank of Investment Bear Stearns, which has survived the Wall Street crack of 1929, collapsed in March. I was the "most admired" in the rankings of Fortune; it was in debt for billions and a leverage ratio of 35.5 to 1. Several managers had to face criminal charges and the Fed granted a loan to JP Morgan to buy Bear.

The End of the Corporations

The crisis of sub- prime papers kept on accruing. The Association of American Mortgage Banks revealed that the number of unpaid was 6 million contracts for $ 6 billion. The prices of living quarters dropped 8.9%, the greatest fall in the last 20 years. Mortgage Bankers Association spoke of a social gravity unprecedented in the history of USA; evictions of families who lost their homes broke all records in history.

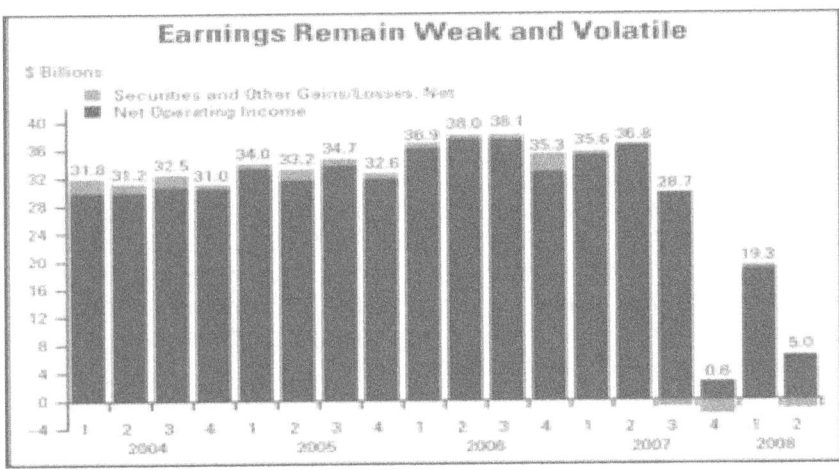

The estimate of profits and losses of the banking system prepared by FDIC by mid 2008 -The nosedive in the 4th quarter of 2007 marks the beginning of the world crisis. Source FDIC

After the bankruptcy of Bear, the greatest bailout in history of the USA carried out with State funds, when the gigantic mortgage conglomeration – Fannie Mae and Freddie Mac were bailed out. Fannie May is the popular name of the National Federal Mortgage Association., created in 1938 when Roosevelt was in the office. Freddie Mac is the Federal Corporation of Residential Mortgage Loans created in 1970. Between both of them, they handled a volume of $ 5 billion, equivalent to the Gross Domestic Product of Latin America with over 50% of the mortgages in the country.

The bankruptcy of the two giants of mortgage credit threatened Sovereign Bank Pimco, the greatest operator of fixed income funds in the world. The State of China, numerous Central Banks and Sovereign Funds of Investments linked to the mortgage colossuses because they have receivables in papers of the USA foreign constituted by Treasury Bonds and Fannie and Freddie. Yu Yongding, Counselor of the People's Bank of China – Chinese central bank – warned. "If the government allows for the Fannie and Freddie to go bankrupt and international investors are not adequately compensated, the consequence would be catastrophic" (The Privateer, 8/08). **(3)**

Bush invested thousands million dollars in the purchase of Fannie and Freddie shares defending the interests of entrepreneurs from USA and the world. The multimillionaire bailout plan was drafted by the president of Federal Reserve, Ben Bernanke, in charge of the Federal Housing Finance Agency (FHFA), James Lockhart, deputy directors of both mortgage institutions and the Treasury Secretary, Henry Paulson. The peace gained by the intervention in Freddy Mac and Fannie Mae lasted one week.

On 15th September an economic earthquake took place: The Lehman Brothers investment bank went bankrupt. This institution had survived the Civil War and the Great Depression but now it was riddled with debts and had lost 73% of its value. Its fall was so great that many regard this date as the beginning of the crisis. That fall of Lehman was a severe blow to world trade, because they emitted hundreds of thousands of millions of short term debts, a fundamental pinion in trade at short term loans are: 30 – 60 and 90 days.

Lehman papers acted as lubricant and fuel of trade, but without Lehman they nosedived. World trade stopped dead and is still finding it difficult to recover. According to information by World Trade Organization (WTO) in their report for 2008: *"the months that followed last September have seen world production and trade come tumbling down: first in the developed economies and then in the developing countries."* By the end of 2008, world trade shrank by 40%.

After the Lehman collapse, there came the collapse of American International Group (AIG), the greatest insurance in the world, following the collapse of their CDS (credit default market) market derived from credit risk, AIG offered counselling in sophisticated techniques for tax evasion, because the conglomerate is closely related to offshore financial centres or "fiscal paradise" **(4)** The USA took over almost 80% of the AIG shares and Nouriel Roubini commented ironically, *"...The USA is now world's greatest insurance company... socialism for the rich... Wall Street, the place where profits are privatized and losses are socialised".*

After the AIG bankruptcy, Washington Mutual followed suit. Until 2008 Continental Illinois National Bank and Trust in 1984 has been the greatest collapse of a bank in American history. But it faded compared to what the greatest American savings bank, Washington Mutual, known as WaMu, did. If Lehman made an impact on commerce, Fannie and Freddie on credits and AIG on insurance, Washington Mutual did the same for commercial banks and sold deposits and branches to JP Morgan Chase, operation that unleashed all kinds of suspicions because that was the second time in six months that JP Morgan Chase took over deposits and assets of a financial institution, which made it the largest American bank in USA as far as deposits go.

The first global bailout by Bush and the G7

So far, the policy of the powers and their Central Banks was to rush to aid the multinationals and corporations as far as they required financial aid and were on the verge of bankruptcy or directly were bankrupts. This policy of "random bailouts", putting fires out that were occurring in Europe, the USA and Japan and insofar as they were occurring soon proved insufficient. Operations of much larger wingspan were needed in order to cope with a crisis of such magnitude.

Between September and October 2008, the first process of coordinated and global bailout took place. This policy put an end to the stage of "random" bailouts and began this new stage in accordance with the Economic Emergency Stabilization Act 110 – 343 of 3/10/08, boosted by Bush for an approximate amount of $ 700 billion. This first bailout was prepared by Treasury Secretary Henry Paulson, who used to be a member of the Board of Directors of Goldman Sachs, together with the President of the Fed, Ben Bernanke and agreed on with 9 of the largest American Banks. (5)

The bailout included the Troubled Asset Relief Programme (TARP) the aim of which was to buy papers in trouble so as to strengthen Banks and recover credit and revive the flow of capitals. Financial Stability Office was created to supervise the bailing out. Paulson appointed another man from Goldman Sachs, Neel Kashkari as interim head of this new Office. With Paulson and Kashkari among the top decision makers, investment banks took over the entire bailout operation.

Europe, Japan, China and the BRICS followed the footsteps of the USA, the FED and Wall Street determined the orientation adopted by all the countries. The EU and ECB had to put out the fires that threatened all of the most important European Investment Banks and multinationals. The first EU Summit held in September 2008, launched a bailout of nearly $ 400 billion to help in several Eastern European countries, such as Poland, Hungary, Ukraine, Latvia and Lithuania.

These were risky measures but even greater perils were those that caused them: if any of those countries declared bankruptcy they would cause the collapse of creditor banks, such as UBS of Switzerland, the Austrian bank Raiffeisen, the Commerzbank, the Deutsche Bank of Germany of the BNP of France. There was also the case of those countries that sought to turn into financial paradise and suffered the shock of capital flight like Ireland. Or Iceland, who's Exchange sank 76% after remaining closed for several days.

The shock of the crisis in China compelled Prime Minister Wen Jiabao to boost a bailout that reached the figure of $ 500 billion mainly to develop public work and credits to reactivate economy. The blow suffered by China due to the slump in their exports was reflected in the closure of factories in the south of the country and the destruction of thousands of jobs. The growth shrank from 11.4% in 2007 to 9% in 2008. As we shall see further on, among other things, Chinese bailout turned into a powerful estate bubble.

The crisis allowed us to corroborate the central role that the USA still maintain as world protector of capitalism. The dollar and the Treasury Bonds became the main haven against the world crumbling down. In spite of the fact that the crisis broke out in the heart of American economy, paradoxically, investors' and countries' reaction was to shelter their assets and reserves in dollars. The dollar became stronger because it was being in high demand with the banks of the whole world after a series of paralyses suffered due to interbank loans.

The BIS, the Central Bank of Central Banks estimated that dollar had become 55% of the assets and liabilities, plus 70% of the reserves, 80% of the transactions, 70% imports and all but the total of oil trade in the world. At the same time Russia, Brazil, India, South Korea and Taiwan became the leaders of the world accumulation of reserves in dollars and so this currency became, according to the definition by BIS "the favourite currency of the Central banks".

At the sharpest and most dramatic peak of the crisis, nothing refuted better those groups of intellectuals and analysts that had begun to pose the thesis about "the loss of hegemony by the USA". The most exclusionary piece of information is that in the middle of the sharpest crisis in the history of capitalism and of economy of the USA, the only thing that thrived was the dollar. All the countries of the G7 and most of the underdeveloped countries rushed to seek shelter and protect their reserves in dollars and assets of American Treasury. The demand for dollars in full crisis is the clearest signal that the great companies, counties and capitalist power regard the USA with its seven fleets, military dominion and arms power as the acme of guarantors in case of any jeopardy that may challenge it.

The G20, an organism that existed since 1990 and had now turned to be, together with G7, an important instrument in the activity of capitalist governments met in Washington on 14 and 15 November. At the Washington G20, the USA imposed the world guideline of bailouts, to give money to the multinationals and investment banks, adding words of commitment in the final document, such as *"establish norms of financial regulation"*, i.e.: determine controls for unleashed speculation, an issue that never happened.

The G20 consolidated the dominion of the USA. They consolidated the bailouts as a policy for saving multinationals and corporation whatever the cost. The Washington G20 included the incorporation minor Capitalist countries such as China, Brazil, India, Russia, Australia or South Africa to decision taking posts. This is a distorted expression of the blow suffered by imperialist countries and the historic degree of the magnitude of the crisis of capitalism that compelled the governments of the G7to appeal to the support from underdeveloped countries to be able to carry out their plans.

The Obama administration and the second global bailout in 2009

Obama continued Bush's economic policy, an orientation that became clear when he appointed Timothy Geithner as Secretary of Treasury number 75 replacing Paulson. Geithner, coming from Kissinger Associates, Henry Kissinger's and Brent Scowcroft's consulting firm **(6)**. At the time of his nomination he was the President of the New York Fed, position to which he was appointed by Bush. Once in his office Geithner actively imposed bailouts on the corporations, which deserved accusations of embezzlement benefiting investment banks.

Obama appointed Lawrence Summers, an economist, Chief of the World Bank and Clinton's Treasury Secretary, who used to be Reagan's adviser. Together with this, he appointed a Board of Advisors where the cream of financial oligarchy had seats. To the presidency of the board, he summoned Paul Volcker, American economist, who used to be director of the Fed during Carter's and Reagan's presidency and part of the Rockefeller Group.

Other appointments of his to the Board are Robert Rubin, connected to Citigroup, William Daley de JP Morgan Chase, Roger Ferguson of TIAA-CREF, Anne Mulcahy of Xerox, Richard Parsons of Time Warner and Eric Schmidt of Google among others. Obama decided to replace the director of the bailout monitoring office appointed by the Bush administration Neel Kashkari by Herbert Allison, a man from the multinational corporations Fannie Mae and TIAA-CREF.

The End of the Corporations

Bush's bailout had prevented multinational corporations from going bankrupt, but the crisis continued getting worse and worse and – slowly but surely - began affecting the entire world economic and political system in its different dimensions and dragging new parts of the capitalist system into the crisis. The generalized collapse, the increasing loss of value of assets, the mistrust in the indicators and measuring instruments, in qualifying agencies, in governments, suspicion, disappointment and confusion reigned in many sectors.

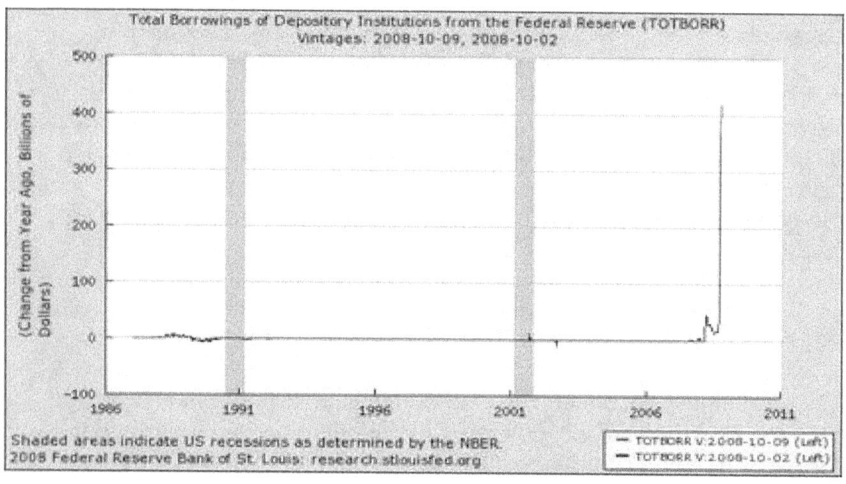

Evolution of loans to financial institutions from the American FED (08/01/1986 – 09/10/2008) – Note the leap in the development of the above since 2007 Source: Federal Reserve Bank of St. Louis.

The fall of all the indicators, the dwindling of American retail sales and the prospect of breakages of great companies forced Obama to launch a new bailout of almost $ 800 billion by means of the Recovery Act of USA and the Act of Reinvestment. In March Geithner presented a "programme of public-private investment" to buy "toxic" and uncollectible assets and loans, which caused euphoria in the Stock.

After the law was enacted, the USA went out to buy the shares of GM that formalized its bankruptcy petition filing in June 2009. Fearing the fall of car industry centred in Detroit, Obama bailed out GM that for the last 77 years had been the world Number 1 in car industry and an emblem of capitalism. The USA was no 60% of the company While Canada and the province of Ontario kept 12% of the shares. The bailout meant a vicious attack on workers, reduction of their dealer network, and closure of factories, with suppression of thousands of jobs. European governments also rushed out to bail their car factories out.

Credit rating agencies: Standard &Poor's, Moody's and Fitch began to have a major role because it was up to them to decide which debts and Paper were worth and what they were worth. In days of great debts, like the one that started with the bailouts, this is of vital import for the future of capitalist enterprises and states. In April, a new G20 summit was held in London and decided to grant another half a billion to IMF to reinforce its role as international money lender.

Due to the shrinking of world trade produced by the Lehman Brothers crack, G-20 decided to inject $ 250 billion meant to reactivate global trade and $100 billion for international development banks in order to recompose it. The London G20 reached no agreement about the reform of financial system and fiscal paradise. During the third and fourth quarters of 2009, the enormous bailing out caused a slight a slight upturn of global economy, but the global misbalance continued. In November, the official company of Dubai Emirate, Dubai World, broke down. Dubai is one of the seven emirates that, since 1971 is part of the United Arab Emirates. The failure was due to a speculative bubble that was bailed out by the Abu Dhabi bank.

The world movement of circulation of capitals continued on its downward trend, If by 2007, the flow was estimated at $1.2 trillion, in 2008, it was reduced $ 707 billion. In its June 2009 report, "The World economic crisis affects seriously capital flows to the developing countries", the World Bank projection envisage international flows of capital in descent until they reach $ 363 billion in 2009 and this, once more placed the perils threatening capitalism on the agenda. In order to avoid the brutal descent in the flow of capitals, with nonetheless continued, the most probable prognosis was another bailout, global and coordinated between the different governments and capitalist powers and central banks.

2010 the third global bailout

Bailouts carried out between October 2008 and April 2009 were dubbed QE (Quantitative Easing) in economists' jargon, i.e.: currency emission with no gold backing. This fabulous injection of money weakly reactivated world economy and many economists spoke of recovery seeking support in the tendency that was reflected in the drawing of the famous V which meant that the rates were climbing once more after a spectacular nosedive of the years 2007– 2008.

But together with the weak rates of growth that developed throughout 2009 and 10, other rates surfaced indicating that the crisis was getting worse. On the one hand, an unemployment and inflation wave broke out in the underdeveloped countries and so did the prices of food; this increased the food crisis in the entire world. The crisis went climbing down from Investment Banks, multinationals and Central Banks to real estate companies, regions, cities and municipalities.

Inside the USA, the crisis of states and municipalities, American municipal bonds, known as "Munis" that serve the purpose of financing municipal infrastructure of transport, health, education and sanitation began to collapse due to the increasing incapacity of the municipalities and states to pay their debts, which in turn affected the financial entities that held the "Munis" in their coffers. All this deterioration of the conditions happened on the base of QE1 was reaching its end and neither American economy nor that of the world had been reactivated. Neither had consumption been reactivated, nor the production or trade.

The weak recovery caused by QE1 ended with the bailout itself. Faced with this critical situation, the summit of ministers of finances and governors of central banks of the G20 at the Busan (South Korea) May gathering and so did the Toronto June G20 summit. The failure of these summits was not only all about the magnitude of the crisis, but also with the development of the crisis in Europe, something that posed a historic unsolved problem of European capitalism.

Unlike the USA that is only one state that prevails over world economy and may emit money in their Central Banks to implement bailouts, Europe is not a sole country but the sum total of countries with very uneven economies. In the EU powers such as Germany and France coexist with decaying powers such as Germany and France, decadent powers such as Italy, Portugal or Spain or underdeveloped countries such as those of Eastern Europe. Even if there is a Central Bank – the ECB – there were no clauses in the treaty of the Union that would permit the different countries to bail out other countries. **(7)**

The magnitude of the crisis forced dominating imperialist countries (Germany and France) to have to cope with historic contradictions and unsolved problems of European capitalism and to establish measures that would permit overcoming them even if precariously. The crisis of the so-called PIGS (Portugal, Italy, Greece and Spain) caused the implementation of the bailouts in order to avoid the collapse of the common currency, the euro.

In May, after a long round of negotiations, wrangling and ups and downs, a bailout of 1.1 billion euros was implemented to help Greece and an agreement was reached to create a European Stability Fund was created through a combination of contributions of different governments and the IMF, consisting of a fund of up total of $ 7.5 billion.

The creation of the Stability Fund was a political change for European institutional structure for it means the construction of a supranational entity that began to make decisions what involved over 500 million inhabitants of the EU; it is an antidemocratic leap in detriment of the interest of the population and in favour of the interests of the bankers. In the days following the announcement of the creation of the Fund, the stocks soared and the euro reached the peak of its profits in 18 months.

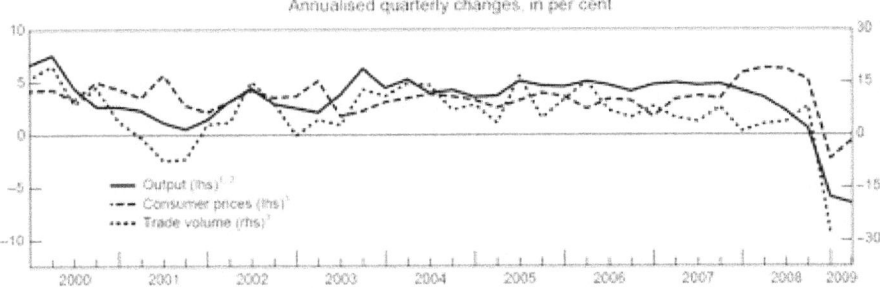

World evolution of production, commerce and consumer prices (2000- 2009) Note the deep fall since the late 2007. Source BIS

The ECB also changed their policy regarding its policy of credit rating and announced that they accept any current debt as collateral, regardless the credit rating. But even so, the rubs between the European countries, Great Britain and the USA reflected not only the unevenness in the development of the crisis but also the beginning of the global political crisis with the G7 governments. A growing pressure of dissatisfaction among the masses and questioning of bailouts of the multinationals and corporation started acting as an increasing factor of pressure.

Dissatisfaction was expressed in demonstrations, and protests of every kind against adjustment plans and cuts in the budgets. These first sign of resistance showed the dissatisfaction of the peoples and were the prelude to a great wave of mobilisations and protests of every kind, in the USA and Europe. From Paris to Berlin, From Lisbon to Dublin, from the USA to Bucharest, From London to Rome: popular and proletarian struggles against the adjustment and budget cuts that affected the old-age pensioners, state employees, students and the unemployed. These first signs of resistance showed the discontent of the peoples and were a prelude o the great wave of protests that spread into the world.

In spite of occasional and conjectural rubs, capitalist governments launched packets of adjustment that affected the budgets for health, education, retirement, public works – with the common agreement that it was the workers and the peoples of the world who had to pay the crisis. After the bailouts, as from May 2010, Portugal, Italy, Greece and Spain announced severe cuts in the public expenditure and increase higher taxes. Even Great Britain, France and Germany carried out their own adjustments.

Poverty and unemployment accrued and so did the deterioration of living standards for millions and aroused indignation against the bailouts for corporations. It was this tidal wave of disapproval for the policies carried out by the governments of the G7 what triggered of the political crisis that began to develop in the USA and caused the first symptoms of erosion, displeasure and disappointment of the population against Obama administration.

This caused the resignation of such members of the administration as Herbert Allison, Larry Summers, Christina Romer and Peter Orzsag. Allison was replaced by Tim Massad, a man from the Cravath firm, Swaine & LLP of New York. The same erosions and political crisis took place in the EU and caused a round of falls of governments of the UK, Ireland, Holland, twice in Denmark, Portugal, Hungary, Czech Republic, in Slovakia twice, also in Belgium, Spain, Greece and Italy from the beginning of the crisis up to now. In Rumania, that received bailouts for 25 million of euros, the prime minister fell in the early 2012.

In November 2010, when all the indicators showed that world economy was once more approaching a collapse, a new round of bailouts, or QE, began. The Obama administration injected $ 1 trillion into economy, the Fed acted massively self-buying Bonds of American Treasury (T-Bond). With this manoeuvre , the FED aggravated the character of their balance sheet that the days of Q1 was loaded with toxic assets bought from banks of investment and now incorporated the self-purchase of the T Bonds with self-emitted money, i.e.: added heaps of fictitious money to the already existing heaps of fictitious capital.

The Bank of England acquired almost $1.5 billion in bonds, Eurozone began a round of bailouts in Ireland, having suffered the bankruptcy of top six banks to finance an estate bubble with losses of $1 billion euros, received a bailout from IMF, GB. Denmark and Sweden 6.5 billion euros, Portugal, in grave situation, also received a bailout of 7 billion euros. In December, European council agreed to modify article 136 of the Treaty on the functioning of the EU, signed in Maastricht 1992 to allow bailouts for countries whose currency is the euro.

The 2011 fourth global bailout

By the early 2011 the round of QE1 and QE2 carried out by the USA, EU, Japan and China was getting near the chilling sum of nearly $ 6 trillion which even then represented one of the most enormous operatives of injecting great masses of fictitious capital in the history of capitalism. After these 2010 rounds of bailouts, analysts and journalist once again started commenting that the crisis of world economy was about to be overcome.

And yet, the truth is that the round of QE2 not only failed to solve the problems of capitalism but also aggravated all its contradictions. QE1 had cropped up in November 2008 and ended in March 2010 while QEII started in November 2010 ended in June 2911, after which between August and September 2011, world economy moved on to another peak of crisis. This peak was more complex because it was the outcome of the combination of 1) the crisis in the USA, 2) the crisis in Europe and 3) the earthquake and the breakage in Japan and 4) the escalation of world inflation in underdeveloped countries.

This peak of crisis made a new impact of China and the BRICS so that the crisis was transferred to all the parts of the world and affected all economies. By the end of the year, this combination of problems aggravated the credit crisis in the EU and made another coordinated and global bailout indispensable. Let us have a look at the complexity of the issues that occurred in 2011.

1) The crisis in the USA: The economy of the USA suffered an economic slowdown after growing at modest rates, demand for great machinery, known as capital goods, dropped 2.6% in April; wages continued anaemic. Unemployment high and recessive tendencies became sharper because of the adjustment plans as those in Wisconsin and California that increased the recessionary bias in economy because they demolished consumption. Those adjustments are so severe that comparatively even the adjustments in Greece and Spain sound like a joke.

At the same time, and with a debt of $17 trillion (almost 100% of the USA GDP), USA reached the maximum of historically allowed by the Congress. This led to heated negotiations between Democrats and Republicans in a parliament where the majority opposed Obama about the raising the roof of fiscal deficit and so avoid the declaration of default. For the first time in history, rating agencies, Standard & Poor's and

Moody's noted down American public debt and of their three greatest banks Citigroup, Wells Fargo and Bank of America.

The occupation of the Parliament and important demonstrations against the governor's plans took place in Wisconsin. As the crisis went deeper, new phenomena began to develop. At Puerta del Sol in Madrid a movement surfaced similar to that of the movement of Tahrir Square in Egypt, the movement of the Outraged analogous to the Portuguese "Postponed Generation"

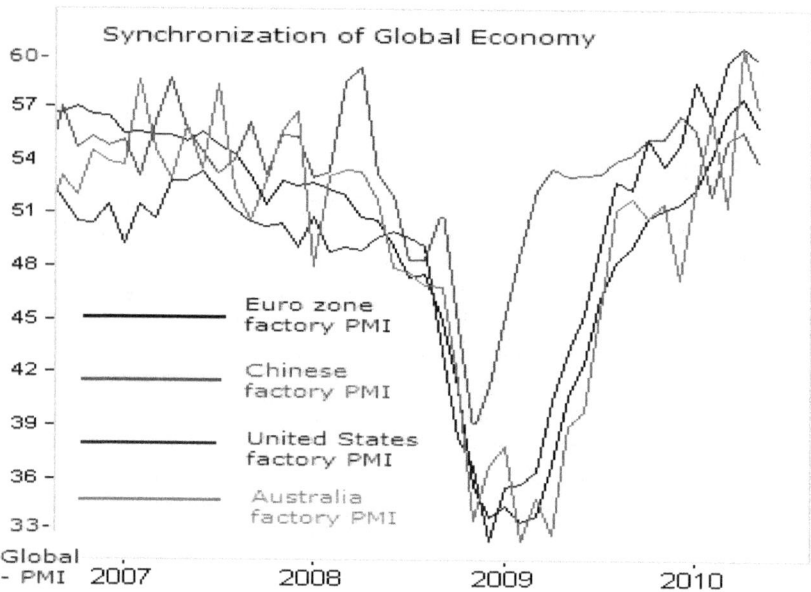

The growth of the world industrial production in 2009, after the bailouts - Note the V form. In 2010 the indicators dipped again (PMI Index) (in black: Eurozone/ in red, China/ in blue USA/ in green Australia. Source: Sir Charlot 05/3010

In the USA the Occupy the Wall Street cropped up, the same as many other movements, with many young people and other social sectors affected by the crisis participating actively. By 15th October, a new movement – with global scope – emerged against capitalism. Even though it was a small movement, it produced the 15-0 the first world demonstration against the adjustment measures of capitalist governments that affected almost all the capitals and major cities in the world; its common denominator was to point out to corporations as main culprits of the crisis.

It has been decades since the last global demonstrations against capitalism, more exactly since the crisis of the 30s, when they were summoned by the Socialist International.

2) The crisis in Europe: On 5th January 2011, European Union created the European Financial Stability Facility (FEES) to issue bonds and papers with the support of German Office of Debt Management with the aim of collecting funds to grant loans to countries of the Euro zone in problems

These bonds that have credit rating AAA by Fitch Moody's and Standard & Poor's were placed on capital markets at an emission of 5 billion euros. In July 2012, the European Council considered the replacement of the EFSB and EFSG programmes by a financing programme of permanent bailouts called European Stability Mechanism (ESM) a plan that implied the concessions of sovereignty of EU with respect to the USA.

The ESM is not only a process of colonisation of the UE by the USA but also the colonisation of weaker European countries by the axis Germany-France. The bailout policy was not only imposed in the EU but also, with the AFSM and EFSF a new mechanism and new institutions meant to aid capitalist states, multinationals, corporations, European banks of European became permanently institutionalised.

By late 2011, Mario Draghi was appointed to the presidency of European Central Bank to replace Jean-Claude Trichet. Between 1985 and 1990, Draghi, a man from Goldman Sachs was executive director of World Bank between 1985 and 1990, vice-president of Goldman Sachs and governor of the Bank of Italy in 2006. The investment bank Goldman Sachs had acted in the crisis of Greece advising president Kostas Karamalis as to the manner of concealing the real size of the Greek deficit, a fraud that was part of the unleashing of the financial crisis in Greece between 2010 and 2011.

On the 13 November, the President of the Republic, Giorgio Napolitano, entrusted Mario Monti the formation of a government after the resignation of Silvio Berlusconi, Monti, a man of the Trilateral Commission, a lobby founded in 1973 by David Rockefeller, was also a consultant of The Coca Cola Company and of Goldman Sachs. In Greece, Lucas Papademos, who used to be the chief economist of the Bank of Greece from 1985 until 1993 and vice-president of the ECB under the mandate of Jean-Claude Trichet, between 2002 and 3008 was appointed Prime Minister of Greece heading a transitory government of national coalition to apply a brutal adjustment against the people.

Combined with the deepening of the crisis in the EU, revolutionary processes broke out in the North Africa and Arab countries. It started in Tunisia and spread like wildfire through the entire region from Maghreb in Algeria, Morocco and Egypt and on to the Arabian Peninsula to Bahrain, Saudi Arabia and Yemen. The revolutionary process affected the entire Middle East regarded as the "back yard" of Europe, including Iran, Lebanon, Jordan, even if in a lesser degree for these.

This process dethroned 60-year-old dictatorships and had its epicentre in the revolution that dethroned the Hosni Mubarak dictatorship in Egypt when thousands of demonstrators gathered at the Tahrir Square. The fall of Mubarak boosted the "Arab Spring" that engulfed Libya where it finally culminated as a civil war that put the end to the Kahdafi dictatorship and developed a process of civil war in Syria against the Assad dictatorship.

3) The crisis in Japan: In 2911, Japan, the third economy in the world, was also brutally hit by an earthquake and a tsunami that left 12 157 fatal casualties, 15 496 missing and 161 refugees. Faced with such tragedy, investment funds and speculators bet on "reconstruction business" about 15 billons of yens, speculating with Japanese insuring companies would repatriate funds to pay indemnities and carry out public works and so the yen began to soar.

The cost of the reconstruction affected the immense public debt of Japan of more than 200% of the GDP, the greatest in the world and triggered the risk of suspension of payments by the State. Two great bailouts came after the tsunami, one of 5 billion yens and the other of 8.9 billion yens by the Bank of Japan to avoid the bankruptcy of insurance companies and of banks. The disaster of Japan affected the USA and China because Japan is the purchaser of 10% of the exports of both these countries.

4) The escalation of the inflation in the underdeveloped countries: The bailouts triggered off world inflation and the prices of food prices that were driven upwards by the high price of oil and commodities and this aggravated the world food catastrophe. This impulse towards the increase of prices expands famine and poverty in all the parts, regions and countries in the world, essentially in the poorest countries. This means that one of the features of the bailouts is that they are brutally inflationary.

Bailouts had inflationary effects because they provided enormous masses of capitals for banks and investment funds that initiated a round of rampant speculations. The purchase and re-purchase of companies and papers linked to food and commodities pushed the prices of food upwards while this did not reflect the reality of production and distorted the prices. The monstrous emissions of capital without gold backing represented by QE1 and QE2 were also inflationary because they increased the proportion of fictitious capital, over-accumulated capital and valueless papers. Let us see the effects of those bailouts on the BRIC´S.

As soon as the bailouts began, inflation kept on soaring in the underdeveloped countries: in China and India, threatening the precarious stability of the nations leaning on the weak growth of world economy, known as BRICS, Brazil, China, India, Russia and South Africa. In the case of India, for example the Central Bank was compelled to increase the rate of interest to halt the increase of prices, and this led to increase the cost of loans even at the cost of reducing the GDP and the growth of economy that had been maintained steady

The Popular Republic of China is going through the same process only more acute. Their growth began to decline from 11.5 in 2007 to 9.5 in 2010 and 8.5 in the 2011/2012. But the $ 5 billion bailouts caused a bubble fed by an even greater real estate credit than what burst in the USA in 2007. Empty flats belonging to families who cannot afford them are becoming increasingly numerous in the provinces after the slumping of the peak of housing purchases. Which left the state and the provinces full of uncollectible due to the massive credits granted the lower levels of income.

The price of a Chinese dwelling is 27 times higher than the average income and inflation has affected the low wages causing great demonstrations of displeasure as those that took place in the province of Guandong, industrial heart of China. Fearing the wrath of the people, the dictatorship of the CP, Was compelled to introduce measures that would push inflation down and decelerate economy pushing the rate of interest slightly upwards making the yuan slightly, the cost of money and the credits and sow diminish consumption of the population that is pushing prices upwards.

This may burst the real estate bubble, because it would cause the same effect as what made the Bush bubble burst in 2007. A more expensive yuan would make credit more expensive and if wages do not go up, people will not be able to pay. Just the way it happened with the real estate bubble in the USA, when the failures to pay begin, a general bankruptcy may be unleashed. Inflation and high prices of food and bread were also the base of the revolutions that broke out in 2011 in the Middle East and caused the rise of the peoples of Maghreb up to the Far East.

This conjunction of the serious problems accumulated in the USA, EU. Japan and China led to hasty decisions in October, November and December 2011 and a new round of bailouts. On October 26th 2011, a 50% rebate of the Greek debt was agreed on as well as nearly one million euros in bailout EFSF funds and an increase of the level of capitalisation of the banks together with other measures that Jose Manuel Barroso, President of the European Commission dubbed *"exceptional measures for exceptional times"*.

This packet was challenged when the President of Greece, George Papandreou, announced a referendum so that people may have the last word, but on November 30th 2011, Papandreou recoiled and withdrew the referendum. On 30th November 2011, European Central Bank, the American Central Reserve, central banks of Canada, Japan UK and the National Swiss Bank, began a new process of bailouts, this time coordinated and worldwide bound on solving the credit crisis in Europe, affected by the interruption of the process of circulation of capitals.

The debt crisis reached a point where banks in the region began to have increasing difficulty in borrowing dollars in the market, because the costs soared and this unleashed fears that credit and flow of capitals may be cut short again. Unlike what happened in 2008, the epicentre of this crisis of circulation of capitals was in the EU and not in the USA. The Fed reduced the rate of foreign central banks to borrow dollars and coordinated the measure with the ECB, central banks of England, Japan, Switzerland and Canada, and that led to getting a level of the ECG of $2 trillion debt with the Fed.

The operation deepened the process of colonisation of the EU by the USA and, on 21 December, thanks to the aid of the Fed, the ECB began the greatest injection of credit into the European banking system in the 13 years of sole currency. Almost 489 billion euros lent to 523 banks for an extraordinarily long period three years at 1%. In this way, the ECB tried to make sure that the banks would have enough cash to be able to comply with maturities worth 2 million euros for the first three months of 2012 and, at the same time keep on operating and lending to businesses an private clients to avoid total bankruptcy of credit that is already much worse for the wear a tear.

In February there was another round of bailouts: the entire operation was called Long Term Refinancing Operation and the measures were described by Mario Draghi, President of the ECB, as a *"powerful medicine"*. Draghi described the bailouts to the German daily Bild as follows, *"...the situation was really critical. It could have reached a dangerous contraction of credit for banks. Many firms would have gone broke because they would have been spinning in a vacuum. We had to prevent that from happening".*

"Time Indefinite Bailout" in 2012- 13 and 14

An important change happened as far as the bailout policy is concerned. Faced with the prospect of recession in world economy and failure of the so-far implemented bailouts, in September the Fed launched the QE3, an indefinite bailout, with no deadline. Let us see how this process developed in 2012- 2013.

The economic outlook of capitalism continued getting increasingly dismal. Early that year, the report "Situation and prospects of World Economy" worked out by the Conference of the United Nations for Trade and Development (UNCTAD) asserted, "World economy is swaying on the verge of a new recession. Anaemic growth is expected in 2012 and 2013"

In January 3012, Standard & Poor's degraded the credit ranking of France and Austria that hot on the heels of Spain, Italy and Portugal, lost their AAA marks. Faced with this situation American Fed launched another kind of bailing out in a plan known as "Operation Twist" after the fashionable dance during the Kennedy presidency. The plan was basically to change inferior 3 year debt securities for assets at 6 to 30 years, a decision that the Fed had not taken for over half a century.

The amount redeemed was of some $ 400 billion until June 2012. But the failure of the operation in the middle of an electoral year, when Obama's re-election was at stake, forced the president of the Fed, Ben Bernake, to prolong the programme for the entire 2012. The objective of the plan was to "set apart" investors of the American debt as refuge value and to boost the flow of investments. And it managed to push down the price of American bonds that reached their historic minimum, but it did not produce the effect of stimulating investment.

In Europe, after a round of bailouts known as LTRO1 of December 2011 and LTRO2 of February 2012 respectively millions of dollars were allocated and the substantive problem was still unsolved. In China, the fall of the economic growth compelled the Central Bank of China to implement a bailout based on a reduction of the reserves in possession of the Chinese banks, implying an important injection of cash into economy.

In 2012, the most dramatic aspect in EU was Spain, after the bankruptcy of the pool of banks wrought after the beginning of the world crisis, called Bankia that required $122 billion bailout to avoid the collapse of European banking system. According to the Bank for International Settlements, in the late 2011, German banks had an exposure of about $ 150 billion in Spanish economy: about $ 53 billion in their banks.

That is to say, between the measures taken by the administrations of the USA, of EU and of China, we are witnessing a veritable "tidal wave of bailouts" spurred by the possibility that would economy would sink into depression. However, the possibility of a depression was confirmed with data world economic growth for Europe, the USA and China and that is what led to September 13th 2012 when the Fed announced the most outstanding and dramatic bailout since the beginning of the crisis of capitalism in 2007.

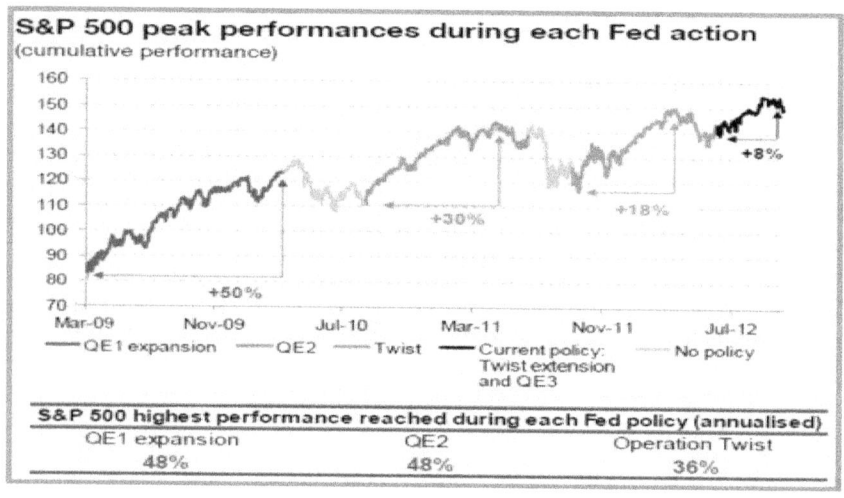

Results in the S&P500 of the different operations of QE - Source: Zero Hedge

It was on that day that the FED announced the so-called Quantitative Easing 3 (QE3), a massive monthly purchase of 85 billion assets in possession of Multinational Corporations (derivatives MBS) that can be extended to another type of assets if the situation of the world economy – and especially of the USA – does not get any better.

The name of QE3 is due to the fact that the round of bailouts that began in November 2008 and ended in March 2010 was known as QE 1 and the round of bailouts that began in November 2010 and ended in June 2011 was QE2. Together with the QE3 of the USA there was the announcement made by European Central Bank (ECB) on 6th September of enormous bailouts that the ECB would buy unlimited debts of countries in risky situation but under very strict conditions of adjustment imposed on countries that receive the bailout.

The QE3 is an altogether different kind of bailout compared to the previous ones because they unlimited proportion and indefinite time, at 0 rate of interest until year 2015. This is something new and it reflects the gravity of the crisis that world economy is going through. They are gigantic bailouts of tremendous proportions; to quote just one datum: adding all the unconventional programmes.

The Fed bought 85 billion dollars' worth in Assets a month from the beginning of 2013. The announcement of the unlimited bailout at 0 rate of interest, is on the one hand the evidence of the magnitude of the crisis and, on the other hand, a number of very dangerous measures that can bring about serious consequences for the already grievous crisis of capitalism because the new gigantic emission of fictitious capital, will bring new imbalance that accelerate the contradiction and new episodes of the crisis of the system, such as the "Fiscal Cliff" in the USA and other that we shall analyse in the next chapter. Furthermore, however, while the effects of QE1 could be perceived for a year, the QE3 had some effect for just a few weeks.

On 31st December 2012 an adjustment plan, known as Fiscal Cliff and is a packet of increase of taxes accompanied by reduction of public expenditure, the combined effect of which is in quest of reduction of the 4% of GDP in 2013, which throughout the forthcoming decade would is said to reach 1.2 billion dollars of reduction of deficit just as the Budget Control Act of 2011 foresees.

As part of the implementation of the adjustment, on 4th of March 2013, President Barack Obama appointed Sylvia Mathews Burwell, Chairwoman of the Walmart Foundation, as head of Budget Office at White House. *"Sylvia knows how to adjust a budget,"* he said. Nobody can be better than Walmart officials to adjust a budget brutally and attack living standards of the toiling masses of the USA.

Also in March 2013 the bankruptcy of Cyprus occurred, so the Central European Bank (CEB) and the IMF intervened the island, broke up the banks and liquidated the little sovereignty that still lingered there in order to save the euro, the German banks and the fiscal paradises. In January this year, Japan started a process of unprecedented in their history bailouts. In order to rescue the Japanese economy (the 3rd in the world) from depression, the Government began execute a plan of injecting 20 billion yens into the economy.

The new Japanese prime minister, Shinzo Abe, leader of the conservative Democratic Liberal Party (DLP) displaced Masaaki Shirakawa heading the Bank of Japan (BoJ) and replaced him by Haruhiko Kuroda, who presented an aggressive programme of bailouts, an operation that was marked by some of the most important analysts and economists in the world as one of the greatest economic experiments in the modern era.

Detroit, a city famous for being the host to the Three Great in American car industry; **General Motors, Ford and Chrysler**, went bankrupt in July this year with debts above $18 billion. Detroit became the biggest city in that country to file for bankruptcy. On 1st of August, the S & P 500, world's most important stock indexes, for the first time since the world capitalist crisis began surpassed the barrier of 1700 percentage points.

Not even at the highest pitch of the sub-prime bubble this index had reached the 1600 points. The S&P 500 collapsed to 700 points in 2008 and as from that moment on, with bailouts a steady climb began until this 1600 peak of today was reached. But these indexes began to show the perils that world economy began to face. Bernanke, President of the FED announced that they can envisage the danger of the formation of bubbles throughout world economy.

The rise of the Wall Street panels to levels above that previous of the beginning of the crisis, ignoring the reality of world economy, shows that bailouts are inflating one or several bubbles of high destructive power and going up simultaneously. And more likely than not, the bubble is developing even in the Bonds of the U.S. Treasury, the financial tool used to develop bailouts.

The fear of an explosion of bubbles in the Treasury Bonds had pushed Bernanke to announce a possible deadline to the "indefinite bailout". But it is precisely due to the severity of the crisis and the effect that the bailouts are causing in capitalism, regardless of whether bailouts are suspended or not in 2014, the contradiction, the problems and the crisis are not to be solved with bailouts; the contrary is true as we shall see in the next chapter.

Bankers and "God's work"

In 2009, Goldman Sachs paid his managers with bonuses as a way of celebrating that he had once more obtained profit after the crisis suffered in 2008. To explain why he paid with bonuses, Lloyd Blankfein, the boss at Goldman's stated, *"We are very important. We help companies to grow because we help them to obtain capital. Companies that grow create wealth and this in turn allows people to have jobs, which in turn spawn more growth and more wealth. We complied with a social mission, God's work."*

In Citigroup, the managers collected bonuses and multimillionaires premiums. The same happened in Merrill Lynch, Bank of America, JP Morgan Chase and other investment banks. While the crisis was evolving and serious consequences of poverty and destitution spreading out all over the world and engulfing more and more countries, regions and branches of production, trade and finances, bankers share gifts of prizes worth millions.

That is to say, after doing "God's work" bankers received divine salaries. But in the meantime, the crisis kept on developing and nothing - not even the ill-omened deepening of it prevented the great capitalists who control world economy from collecting rich premiums and benefits. While the bankers practice their frenetic dances of granting themselves rewards, a worldwide debate broke out about the nature of the crisis and it's prospective. Questions arise and seek answers. Where is this crisis going? Why did it happen? Can capitalism overcome it?

We shall pose answers to these questions one after the other. The future panorama of the crisis of capitalism, beyond its conjectural movements, the deep processes that are unfolded and the fundamental tendencies are motives of analysis in the following chapter.

Notes

(1) As George Soros pointed out, "The outbreak of the economic crisis in 2008 can be officially determined in August 2007 when the Central Banks had to intervene to provide liquidity to the banking system". George Soros – The new paradigm of financial markets. Taurus 2008

(2) Walter Bagehot, 1826-1877. English economic journalist. He was among the first editors of The Economist. In his book *Lombart Street,* Bagehot defended that the fundamental mission of the Bank of England was to use all its gold reserves so as to – in times crisis of liquidity – acquire as many assets as possible from commercial banks and so restore credibility to banking system – Source: http://www.junademariana.org/estudio/

(3) There are various versions regarding why the government did not bailout Lehman and did bail out Merrill Lynch, Bear Sterns, Fannie and Freddie. The behaviour of the Fed and JP Morgan after the bankruptcy of Lehman gave room to suspicions among analysts. Be that as it may, it was JP Morgan – who had an exposure of nearly $90 dollars in derivatives – benefited from the operation, was technically broke and actually underwent a process of concealed recapitalisation

(4) Also the Wall Street Journal indicated that the real beneficiaries of the successive bailouts of AIG were two dozen great financial entities who received $50

The End of the Corporations

000 million since September, when the bailouts of the insurance agencies began. Deutsche Bank and Goldman Sachs are the top of the list, but further down se can also see Merrill Lynch, SG, Royal Bank of Scotland, Morgan Stanley or HSBC, etc. The legislator Christopher Doss, a Democrat of Connecticut, protested, ""It is not clear whom we are bailing out". Source: http://77edicion4.com.ar

(5) Investment Banks JP Morgan Chase, Bank of New York / Mellon, Merrill Lynch, State Street, Morgan Stanley, Goldman Sachs, Bank of America, Citigroup and Wells Fargo were part of this agreement.

(6) Henry Kissinger was State Secretary in the Richard Nixon and Gerald Ford administrations. He had an outstanding role in foreign policy of the USA, in the Vietnam War, in the bomb raids on Cambodia and the relations with China. Brent Scowcroft was National Security Advisor under Presidents Gerald Ford and George Bush. He also served as military assistant for President Richard Nixon and as assistant to the President for National Security Affairs in Nixon and Ford Administrations and assisted President Barrack Obama in the election of his national security team.

(7) On 1 of June 1998, the ECB was constituted by Belgium, Germany, France, Ireland, Italy, Spain, Luxemburg, Netherlands, Austria, Portugal and Finland. As from the 1st January 1999, the economies of the member states adopted the single currency, the euro

The End of Corporations

An explanation from left to the capitalist world economic crisis

CHAPTER II

Trends

The End of the Corporations

CHAPTER II: Trends

"The real Internal Connections of the capitalist process of production is an extremely complicated process... it goes without saying that ideas about the laws of capitalist production must be formed in the minds of the agents of production and circulation that would be totally different from these laws... the ideas of a merchant, a stock speculator, or a banker are necessarily completely wrong."

Karl Marx, Capital, Chapter XVI, Book III

After the Bailouts, the world has literally changed. It has changed not only in the economic scope: bailout have made an impact on social relations, on the relations of production, political and economic relations on location and agreements of social classes and between different sectors of classes and their relation with the whole world. Definitely, everything has changed.

And yet, even if in the essentials everything has changed, everything seems to go on as before: multinationals move, the population consumes; everything continues except for occasional announcement of a bankruptcy and some companies missing. Furthermore, at times there is economic growth. This outer shell of the crisis is one of the elements that cause the greatest confusion among the economists and analysts in the world.

Most of them are at a loss. They show their perplexity permanently in the face of a reality they ignore; there is no doubt that they are wandering through a unknown land. To find answers, they seek parameters. They compare this crisis with others, "It is just like that of Nasdaq of the year 2000," say some. "It is the same as the crisis of oil in the 70s," assert others. Every time statistics manage to confuse them. *"We are coming out of the crisis,"* some will claim, but then data prove them wrong. *"It is part of a long cycle of growth,"* other put in. Others refute, *"It is the end of a long cycle of growth"*

Statistics themselves provide data to say one thing as much as the other. The same statistics lead analysts and economists, even some of those that are regarded as Marxists, to such a state of confusion. It is important to compare this crisis with the other ones that took place during capitalism, but we cannot pretend to find answers in comparisons alone, because this current crisis has elements of all the previous ones.

Statistic data cannot explain the profound laws of economy; they are very important, but they are useful only as supports. It is a dismal panorama in the land of Marxism, where most of the economists run aground in the attempt to explain the crisis asserting if of the overproduction type. They commit the same error as the capitalist analysts who restrain themselves to describe market statistics. It is true that there are millions of goods on the market that cannot be sold, but this does not explain the crisis or the bailouts, because overproduction is the outer expression of the deep phenomena of capitalism.

Those who qualify this crisis as of overproduction take appearance for essence. Actually, this is a very complex crisis; it is no coincidence that the interactions of conjectural, structural and historic elements of capitalism have found an intersection in the first decade of XXI century. This is the only mitigating factor we can grant our analysts to justify their confusion. And as for those who defend capitalism, they commit the additional and recurrent error of confusing reality with their wishful thinking and defence of their interests.

But changes loom in front of them steady and unmovable for they, have come to stay and have drastically modified reality and economic prospects of capitalism. Since the bailouts and the fabulous masses of capital injected into economy as a whole, nothing will ever be the same. Even the data of the early years of the crisis acquired such dimensions what we have to look many years back to find antecedents of similar magnitude, unregistered for decades or even centuries.

The main ECRI indicator produced by the Economic Cycle Research Institute has shown falls in American economy hinging round -6.9 aiming at a contraction and drop rate that the most important capitalist economy has no news of since the post-war. In 2009, all the economies of the G7 registered a simultaneous negative growth, something that has been unheard of for the last 200 years.

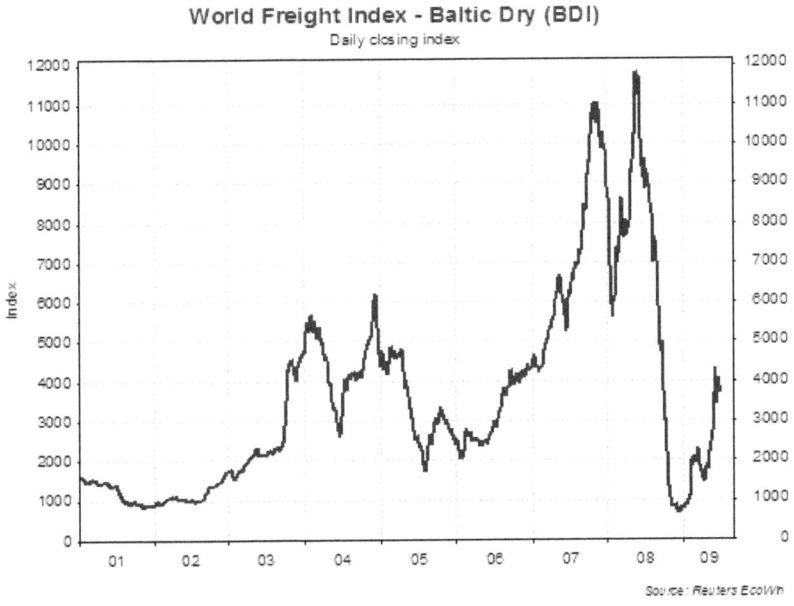

Baltic Dry Index shows the spectacular fall of trade after the bankruptcy of Lehman Brothers. After bailouts world trade recovers slightly. Source: Baltic Dry Index

Also in 2009, over 100 nations registered growth zero or negative for the first time in the history of capitalism! The Indicator Baltic Dry, that reflects the evolution of world trade neared 12000 points in May 2008 but by May that year there was a historic fall and it collapsed falling apart to 660 points only to start climbing slowly and finally reach 4 500 points in the late 2009. Ever since then the descent has been steady and in early October it reached 2478 points, a clear signal that economy was still moving far from the expected rates for the crisis because in relation to the period 2006 – 2007 the volume of global trade fell 25%. This has been the worst fall since... 1945!

The fall of the prices of oil and other commodities was the fastest and the deepest since the first registers were made in 1956. If in the

The End of the Corporations

days of the Great Depression of 1929 In the USA, was 186the percentage of the debt over the GDP was 186%, during the current crisis, the percentage of the debt is estimated at …379%: more than the double of the days of the Great Depression! And if we add to it the debts for future old-age pensions, the percentage will stand at 800! The 2009 GDP of Japan is swaying between -6% and -10. These are the worst data since 1945.

Ever since the beginning of the crisis, the American rates of interest are practically at zero and nearly all major economies are at their lowest in the last… 100 years. But it was the British rates of interest that have reached their lowest pit in over three centuries! That is precisely since the Bank of England was founded: in 1916. In 2008, the Caisse des Dépôts, the financial arm of the French State since 1816 and under all the regimes (monarchy, empire, republic…) suffered its first yearly loss… in 193 years!

We can summarise the fundamental trends that occurred in the capitalist system as from the bailouts, grouping them in 4 items that incorporate a series of issues that in turn are linked to each other:

1) **Leap in the levels of poverty and inequality in the G7 and the world**

2) **Devaluation and decomposition of world economy**

3) **Crisis of credit, money and general bankruptcies of companies and states**

4) **Permanence and institutionalisation of bailouts**

1) Leap in the levels of poverty and inequality in the G7 and the world: The indicators of world poverty and inequality have already been serious but after the bailouts they soared to unprecedented limits. By 2012, over a total of 6.7 billion world inhabitants, 1 billion "survive" on an average $ 2 a day; 70% of them are women. 3 billion cannot afford to cover their basic needs in food, housing and health. More than 24 billion starve a day; 840 million people are undernourished out of which 200 million are children under five.

More than 1.8 billion human beings have no access to drinking water. More than 1 billion have no dente housing; 2 billion people suffer from anaemia due to lack of iron; 880 million have no access to basic health service and, 200 billion people lack access to essential medicaments. In the other extreme, those who keep on pocketing money

The End of the Corporations

from the bailouts, the top twenty millionaires of the Forbes list calculate between them an amount estimated at $109.5 billion **(1)** This is more than enough to put an end to famine and poverty in the world.

The elite club ranking Forbes switched from 1125 members in 2008 to 793 in 2009. These $109.5 of wealth accumulated in the hands of millionaires outstrips the world's GDP, which stand at about $100 billion. Such data prove that bailouts have exacerbates the inequalities which are becoming increasingly serious as days go by. After the bailouts, social inequality, human impairment and the damage done to nature soared sky-high and this heralds the peril that his phase of capitalism is leading us to.

The demolishing data of world economy are so serious that we can assert that there has not been so far any phase, any stage or period of capitalism that could mean such grievous fall in the living conditions of thousands of millions of people simultaneously as what we are witnessing now, after the bailouts. With these chilling ratios at hand, and comparing them with the days of 25 years ago, we could perfectly well declare Ronald Reagan and Margaret Thatcher, benefactors of mankind.

This is what officials, defenders of capitalism as who was in 2009 the Managing Director of the IMF, Dominique Strauss-Khan, *"Since the beginning of the crisis in the USA, in 2007, 30 million jobs were lost in the world... we are really running the risk of losing a generation."* At the 2010 Jackson Hole Conference, the analysis of the economists Carmen and Vincent Reinhart addressed to the Central Bank in the world was, *"Ten years may pass before the economic growth in the USA and other countries will be back at the levels previous to the recession."*

The bailouts unleashed economic, political and social forces that are not only modifying social relations between classes and sectors of classes but also affect and modify the relations between nations and states. Before the bailouts we knew that there was a "First World" consisting of 7 countries: the USA, England, France, Canada, Germany, Italy and Japan separate from a "Third World" integrated by the remaining 192 countries that, regardless all the difference between them have always shared higher rates of poverty.

The inhabitants and citizens of the countries of the so-called "First World" have always enjoyed better living standards than those of the remaining countries of the planet, including social classes and sectors of classes of a lower purchasing power. After the bailouts this changed definitely. After the bailouts the countries of what used to be called the First World, poverty and unemployment accrue very fast spurred by the adjustments and austerity implemented by their governments.

Even if the rates of poverty and unemployment are not yet the same as in the countries of the Third World, they tend to equalize and get nearer to those standards. That is why, and considering the definition of a country as a social formation consisting of social classes and sectors of classes at a given moment of a historic process, we can now assert that in the countries or social formations of the USA, France, England, Canada, Japan and Italy rates of poverty and unemployment, so far regarded as specific for social formation of the countries of the Third World, tend to increase.

The situation is different when it is all about states. After the bailouts the existence of some few states, qualitatively richer and more powerful from the military and economic point of view than the remaining 192 becomes stronger and deeper. These imperialist states are the richest on earth not only because of the accumulation of wealth they have been grabbing historically from colonial and more underdeveloped countries, but also due to their control of trade, industry, distribution, finances, and communications in combination with their military and technologic power.

Relation between States and Multinationals

There is greater overlapping between the immense bureaucratic and military machinery of these states and the multinationals. Bailouts have implied injecting gigantic masses of capital into them and this goes together with a closer and more intimate union of the constitutive elements of the states and the multinationals. Ever since the bailouts, the situation of the imperialist states and the multinationals is even more deeply interrelated; the future of the multinationals depends on the future of the states and vice-versa.

Blending states with their multinationals is a permanent trend in capitalism and has already been expressed in the fascist states of Hitler and Mussolini, in which deep unity has been reached between the great corporations and national monopolies on the one hand and the states on the other. Though the multinationals were not predominant in those days, the tendency is the same and an analogy can be perfectly well established even in very different social and political contexts.

According to Trotsky, *"The corporative state... is nothing but an agent of monopolist capital...Mussolini makes the State run all the risks of the companies and lets capitalist enjoy the benefits of the looting"* (2) What we are analyzing is a tendency of which bailouts are the best expression. What stems out of the generalized collapse of mega-corporations affects imperialist states; the deep overlapping the former with the latter implies that the fate of the states is also the fate of the corporations.

This unity between imperialist states and multinational corporations spawns changes in the relations between states, economies and nations. A study carried out by Sarah Anderson and John Cavanagh of the Institute for Political Studies, finds that among the top 100 economies in the world, 51 are corporations and 49 are countries. A comparison of the corporative sales and the GDP of the countries reveals that General Motors is greater than, for example, Denmark and that Wal-Mart is greater than countries like Norway and that General Electric – also associated to JP Morgan – is greater than, for example, Portugal.

This tendency of the states of the G7, their role as imperialist states, their deep overlapping with the multinational corporations, their interweaving with armies that depend on them, their renewed arms development and the existence of the bourgeois class and bureaucratic caste components of the imperialist state machinery develop another trend.
These states will tend to split away from the social formation that they dominate and will try to modify relations of production and structure of that social formation to gain stability and impose new balance of power between the classes.

That is why the development of the rich imperialist states goes together with social formations of accruing poverty, contrasting with what used to differentiate the "First World" from the "Third World" and will now be the contrasts between the states of G7 and the social structure they dominate over.

After the bailouts, the population of the countries of the G7 and fundamentally their working class and popular sectors are beginning to go through phenomena and situation unknown for the inhabitants of European north, the North of America and Japan though they have always been habitual for any citizen of the "Third World".

At the same time and according to what we saw in Chapter I, with the bailouts the relations between the imperialist countries are changing drastically while there is a rapid process of colonization of the EU and Japan by the USA. The colossal infusions of Fed capital are acting reinforcing American hegemony that imposes their policies on EU, Japan and BRIC's

Accruing poverty and changes in social structure of the G7

Poverty has been accruing at tremendous speed under the Obama administration due to recession that determined important growth of poverty equivalent to 14.3% of the population, the greatest figure in the last 51 years according to the report of the Census Bureau. In 2009, the amount of paupers in the USA reached 43.7 million people, one out of every seven Americans and this implied almost 4 million people compared to 2008.

The number of Americans without any medical insurance increased to 51 million in 2009 as loss of jobs means loss of health insurance. These rates soar sky-high among minorities. The proportion of poor people climbed alarmingly among the Hispanic population, Afro-Americans and immigrants, youths under 18, women, Hispanic children, old-aged; American poverty is moving towards a new record of people of working age without any resources and is nearing the figures of the days of Great Depression.

Poverty rates are the most important since 1959, when the government started the accounting of this issue and has now outstripped previous high peaks in 1965 and 1980. More than 2.8 million people lost their homes in 2009 because of foreclosure or bank repossessions. This stands for nearly 8 000 a day, the highest figures in the last two years when the sub-prime began to cause other millions of people to lose their homes.

At present there are over 17 million people out of job in G.B. and further millions have only part-time jobs. A research published recently by the British newspaper, The Independent reveals that the level of poverty in England is similar to what it used to be in Victorian days in the years 1837 to 1901: about a fifth of white children are classified as poor, a fourth part among Caribbean's and Indians (of India) and more than half Pakistanis and Bangladeshis. White people earn more; rates of employment among them are higher and they draw benefits from discrimination.

Housing is one of the most serious problems of the toiling masses in Great Britain; it is much more serious now that the government has taken steps that made houses private one third of which used to be in the hands of the State in 1982 and now, 20 years later, this amount was reduced to 14%. In Germany, the number of unemployed reached 341 million citizens in 2010 according to reports of the Federal Employment Office in Nuremberg and 1 out of every 4 immigrants living in Germany is on the verge of poverty if not deep in real poverty. Young

The End of the Corporations

people and children are the most affected. German Institute of Economic research (DWI) estimated that 1 out of every 7 Germans lives on the verge of poverty; those numbers are similar to those in the USA. The situation is not much better for families and actually the risk of becoming poor is greater as the number of children increase: 22% of homes with three children are on the verge of poverty and the percentage increases to 36% when there are four or more children. 40% single mothers or fathers live in situation of poverty. Practically 1 out of every 4 single Germans aged between 19 and 25 live endangered by poverty.

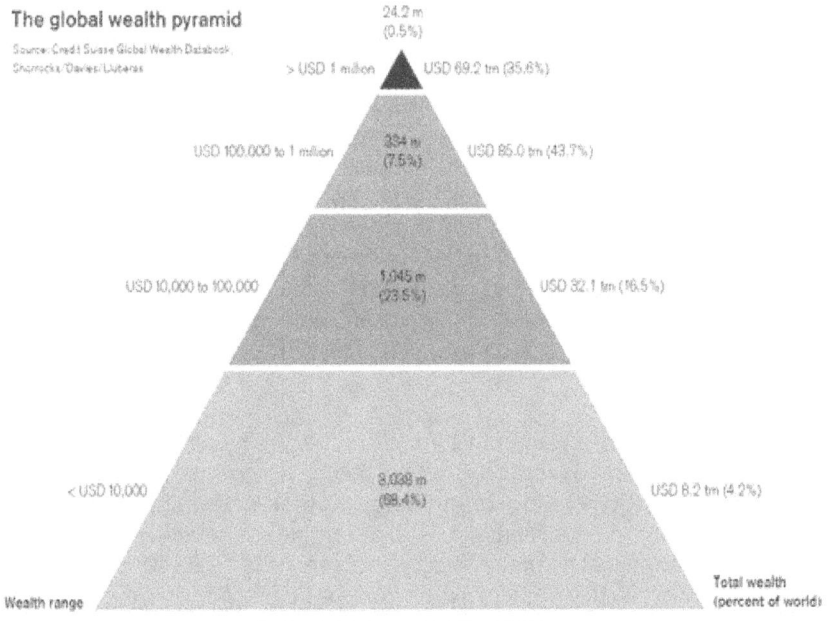

Pyramid of world wealth according to data of Credit Suisse 8/10/10 - 0.5% of the population concentrates almost 40% of world's wealth. Between 0.5 and the following segment of the following 8,2% i.e.: 10% of the world population hold 82% of the world's wealth. Source: Credit Suisse

In Japan, the end of lifetime employment and the deterioration of social security are the main factors of impoverishment of important social sectors in a country that was regarded as immune to poverty. According to data from the Labor Ministry, after years of economic stagnation and increasing disparities of incomes, there are 20 million poor people. Authorities consider the limit of poverty in about $ 22 000 a year for a family of 4 members; in Japan this stands for half the income of an average home.

The End of the Corporations

Over 80% of those who live in poverty are poor workers on temporary basis with no insurance and few benefits. There is a marked headway in labour precariousness; this has opened an enormous crevasse through which millions of Japanese have slid down and, according to official data, Japan is the fourth highest rate of poverty among the developed countries.

In France, poverty advances hand-in-hand with unemployment, fragility and instability at work that affect over 4 million people. In 2010 there were 8 million Frenchmen and Frenchwomen living under the poverty level and once they have paid their rent, gas, electricity an insurance they have only $2.70 a day per person to eat and clothe. With a population of 65 million inhabitants, unemployment affects 2.7 million, equivalent to 10% of active labour force. This percentage is particularly high in homes of immigrants: it reaches 36%

Inequality and poverty also accrue in Canada, essentially among the thousands of immigrants estimated at over 10000 Hispanics that migrate to Canada every year and the demand for residence visa is still increasing. Anyone who lives alone in Toronto or Vancouver and earns about $30 000 a year may just make ends meet. In Vancouver, Toronto, Montreal and Ottawa the sector known as "working poor" – people who work but do not earn enough to stay above the level of poverty – accrues.

According to a research by the United Way, 30% of the families in the municipality of Toronto are poor, taking as parameter households whose income is 50% below the average in their community, and using the LIM – Low Income Measure. For example, a family with mother, father and two children and a yearly income of $ 275000 or under is considered poor. In the case of only one head of family and two children under 17 the figure would be $23 375.

For these families, considering that the cost of living in Canada is high, incomes are considered precarious if they barely cover the cost of strictly basic living and there is access to social assistance such as Food Banks and grants for housing or services that exist but are insufficient.

In Italy, almost three million people live in absolute poverty – 4.9 of the population according to reports of Italian Institute of Statistics (ISTAT) and 13. 6% of the population, 8 078 000 citizens live in conditions of relative poverty. Absolute poverty in the south of the country shifted from 5.8% to 7.9% and got worse among the families of four members, particularly those consisting of the couple and two children more often than not underage, and among families headed by a person of scarce education and under 45, by a self-employed worker or among families in which at least one of the members is looking for a job. In this way, the phenomenon of relative poverty in the south is equivalent to nearly five times that of the rest of the country.

ISTAT reports that the map of poverty in Italy has never overcome the division between the more industrialized north and the underdeveloped south. In the south poverty reaches 32.8% of the population, five times more than in the rest of the country. This situation worsens for families living in Sicily, Campania, and, above all, in Calabria: all of them are in the south of Italy. Absolute poverty is more frequent in numerous families, three children or more, where the rate is 9.4% of families where none of the members of the family works 33% and families whose head is looking for a job 26.7%.

These modifications are taking place very fast in the social formation of imperialist countries with elements that are repeated constantly in practically all of them: poverty accrues, health, education and housing rated fall and affect the weakest and most defenceless sectors of the population. Immigrants, the most displace racial sectors such as Afro Americans, Hispanics and Muslim, women, children and old people that are affected by the cuts in the budget of social aid and the attacks that the G7 administrations are launching when they dismantle education, health and grants for housing that cause the entrance of greater contingents of poverty and destitution. But these attacks and the accruing poverty is what spawns the major political and social processes of the XXI century.

FMI: "Old people live too long"

The slumping of the living standards in the whole world and particularly in the countries of the "First World" is the outcome of the way capitalist governments respond to the crisis, economic plans of the governments and international economic organisms. But while capitalist governments reach their targets, they cause the exacerbation of all the political and economic contradictions and the toiling masses of the world have started confronting the offensive. The plans of the G7 offensive are to go on with the adjustments against the peoples for a long time just as the British Prime Minister David Cameron stated at an interview for Daily Telegraph. Cameron said that the cuts duration in the budget cuts will be prolonged from the initially foreseen 5 years until 2020. The other countries of the EU have to face similar prospects.

There is no doubt that the ideal of an economic model that those capitalist governments can hope for is a front with the multinational Wall

Mart as well as the State of China, who are the vanguard of super exploitation of workers, precarious character of labour, low wages and elimination of the most elementary democratic rights. Organizations such as IMF express their objective in the most brazenfaced manner. In their annual report of World Financial Stability 11/4/12, the IMF stated, *"Old people live too much and that is a risk for global economy... a financial risk for the world economy is the increase of longevity in the countries on the globe, and this is the reason for which we recommend to diminish pensions and increase the retirement."*

It is hard to guess the forms that world economy would take if the offensive that capitalist governments are carrying out against the toiling masses obtained definite success. But we can have a guess at the contents: unprecedented aggravation of social conditions and living standards among the peoples of the whole world. Capitalism seeks to solve the crisis and get out of it by means of a brutal offensive against the masses in Europe, the USA and the whole world. Will capitalism succeeds at getting out of the crisis by imposing a brutal adjustment on the conditions of life of global toiling masses?

This is what is at stake in this process of strikes and mobilizations that are now sweeping across the USA and Europe and are budding even in China challenging the model of super-exploitation and dismantling social achievements embodied in the Chinese state. If capitalist governments defeat the struggles of the workers and peoples of Europe and the USA then we might consider the hypothesis of capitalist states imposing a world-wide adjustment and so overcome the crisis. These are the tendencies cropping up along the path towards the solution to this crisis, a target they may reach if their offensive proves to be victorious.

That is to say: two sets of tendencies and prospects are possible: one is by increasing the super exploitation of the masses, pushing down the standard of living especially in the G7, this heap of papers and over-accumulation of capital that the bailouts represent will be valorised and a possible solution to the crisis will become feasible as well as the opening of a new expansion and economic expansion and growth will become possible.

The other possibility is that the high rates of exploitation, of creation of necessary value and surplus value will not be reached nor will the production of real wealth spawning the prospect of growth of enormous masses of capital dedicated to speculation, something that may produce one or more financial bubbles of colossal dimensions and powerfully destructive that may further aggravate the crisis of capitalism.

Both tendencies are developing simultaneously and in an interrelated manner.

Devaluation and decomposition of world economy

Bailouts spawn "zombies" or "living dead". What are they? This is how Global Anticipation Bulletin defines them, *"Along the streets of the great American and European cities ... one can verify the existence of a significant amount of trademarks that continue shining to attract buyers but actually they are nothing but deceitful appearances of broken businesses, kept artificially alive by means of public money or of restructuring of uncertain future, such as CIT, GM, Chrysler, Sarah, Opel, Karstad, Wuelle, Iberia, Alitalia, etc., they look as if they were functioning normally but as for economic health, there is an illness that undermines more and more deeply all the tissue of the companies... veritable zombies. All of them are economic living dead."* (Global Europe Anticipation Bulletin 39)

Several economists dubbed these companies "zombies" or "living dead"; some of them are among the biggest multinational mega-corporations that dominate world economy and that, even now that they are broke, still exist. After the bailouts, these zombies have become a more general phenomenon. Due to the size of the bailouts, the magnitude of these corpses dragged by capitalism is also enormous and of great weight and importance in relation to the GDP and world economy as a whole.

This is the way that David Troman, chief of financial services in PA Consulting a Consultancy of the industry of informatics: *"The simultaneous existence of zombies is not something that has ever happened before in the working life of any of the financial services... the combination of all these factors means that the banks, in spite of all the appearances, can only shamble in a half-alive state. Their capacity of lending money and to boost economic growth will still be low for several years... We shall al learn how to coexist with zombie banks."* (3)

In many ways, bailouts open an unprecedented situation, with many entities, companies, states, banks, etc, that are broke but they do not declare bankruptcy and a new situation surfaces in which these entities, whose economic operations have proved to be a failure, do not disappear and, up to a point, they still participate in the process of distribution of profits and claim part of the capitals and claim part of the existing capitals and of the surplus value.

The effect of the existence of these corpses that capitalism drags is that it maintains the high organic composition of capital, an enormous mass of fixed capital, machines, workshops, infrastructure and capitals that do not obtain a rate profit and therefore act as capital for the attainment of new value. The increase of the organic composition of capital caused by bailouts, acts like an obstacle preventing capitalism, from overcome the crisis.

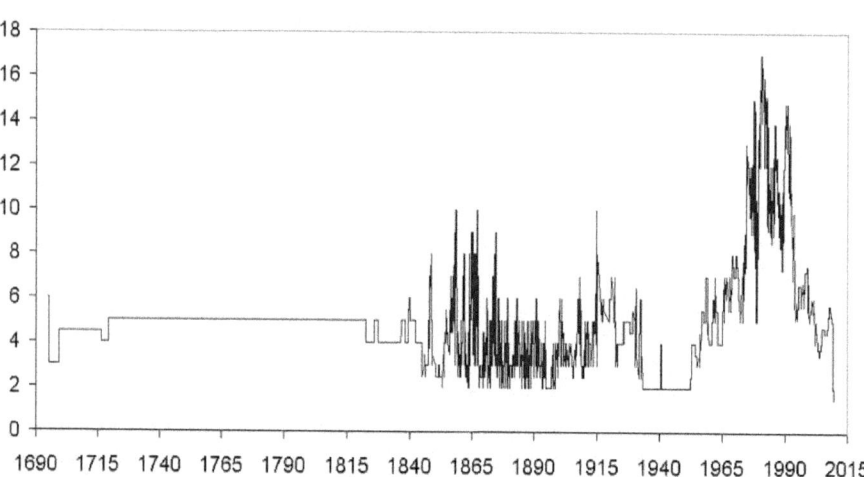

Evolution Rates of interest of the Bank of England. After the beginning of the crisis, the rates descend to the levels of 1690, Source www.geab.org

Historically, each crisis of capitalism is solved through a process of bankruptcies, auctions and embargoes which means that only the strongest capitalists survive, companies and banks that have been operating unsuccessfully disappear and wrong investments are liquidated. This is how Karl Marx put it. *"... The conflict between the antagonistic driving forces is relieved periodically by means of a crisis. How then would this conflict be solved and the conditions for sound capitalist production be restored? This includes laying fallow and even annihilating a part of the capital... but regardless the circumstance the balance would be established by inactivation and even annihilation of capital up to a greater or smaller degree"* **(4)**

Marx says that the solution that capitalism provides for the crisis and to find a new balance that will allow the development of economy is the outright destruction of a sector of capitals. This is the historic mechanism that capitalism has used in order to overcome the crises for a new capital to invest and for a certain functioning can be re-established and for capitalist system to attain a certain balance. The crisis that broke out in 2007, the process of annihilation of capitals that Marx was talking about developed partially insofar as a very important sector of the great capital went bankrupt and disappeared.

"Too big to fail"

But there is no doubt that - were it not for the bailouts - the annihilation of capitals that took place would have been qualitatively superior and would have reached the multinational corporations and a sector of the banks. This massive intervention of the G7, fundamentally of the USA, actually perturbed and altered the process of annihilation and destruction of capitals that would have allowed capitalism to recover part of the lost balance.

As there has been no process of "natural selection" of capitals and capitalists, bailouts prevent the destruction of surplus capitals. Obstructing the burning of capitals obstructs the solution to the crisis and the bailouts turn into another structural factor that makes the admittance of investments meant to pre-launch world economy more difficult. From the point of view of the process of burning and annihilating capitals that Marx analyzed, we can now answer the question, why were there any bailouts anyhow?

And the answer is: this can be explained by the magnitude of the crisis that was such that it could have triggered off a process of destruction and annihilation of capitals that it would have jeopardized the very existence of capitalist system. For example: General Motors (GM) should have gone bankrupt, but if GM disappeared this would have been an impact on the production of millions of cars and lories in 34 different countries, of 463 subsidiaries and 234 500 labour force, 91 000 in the USA that provides for health insurance and old age pensions of nearly half a million of retired workers.

And several multinational corporations, the size of which in relation to GDP and proportions of the branches and sectors is such that their disappearance would affect the very core of world economy. That is where economists who defend capitalism coined the expression "too big to fail". The problem is that now, after all the bail outs, many of these "too big to fail" have become "the living dead" and their survival depends on enormous and increasing masses of capital.

And what is more: because the burning of the capitals did not go deeply enough to stop the crisis, the overcoming of it is turning increasingly difficult and the dead bodies spawned by bailouts become obstacles. The definition of zombies is now extended to countries, some of which have become according to the international credit organizations "unviable" – even those that used to be powerful, such as Spain, Italy, and Portugal and are now regarded as zombies.

Bailouts make the devaluation of world economy even worse

"Bailouts" were useful to save the great world banks, but according to what Marx wrote, the capitals contained in the banking industry and express created value lose their value in the crisis- That is to say, if the banks estimated future profits that never occurred, this would produce immediate loss of their assets. Marx explained it as follows, *"the part of the value of the capital that is to be found only as allocation on future participation in the surplus value; in the profit as such as mere titles of debt on the production in diverse forms, immediately loses value due to the dwindling of the inflow that was the base for the assessment"* (5)

It was not the banks alone that the bailouts were aimed at but also key industries such as cars, steel, shipyards, airplanes that also suffered partial destruction of their value as crisis delivered its worst blows. In the shipyard industry, for example, the contraction of world trade caused them to have idle capital.

That is how in 2009 *The Economist* analysed, *"453 container ships, 11% of its global capacity, are now moored in Hong Kong, Singapore and other ports in the South of Asia. Only five years ago, the high demand from China meant that all those ships and more than that would be desperately requested. Between late 2006 and July 2008, ship builders received enough orders to double the global merchant fleet. Right now, these new ships are being launched – more than 9000 of them, just when the demand is sinking… orders of new ships… as it was to be expected, have collapsed and the concern no longer seems to be what is to be bought but rather how to cancel orders".*

The collapse of shipping industry has hit the south-east of Asia, especially South Korea where seven out of the ten largest shipyards in the world are to be found and analysts predict a slump in placing orders for ships to levels far below those of previous years and with poor prospects for 2011 and 2012. Another element caused by zombies is that they make the restitution of the rate of profit more difficult. Since capitals doomed to go bankrupt, the destruction of surplus capitals and that is a fundamental process to counteract the fall of the rate of profit.

The high organic composition of the capital causes the slump of the rate of profit because if the percentage of fixed capital remains high in comparison to the variable and is not destroyed, it is an element that favours destruction. In order to recover the rate of profit, the process of bankruptcy of a sector of capitalists plays an important role, reducing competition it allows for optimizing the profits of surviving capitalists.

Bailing out aggravates the dangers stemming out of super-accumulation of capital

Since wealth granted ahead of time, which is what bailouts stand for, is not created within the scope of production and values, it is nothing but a heap of papers, bills and worthless bonds. Accumulation of capitals on top of accumulation of capitals, if not producing new wealth may spawn a new speculative bubble or several of them at the same time. And if still no value is generated, a tendency towards general devaluation of economy is spawned and the subsequent symptoms of inflation, a new wave of bankruptcies, default and crises with economy already badly affected.

We can validate all the tendencies heading for devaluation, decomposition, concentration and financial speculation by verifying how the enormous injections of bailout money not only allowed Investment Banks to survive but also spawned other "monsters of high speculative and destructive power for economy. For example, BlackRock, an investment firm sited in New York that manages a portfolio of $ 3.35 billion, equivalent to the nominal GDP of Germany, is today the greatest manipulator of money in the world.

Seemingly, BlackRock is controlled by BofA (Bank of America with 34% of its assets and the British Barclays PLC, with 19.9% of its assets. The tendency to decay of world economy is expressed in the way gigantic global banks, such as BofA and Barclays triangulate operations using a financial entity, such as Black Rock, Where Lawrence Fink, creator of the MBS (Mortgage Backed Security), is CEO.

Black Rock has inaugurated the euphemistic term "opacity" to refer to entities that you cannot really know, and you cannot observe with absolute clarity how the money is handled. The euphemistic term "opaque" entities goes together with "creative accounting" or "toxic assets" not to use the straight forward terms such as money laundering, thieves in white gloves, professional con men, rotten commodities, etc., terms that would perfectly well fit these activities.

Other entities that show the tendency to decomposition of economy are the so-called "dark pools", kind of black holes that suck up operations at dazzling speed and keep on reducing space for the once-predominant New York Stock Exchange and are now turning into its major jeopardy since its foundation in 1792. Since the "dot.com" bubble in the year 2000, Wall Street has been shrinking and Dow Jones 30 had to try hard before overcoming the 10 000 percentage points.

Since the beginning of the 2007 crisis the latest important Dow Jones marks the 13 000 in May 2008 but this is still very far away from the 14.150 points in October 2007. What is so striking is that the rivals who are ousting Dow Jones are not the New York Stock Exchange, or the London or Sao Paulo or the Malaysian or that of Beijing. This is the produce of the Dark Pools, headed by a generation of young, agile, the new "yuppies" who offer the great banks and the speculative funds advantages over the common institutional investors who used to be very popular during the globalization of the 80's and 90's.

Now, these dark pools are in fashion largely because they are practically invisible for regulators, those who control these activities and let alone those who propose the "Tobin rate", a sort of tax on world speculative operations. The Dark Pools have stealthy and refined gamblers allowing for great-block dealers to work with the speed of light and have already caused discussion and controversies in SEC (Securities & Exchange Commission) that is the federal commission of values regulating financial activities.

This has caused changes in speculative activities that prove the high degree of decay of capitalism. Only 35% of the daily transactions in New York are actually carried out in the traditional Stock Exchange, while 5 years ago and before the bailouts it used to be 75%. At present speculating by electronic dark pools is the favourite for most even if in a defensive movement against the black holes, NYSE established alliance with European panels and established the NYSE/Euronext panel.

The way that capitalist system tends towards decomposition can also be observed in the way that the hedge funds and the CEOs, a caste of parasitical millionaires who made 253 billion in the year 2009, establishing a new record for industry. Hedge funds sharpen social unevenness and their investors are required funds to produce sums between $ 500 billion and $ 3 trillion. After the bailouts they still spawn enormous speculative hazards, cheating millions of people and seeking for a way to evade taxes legally.

That is why after the bailouts scandals, swindles, usurpations and embezzlements accrue and expose all the distress, excrescence and the high degree of decomposition that world capitalism is going through now. On 12 December 2008, financial scandal perpetrated by American finances Bernard Madoff, who used to be the chairman of Nasdaq of New York. In the USA, in 2008, $18 billion in bonds were issued. If we regard the entire world economy, the estimate will show that by 2010, bankers entitled themselves to some $40 billion in bonds.

Hot on the heels of reports on Geithner for deviating funds for bailing out AIG to the French bank Societé Generale and to Wall Street such as Goldman Sachs, Merryl Lynch, Barclays and Bank of America. Madoff, who was sentenced to 150 years in jail, there came those against Madoff. There were also reports on JP Morgan Chase and UBS for frauds committed in the "warranted investment contracts" that states, communes and school districts perceived. The multimillionaire investment banks did not hesitate at double-crossing states, municipalities and educational institutions paying lower interests to these entities.

Scandals about financial fraud of the pyramidal kind accrued four times over in 2009. The quantity of criminal deceptions grew from 40 in 2008 to 150 in 2009. The analysis of the files of the district attorneys and of the FBI, apart from civil and penal court actions at state and federal level show that in 2009 there had been swindles of all kinds, from the criminal deception against international for $7 billion, organized by the executive Allen Stanford down to swindling of $1.2 billion orchestrated by the lawyer Scott Rothstein.

The explosion of unlawful proceedings such as smuggling, drug dealing, trafficking of weapons, etc also constitute part of these signals of decomposition that operate together with elements of fraud that come together with the bailouts. All the tendencies towards a solution of the crisis, such as the overcoming of it are combined with and influenced by many of the symptoms that express the problems with economy and affect it, such as the paralysis of credit or the generalized bankruptcies of companies and estates.

3) Crisis of money, of credit, and generalized bankruptcy of companies and states

As we could see in Chapter I, the process of circulation, money and credit system suffered consecutive collapses. As Marx had said, *"This perturbation and standstill paralyses the functioning of money as means of payments, function granted simultaneously with the development of capital and based on such relations as foreseeing the prices interrupt the chain of obligations of payment at determined periods..."* (6)

But ever since the 80´s, capitalism increasingly depends on financial scope, on credit and especially credit for consumption. The credit crisis is the key issue because, apart from being one of the fundamental institutions of capitalism in this era, it has also been the privileged tool to which capitalism has been resorting in the last decades to achieve growth of GDP. A situation where money proves to be increasingly "paralyzed in its function", as Marx put it, its absence occurs due to permanent interruptions in the flows of capitals.

Bailouts are meant to restore the flow of capitals, but as the investment process does not depend merely and solely on economic factors but also on political ones, what the "bailouts" achieve is a partial, precarious recovery that prepares a new crisis. The interruption of the flows of capitals and money is intimately related to the crisis of credit. The crisis of credit is the outcome of the tremendous impact produced by devaluation and debasement suffered by this activity that reached its zenith during the crisis of the "second class" mortgages but that has been developing as the main tool for development of economy for the past 25 years.

Banks find it increasingly difficult to lay their hands on money and bailouts are practically their fundamental source of income. There is a moment when attempts at upholding amplified reproduction by means of successive bailouts and injections of money halt all credit expansion because banks no longer concentrate on granting credits as this activity is no longer profitable at determined segments. At the same time, fear of bankruptcy prevents banks that dominate over world economy from lending to each other and as soon as the circle of credits is closed, all the wrong investments or overvalued assets begin to surface.

As soon as the growth of the circulation of fictitious capital begins to slow down, stops or begins to decrease, the credit pyramid also decreases and it is then that the bailouts and the direct purchase of bonds and assets by the Central Banks are only a temporary patch to avoid the collapse and postpones the outbreak but does not solve the crisis. Once the chain of payments snapped inside the USA due to the crisis of the sub-prime, the thing spread to the entire world. The unpaid credits together with the slump in the tax revenue and the increase of the deficits of the governments and the bailouts lead to the devaluation of currency and masses of capital.

Once this point of economic emergency is reached, unless capitalism manages to smash workers' resistance and so modify the relation between the classes qualitatively, they must keep on patching up and issuing more money and wait and see. The banks and investment funds that placed the sub-prime bonds of the "real estate boom" on global financial markets belong - through endless communicating vessels – to the same groups that control the Federal Reserve and the Treasury of the USA apart from being associated to the risk rating agents and the

Multinational Corporations who concentrate financial information throughout the world.

By means of the bailouts, the State backed financial speculation allowing the network and all the private banks that are part of the Federal Reserve to act as a borrowing supra-entity that handles a billionaires fund oriented to do business after the 2007 collapse in the USA. This is the monetary expression within the banking scope and capital flows, of the increasing overlapping of the international corporations with the states of the G7. The same process is used in the underdeveloped countries where capitalist governments reproduce the same schema. Using public money in order to bail out banks and private companies and this adds the economies of the underdeveloped countries to the world speculative bubble.

As the Wall Street Journal points out. *"The governments of the world are injecting money into their economies at a tremendous speed. Because companies cannot invest thousands of millions of dollars in such a short period of time, funds have begun to reach financial markets. Some investors are beginning to talk of a 'bailout bubble' on certain markets"*.

That is why this process of crisis of money, credit and loans – inasmuch as the crisis is not solved – will continue perturbing the process of amplified capitalist reproduction. According to Marx, *"... within determined terms they become intensified even by the consequent collapse of credit system developed simultaneously with the capital, and so lead to violent and sharp crises, sudden forced devaluation and stagnation and real obstacle for the process of reproduction as well as effective decline of reproduction."* (7)

Financial indicators are so distorted that the rates of interest that should not be at 0% but at -5% according to reports of San Francisco Fed. Credit for consumer is reduced where world sectors of lower income, whose restrictions accrue, come into account and this becomes manifest in slumping consumption in some segments of the population and affects the possibilities of a solid economic recovery.

Credit risk rating agencies such as S&P, Moody's Investor Service and Ritch Ratings, who gave excellent marks to values that they declared secure but were not so and yet – in spite of their lies – earned millions of dollars. Moody's, for example, made a profit of $ 3 billion between 2002 and 2005 for rating values based on mortgage loans. The same goes for other risk assessors who gained multimillionaire figures by telling blatant lies about the reality of companies they assessed.

The End of the Corporations

The money crisis expresses that the mass of bank notes circulating round the world are suffering permanent devaluation due to bailouts. For USA, devaluation of their currency is the outcome of emission of currency without the gold backing and that is why the bail outs are a brutal and persistent devaluation of dollar. On the other hand, EU currency moored to the euro and the euro zone countries must have plenty of money in their central banks if they are to remain in the euro zone. In order to accumulate reserves in their central banks, these countries must receive endless loans and apply strict adjustments to their expenditures.

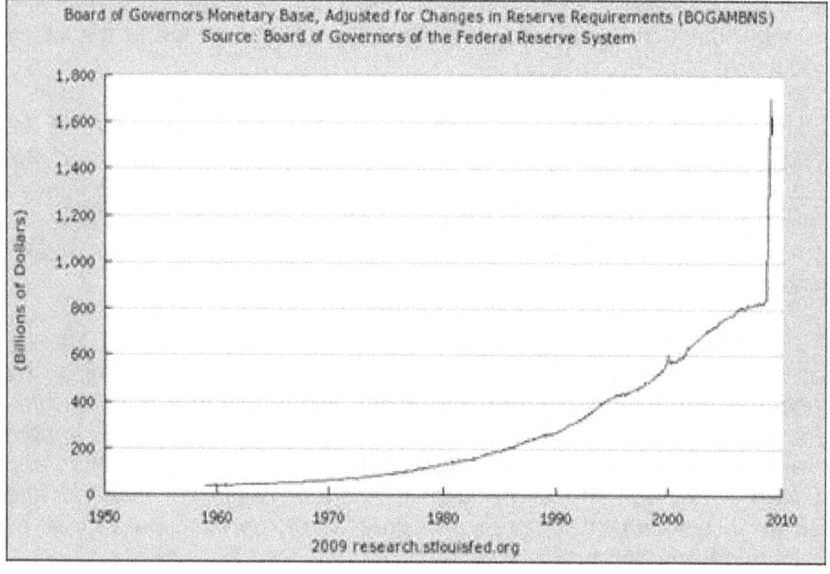

The graph shows the evolution of monetary mass in the USA leaping forward with the bailouts. Source: Federal Reserve of the USA

The crisis of the euro expresses the contradictions of European capitalism. As we have seen in chapter 1, Europe is a complex of countries with very uneven economies, dominated by Germany and France, where decadent powers, such as Greece, Portugal or Spain and very underdeveloped economies – such as those in the East.

The money crisis in the EU can become manifest in the fact that if the plans of adjustment in the underdeveloped or poor countries fail, convertibility with the Euro snaps and the old and devaluated local currencies come back into use.

Generalization of bankruptcies

Together with the crisis of money and credit, a process of bankruptcies was also detonated: it started in 2007 but it is still on the increase and engulfs not only banks but also companies and states. Alongside with the development of the bank bankruptcies the process of purchase of bank shares blooms. In 2010, the FDIC (Federal Deposit Insurance Corp.) took over 118 banks and, in 2010 the pace of bankruptcies of financial entities was greater than that of 2008.

The 2009 bankruptcies cost the FDIC nearly $ 30 billion and it has been estimated that between 2010 and 2015 they will have to disburse further $ 60 billion intervening in financial entities, because the list of bankrupt banks is still growing. Countless banks have been engulfed by the FDIC such as in the case of Butler Bank of Lowell of Massachusetts, the Lakeside Community Bank of Sterling Heights in Michigan, the Innovate Bank of Oakland in California, the City Bank of Lynnwood in Washington, Transpais Bank of San Rafael, the First Federal Bank of North Florida, the American First Bank (90, 5 million) and the Riverside Bank to mention just a few of them.

Bankruptcies of companies also accrue: according to The Economist of 6/9, 20251 companies went bankrupt, a 52% increase compared to an equal period in the previous year, with some resounding examples such as the film studio Metro-Goldwyn Mayer (MGM) of the Blockbuster chain. Also in 2010, CIT, the American financial group specialized in loans for small enterprises, being the 5th top bankruptcy in the history of the USA after the Lehman Brothers (2008) Washington Mutual (2008), Washington Mutual (2008), WorldCom (2002), and General Motors (2008).

Together with the bankruptcies of enterprises, states also begin to go bankrupt including countries, provinces, townships, counties and all kinds of national and local administrations. Among the most outstanding ones we can find the bankruptcy of the Holding Dubai World of the city-state of Dubai and in charge of some of the mammoth estate projects that this city-state had undertaken.

Dubai declared default of their nearly $ 22 billion debt, which triggered off the unpaid insurance prices of the sovereign Dubai debt. Standard & Poor's and Moody's diminished the ratings of 6 estate-owned enterprises down to the level of junk bonds and placed the entire debt of the city state at $ 80 billion.

Dubai world is the main financial and commercial centre in the Middle East and its crisis affected 4 British banks: Royal Bank of Scotland, HSBC, Standard Chartered and Lloyds as well as Emirates NBD and First Gulf Bank of Dubai, Barclays, NPB Paribas and several Asiatic banks. The government of Dubai stated that they would not warrant the debts of the conglomerate, whose total commitments were assessed at $ 59 billion and constitute an important part of the total debt of the emirate $ 50 billion will be due between 2011 and 2013.

Bankruptcies are now engulfing European states and have unleashed serious crises in Greece, Ukraine and Portugal. According to data of the Fiscal Affairs of the IMF, by 2014, the accumulated debt of developed countries of the G20 will have reached an average of 118% of the GDP. If the aim were to reduce the debt by 60% by 2030, next year adjustment should be 8 points of the GDP, and such level of the public debt has not been registered in times of peace and only surpassed by what was registered in the immediate aftermath of II World War.

Bailouts caused a leap forward in indebtedness of states and fiscal deficits. Public debt of USA, for example, changed from 40% to 100% of their GDP while the public debt of Japan has reached 250% of their GDP. Instead of "wiping" their irrecoverable "toxic assets" off their balance sheets, banks incorporated new assets, now in the shape of public deeds. In Europe, the banks with the greatest proportion of irrecoverable credits are the German, French and Spanish ones; the toxic assets" of the German banks reach thousands of millions of euros.

The volume of banks' "toxic assets" and short or mid-term financing of short term debt contracted, which means that the crisis became more serious and affected Central Banks. What the gigantic injection of funds provided by the bail outs really stood for was a tremendous injection of credit, which paradoxically annihilated credit globally. This level of debts made the prices of insurance papers for debt soar sky- high.

For example, in EU before the crisis, credit default swaps (CDS) Germany as well as in Spain, Ireland or Greece oscillated about 15 points. By 2009, Greek CDS stood at 180 points; Spanish at 82; Irish at 150 points and German at 22. Each point of those that measure CDS means insuring $10 million and implifes a cost of $1000 a year. In the case of Germany, this meant $ 22 000 as compared to 180 0000 of Greece.

Unlike what used to be habitual in crises, the process of the crisis of foreign debt is getting inverted. In the 80s, when this process began, it would hit the "Third World" countries, but after the "bailouts", the tendency is for the debt crisis to hit the developed countries harder and in a more generalized manner than the underdeveloped. "At present, Eastern Europe is like Latin America in the 2000," admits Eduardo Ley-Yeyati of Barclays Capital.

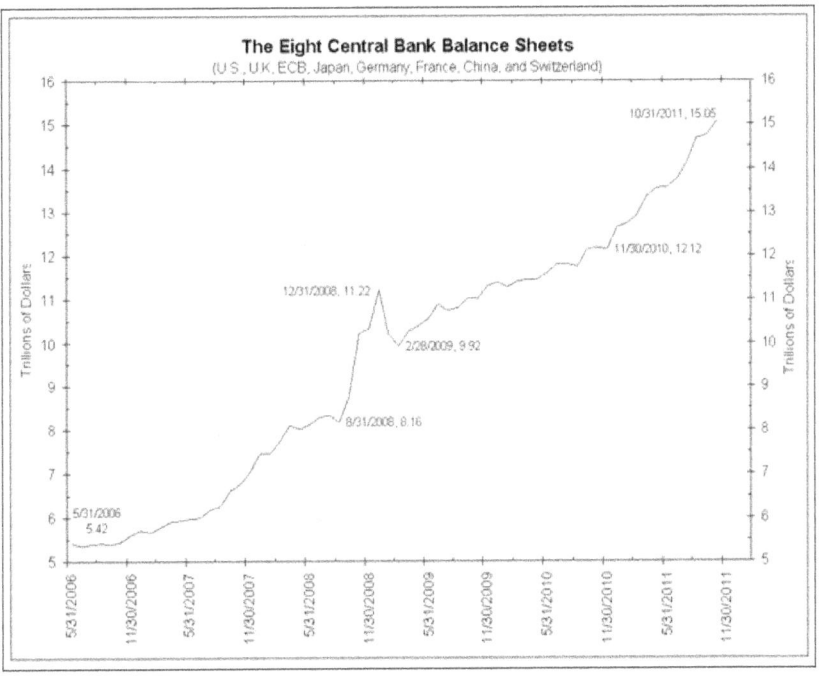

The graph shows the evolution of the 8 Central Banks. From 2007, the beginning of the crisis, the balance sheet was trebled due to bailouts. Source: ritholtz.com

But all through 2010, World banks have been buying masses of public debt papers for $1.1 billion, and this causes two tendencies: one is towards increasingly brutal adjustments against workers and people to pay off the debts emitted by bankrupt states; the other is a wave of bankruptcies of great banks according to some of these economies declare default. That is why the cuts and adjustments become tougher, leaving millions of people without any social aid. California must reduce expenditures by $19 billion, an amount similar to the joint amount of Greece, Portugal, Ireland, Hungary and Rumania.

The crisis in Greece can be regarded as an example of the development of these tendencies on one hand and on the other hand, the brutal adjustments and the dismantling of all achievements by the Greek administration, an on the other hand the process of speculation thriving around the papers of the Greek debt and the corresponding denunciations of corruption in the ladling of these papers., above all in the Goldman Sachs investment bank. Of course, it is the administrations of the G7 states that stand behind these new manipulations of debts of countries in trouble.

In Europe, for example, the Central Bank of Europe (ECB) has placed unlimited funds at an interest rate of 1% at disposal of capitals and so has the Fed at 0%. The same problem is developing in countries such as Ireland, Portugal, Spain and Eastern Europe, such as Hungary and Ukraine. And it is beginning to develop in some countries of the G7, such as Italy and England.

Imperialist countries are not free from these tendencies. And even if USA is broke – just because it is the state that dominates over world economy – it can go on emitting indefinite amount of paper bank notes and never declare bankruptcy. In a speech of his titled "Deflation: how to make sure it does not happen", the manager of the most important bank in the world, Ben Bernanke put it very simply as follows, *""The government of the USA have some technology called printing machine that allows them to produce as many American dollars as they please and essentially with no cost at all."*

Even if USA as a national state does not declare bankruptcy, the insolvency is being declared by the constituent states and this becomes very strong downwards as the situation of municipalities and counties is studied, just as we saw in Chapter 1. California's deficit has accrued up to $ 40 billion and this led to printing promissory notes to satisfy the debts of the state with the tax-payers – private and companies. Even if it is not officially declared, California is a bankrupt, the same as New Jersey, one of the richest states in the USA, where the governor has declared a state "of Fiscal Emergency".

4) Permanence and institutionalization of bailouts: Bailouts are credits. The G7 administrations make use of injections of credit into economy and this is a latent and constant tendency inasmuch as world economy cannot overcome the crisis. And they constitute the fundamental strategy of the USA and the states that dominate in capitalist world economy to palliate the crisis.

At the round table of the magazine Barron's of 2010, the CEO Felix Zulauf of Zulauf Asset Management expressed it as follows: *"Governments and Central Banks are injecting money into the global economy. We do not know what the real situation of economy would be without this help."* What we understand by bailouts is all kinds of credit and creation of fictitious capital meant to uphold bankrupt companies, states and banks that dominate world economy, especially multinational corporations. This means that bailout have various mechanisms.

The following can be grouped as bailouts:

1) The QE, or the gigantic emissions of money by Federal Reserve of the USA or other Central Banks or international organisms of credit as well as bailout packets promulgated by law or by decree of any of the governments;

2) Such variants as swaps of bonds via primary dealers of the Federal Reserve (8) or other variants of obtaining money from different informal windows making economic packets voted by the Parliaments unnecessary;

3) The massive injections of money destined for credit, known as "stimulus": these are operations with low rates of interest for the loans of Fed to The European Central Bank or other Central Banks, the swapping of bonds and different kinds of credit such as the injection of billions to stimulate economy, as in the case of "operation Twist" in the USA or the loans for housing or the lowering of legal banking reserve as in the case of China.

4) Purchase of shareholder packets of multinational corporations and great enterprises or national monopolies by capitalist governments in the First World as well as in the Third World. These are the so-called "nationalizations" or expropriations by economic agents and governments, but actually are nothing but coordinated action of states and banks to defend private property and multinationals.

In Latin America as well as in the Asiatic southeast and all the remaining underdeveloped countries, technically speaking there are no bailouts, because they are not head offices of the multinationals. Consequently the states of these countries do not rush out to help the multinationals directly the way the G7 states do. However they do act indirectly, for the purchase of shareholder packets of companies means state contribution of the governments of capitalist underdeveloped countries to facilitate the arrival of the investments of the multinationals.

Deceitful effect of bailouts

At first, bailouts were unanimously supported by the population that, in view of the gravity of the crisis, actively supported fast and blunt actions of governments willing to halt it. But after the initial enthusiasm, the population of all the countries began to feel disappointed and regarded the bailout packets granted to the corporations while their own problems kept on getting worse and worse and bankers´ and great entrepreneurs´ fortunes accrued.

Since those days, the bailouts policy became more consolidated and diversified. Since the beginning of the sub-prime crisis in the mid-2007, the aggregate balance sheet of the top 8 Central Banks shifted from slightly over $ 5 trillion onto over $16 trillion. Four years ago, the balance sheet of the top 8 Central Banks represented 10% of world's markets but after the bailouts it now stands for about 1/3 of the assets of Worlds' Exchanges. Different theories surfaced and have been hatched since then in relation to the role of states in economy.

After decades when analysts and governments of the world alike repulsed state intervention in economy, massive intervention by means of bailouts gave the impression that the G7 administrations have turned "state-lovers" and so forsaken the "privates" values pertaining to globalization.

Different trends of opinion are talking about "back to Keynesianism" or state interventionism aimed against globalization. In the G7 countries, governments buy packets of shares of the great banks and enterprises in the name of "defence of jobs", such as the case of General Motors and call this nationalization and stratification.

The governments of underdeveloped countries also carry out purchases of packets of shares of strategic importance: food or energy and these measures are also dubbed "nationalizations" This purchase of packets of shares of enterprises is regarded by many analysts as the verification of the "Theory of Uncoupling". According to this theory, the world is shifting towards a kind of "uncoupling" of countries from American domination because the "hegemony of the USA" is said to be recoiling and the BRICS (Brazil, Russia, China, India and South Africa) – or some of these countries are said to occupy their place.

According to this theory underdeveloped countries are splitting away from the domination of the USA and the G7. Partial "nationalizations" are regarded as a confirmation of this tendency. The Uncoupling Theory poses the end of dollar as currency and the beginning of a basket of currencies to replace it. Some variants of this theory even insist that China is to become the new "empire" to rule over the world.

All those premises and theories are based on real facts of life for all the capitalist countries in their effort to halt the crisis have been practicing state interventions at a rate rarely seen before. On January 27th, James Bianco, of the investment analyst firm, Bianco Research LLC, wrote as follows: *"The degree up to which Central Banks of the entire world are printing money has no precedents... Central Banks are governing markets to an extent never seen by this generation. Collectively, money is printed up to a degree never seen by human race."*

However, nothing is farther from truth than saying that bailouts stand for uncoupling or that they mean the emergence of new states that will dominate world economy instead of the USA, or that they anticipate tendencies where governments will take measures against the multinationals or a new wave of "nationalizations" that will foretell the return to a Keynesian regime. There is no fact of real life that will indicate this.

Far from the deceitful effect, bailouts appear as a mirage that the facts of life soon belie. All the data of economy indicate that the policy of bailouts has reasserted the hegemony of the USA has aligned all the capitalist governments with a common policy under their supremacy and has caused a world-wide wave of privatizations of a magnitude superior to that of the 90's.

The difference between that privatizing wave and the present-day one is that the epicenter of privatizations today is not in the underdeveloped countries but, for the first time in history, the crest of this wave is sweeping the G7 countries, essentially the USA, who is now the world leader in privatizations.

In 2009, the total amount spawned by the sale of public companies broke another record with $256 billion, which made the USA the most privatizing country for the first time in history. The key is TARP because the mass of capital offered to the investing banks valued the purchase of assets of public companies.

Second on the list of privatizations is the EU for there is a rarely seen before privatizing wave sweeping across Spain, Portugal, Ireland, Greece, etc. We shall mention just a few Third World examples so as not to overwhelm the reader with data. In underdeveloped countries the tendency is to use part of the state-owned funds - which ought to be used for health, education or old-age pensions – to buy shares of companies.

The End of the Corporations

These measures allow the multinationals to save on expenditures for personnel, debts and investments for which now the states of the underdeveloped countries are liable and in this way somehow improve their own balance sheets.

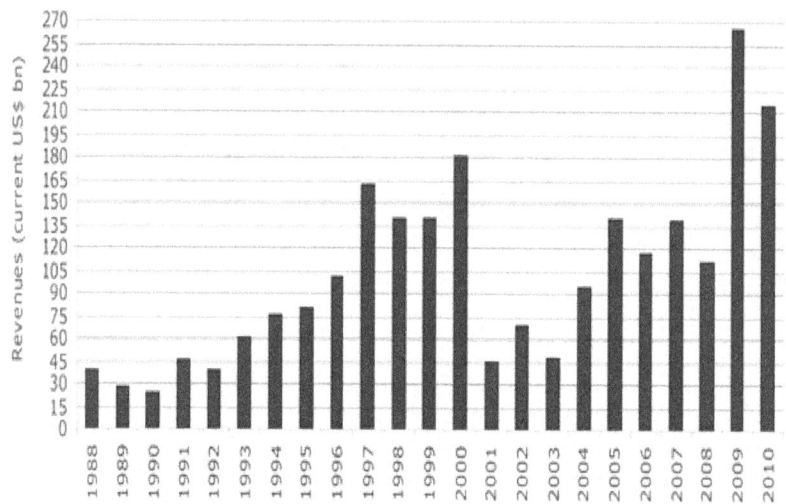

Figure 1. Worldwide Revenues from Privatizations 1988 - 2010

Source: *Privatization Barometer*

The graph shows the tremendous leap in privatizations in the World in 2009 and 2010, due to bailouts and measures taken by the governments in underdeveloped countries. State interventions, far from being nationalizations, have caused a wave of privatizations, the rates of which double or treble those of the 90s.

The conclusion is that the purchase of shares by the governments of Third World countries, far from being nationalizations, is merely a set of measures that are complementary to the bailouts of capitalist governments of the G7 countries. And the data related to the outcome of the bailouts bluntly belie that the measures of the capitalist governments in the developed countries as well as in the Third World, may mean anything different to the privatizing wave of the 90's.

They also belie the assertion that these measures stand for anything like uncoupling from American hegemony or that the purchase of shares may deeply affect the interests of the multinationals. The contrary is true. Bailouts make the deepest tendencies towards privatization and concentration of branches of production and trade in the hands of the same economic groups that spawned the crisis.

Bailouts do not only continue but they also tend to become institutionalized as the creation of FEEF o MEDE seems to indicate, of the supervision offices TARP in the USA. The surfacing of supranational entities that decide about the fate of the billionaire funds, which in turn decide about the lives of millions of people in Europe, the USA, Japan or developing countries, they are the institutional expression of the so-far privileged political strategy used by the G7 administrations and states.

Bailouts produce an impact on the awareness of millions

Due to its magnitude of historic character, bailouts have caused an enormous impact on the awareness of millions just as important as all the transcendental events, such as the Great Depression, world wars, the Russian Revolution, the fall of the Berlin Wall or the fall of the Twin Towers. Bailouts expose what for decades has been concealed to the eyes of millions: the contribution and support of imperialist states have been the base for the development of capitalism ever since II World War. Bailouts expose the lies about the existence of "democracy" in the USA.

The same financial oligarchy that dominates over world economy is perfectly represented in both parties: Democrat and Republican, both of them consist of patrician families, veritable dynasties of multimillionaires who interpret the needs of the world dominating class perfectly. As a rule, the careers the professional politicians are financed by the multinationals so as to control the oligarchic two-party political system of the USA. Now millions of Americans, Europeans and inhabitants of the Third World can now clearly perceive the governments of the richest countries rushing to the aid of the capitalist system.

That is why the bailouts are the end of the "American Dream", the end of the dream of social ascent, while poverty and destitution spread relentlessly. Capitalist state so far favoured the rich and the powerful in a veiled and discreet way but now, with the bailouts these contributions have become shamelessly public. They stand for the end of the propaganda for "triumph of capitalism" and "failure of socialism".

Today, 43% under 30-years old have poor opinion of capitalism and such minorities as Negroes and Latinos react positively to socialism at an even wider scope within the entire American territory. Bailouts make the younger generations associate the word capitalism with injustice, unemployment, poverty, loss of right and future. This represents the end of the propaganda of the "triumph of capitalism" and "failure of socialism".

Bailouts are an irrational immorality that can only be explained by the decadence of the dominating oligarchy of the world capitalist economy. Considering that world famine will earmark barely 1% of what has been contributed by the governments to bail the multinationals out. Bailouts cause outrage among millions because they take place while governments apply cuts to wages and jobs. Bailouts impose capital's harsh conditions on millions of humble people around the world and at the same time they affect their awareness showing them the crudest spectacle possible: that of politicians, even those considered to be "progressive" and "liberal", working brazen-facedly for the corporations, desperately trying to maintain capitalist order shaken by contradictions.

We, the Marxists, know that the definite solution will not come from bailouts; these constitute the policy that the great states that prevail over capitalist economy put into practice as a result of the little room that world political situation leaves free for them. We shall see if the imperialist states manage to achieve other room to provide a solution to the crisis. As long as they have not yet achieved this goal, their central strategy will continue being that of the bailouts.

But as soon as they find that different relationship of forces may be feasible all over the world, capitalist governments will appeal to other solutions to the crisis. Are there other ways for capitalism to get out of the crisis? Actually there are. In order to become acquainted with them we must begin to sink our analyses in previous significant crises suffered by capitalism throughout history. Our analysis will begin by studying the '29 crisis and we shall analyse its nature and development in the next chapter.

Notes

(1) Report on World Wealth Boston Consulting Group (BCG) 2000

(2) Leon Trotsky – Revolution betrayed – Chapter IX What is the USSR

(3) PA Consulting Group "Zombie Economy: leadership in uncertainly times"

(4) Karl Marx: El Capital, Book III, Chapter. XV. Internal contradictions law development.

(5) Karl Marx: El Capital, Book III, Chapter. XV Internal contradictions law development.

(6) Karl Marx: Capital, Book III, Chapter. XVInternal contradictions law development

(7) Karl Marx: Capital, Book III, Chapter. XV Internal contradictions law development

The End of the Corporations

(8) The "primary dealers" are the banks that trade in bonds of the USA Treasury in the world. They are: Bank of Nova Scotia, New York Agency, BMO Capital Markets Corp, BNP Paribas Securities Corp, Barclays Capital Inc., Cantor Fitzgerald & Co, Citigroup Global Markets Inc., Credit Suisse Securities (USA) LLC, Daiwa Capital Markets America Inc., Deutsche Bank Securities Inc., Goldman Sachs & Co, HSBC Securities Inc. Jefferies & Company Inc., J.P. Morgan Securities LLC, Merrill Lynch, Pierce, Fenner & Smith Incorporated, Mizuho Securities USA Inc., Morgan Stanley & Co. LLC, Nomura Securities International, Inc., RBC Capital Markets LLC, RBS Securities Inc., SG Americas Securities

The End of the Corporations

The End of Corporations

A Marxist explanation to the capitalist world economic crisis

CHAPTER III
1929 & 2007

The End of the Corporations

CHAPTER III: 1929 & 2007

"Since 1948, capitalist production became increasingly rooted in Germany and now it has already transformed this country of dreamers into a nation of swindlers"

Karl Marx, The Capital, Tome I Preface to first German edition

Any observer of this grave crisis in world economy may wonder why this has happened. What has spawned it? Is it like that of 1929 or is it superior to it? Can capitalism find a solution to it? It is important to pinpoint similitude and differences between the current crisis and that of 29 and so be able to respond to those simple questions that have complicated answers. The first answer is that both crises are the outcome of a long stage of decadence of capitalism that we dub imperialism, which started in 1903 and is more than a century old now.

Capitalism began its ascent and the battle to displace feudalism in the XIV century and stemmed out of the depletion of the feudal mode of production, 7 centuries ago. The imperialist stage includes the last phase of its existence and together with this, the two most important crises that capitalism had to face: that of 1929 and the current one so it is not useless; it is meant to go in quest of comprehension of the changes that took place in the capitalist system between both crises.

In this chapter we'll see the concept of Forms of Accumulation, Regime of Accumulation, Pole of Accumulation and Axis of Accumulation. Let us have a look at some comparative data: in '29, economy fell 33%. In the current crisis the fall is similar – it also oscillates round 33%. As for commerce, in '29 it fell 66% while during this current crisis the fall is slightly more significant: the average is 69%. As for the volume of financial assets in relation to GDP, in '29 financial assets doubled the GDP while in the current crisis financial assets quadrupled world GDP.

This is the way John Kenneth Galbraith, American economist and a scholar of the 1929 crisis, described the beginning of the crisis in his book published in 1954 "The Great Crack": *"At eleven o'clock in the morning, the market had degenerated into a wild and crazy crowd of vendors. Inside the halls with indicators installed throughout the country, the ticker informed the terrified and huddling spectators that a dreadful collapse was taking place."*

There is a myth about the immense majority of American population participated in the Stock Exchange. Galbraith refutes this fact. He estimates the total amount of participants as under a million in a total 120 inhabitants, which stands for less than 1% of the population of the country participating in the "speculative" festival. The issue of *"everybody is nowhere near the truth...At any rate, purchasing securities on instalments was an event as far away from real life of the mass of the population as gambling in Monte Carlo Casino"* **(1)**

There are elements that allow us to establish analogies between the 1929 crisis and the current one. For example, both crises were preceded by a spectacular speculative development in the real estate sector. In the current crisis, it was the sub-prime bubble of the housing credit that developed between 2002 and 2006; in the '29 real estate bubble the state it was the '29 real estate bubble of Florida that swelled between 1925 and 1929.

Galbraith mentions the participation of Carlo Ponzi, well-known creator of the scheme that bears his name, as a kind of pyramidal economic fraud in the sale and purchase of land near Jacksonville (Florida).

Precisely, swindling was another analogous element: the existence of numerous frauds in 1929 was verified just as in the 2007 crisis spawned a great number of crooks as is the case of the financial scandal perpetrated by the American financier, Bernard Madoff, ex president of the New York Nasdaq index that also put into practice the classical Ponzi scheme.

Another element of this analogy is that both crises had their epicentre at the New York Stock Exchange. There was cheap credit and high profit on the stock exchange in 1929. This led many American and foreign investors in the USA and in the world obtained credit to speculate on Wall Street at Wall Street.

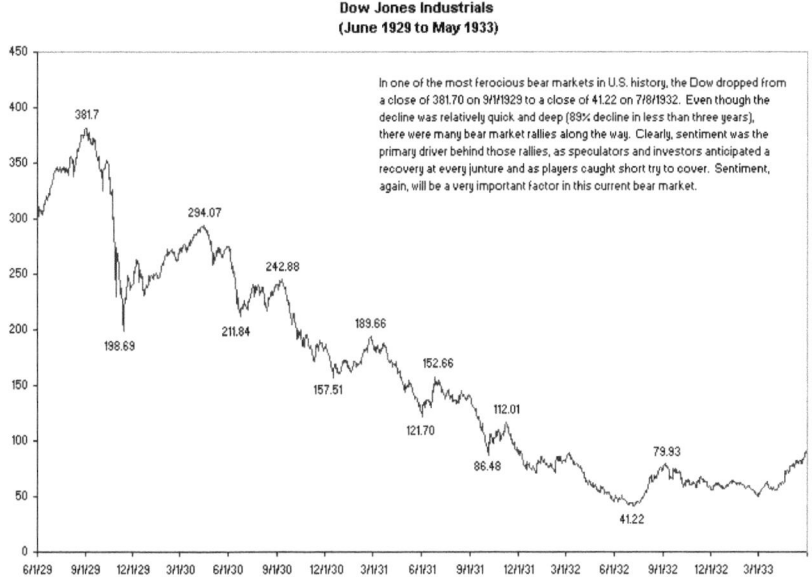

The graph shows the fall of the industrial Dow Jones as from the beginning of the crisis in 1929 until 1933. Source: Market Thoughts LLC

A powerful flow of capitals from Montreal, London, Shanghai, Hong Kong and other capitals set off towards New York and the average PER (Price to Earnings Ratio). The price of shares above the value of the company was 32.6 points in September 1929, a similar range in historic terms to August 2007 PER which stationed at 28.5 points. Another common element between both crises is the absolute state of bewilderment of economists, officials and rulers as to the diagnosis and he course of the crisis, also observed in 2007.

In 1929 reputable voices claimed that there would be no depression of economy. Among them there was the President of the USA, Herbert Hoover and the Harvard Economic Society (HES) that grouped some of the main economists of the Harvard University. As late as October 1931 – with depression well advanced – that economic situation would soon get better. But the Great Depression that got unleashed in 1931 mortally wounded the reputation of infallibility of the HES and it dissolved.

Galbraith was determined to study how far the stock market crash was what spawned the Great Depression of the 30's. The author claims – against the general opinion – that the economic situation in 1929 was extremely weak and the crash was nothing but the detonator of the situation.

The causes of the crisis of '29

What caused the '29 crisis? Galbraith seeks explanations rejecting those he considers useless for the comprehension of the crisis. The first explanation he rejects is that the crash was caused by the facility of obtaining credit. In his opinion financial speculation is the expression of the problems, not their cause. He also rejects the Theory of the Long Waves that explains the crisis referring to the inevitability of economic cycles with consecutive periods of expansion and contraction.

According to Galbraith, the causes of the crisis of 1929 are to be found in the depletion of productive factors in the 20's. This depletion of the productive factors spawned tendencies that caused serious changes in economy: firstly serious social inequity and unfair distribution of revenue which made a third part of American revenue to remain in the hands of 5% of the riches population; secondly there was the structure of monopolies that dominated the economy of that time.

Analysing the holdings and the trusts, Galbraith understood that these companies caused serious maladjustments and perturbations in economy and instead of serving as stabilising factors they benefited speculation and acted as an obstacle for the development of production, *"...American enterprise of the twenties had spread its hospitable arms to an exceptionally vast number of promoters, social climbers, crooks, scammers, impostors and all the wiles. Seldom if ever in the long history of such activities could we witness like a tidal wave of corporative larcenies of such vast proportions".* (2)

Thirdly, Galbraith found that the banking structure in the service of holdings and trusts and financial speculation was favourable to the surfacing of dangerous speculative manoeuvres that caused chain bankruptcies of entities.

In the fourth place, Galbraith discovered that the problem of the growth of the debts of the states, a bad situation of the Balance of Payments which grew and drove the debtor countries to find more and more difficulties to cope with maturities and this was transformed into unpaid debts and bankruptcies.

In the fifth place, Galbraith saw that the measures adopted by the governments and the political orientations of officials and economists were another factor that caused the aggravation of the crisis. *"Economists and all those who offered economic advice during the late twenties and early thirties were as a rule bad economists and perverse advisers. In the months and years that followed the crash at the Stock Exchange, the honourable economic advisers of the professionals loaded their orientation towards the type of measures only meant to make things worse."* (3)

Beyond any political, ideological and methodological differences with Galbraith, including his vision that the policy of officials in the administration and of economists aggravated the crisis due to their scarce knowledge of economy, we must admit that Galbraith sought the explanation not in statistic or superficial data of capitalist economy, such as financial movements or search for "cycles" in the growth rates, or on the production of commodities in trade.

Galbraith sought the answers in the motives that caused the '29 crisis in the study of the structure of the forms of accumulation of production and capital that predominated at that time, trusts, holdings and banks. Galbraith regarded the root of the explanation is rooted in the process of accumulation.

His critical analysis of these enterprises that dominated over world economy in those days and his definition that after an expansion they suffered a process of depletion are the correct methodology to find an explanation of the 1929 crisis and its subsequent development.

Differences between 1929 and 2007. Concepts of Forms of Accumulation, Regime of Accumulation, and Pole of Accumulation

However next to the analogies between the '29 crisis and that of 2007 there are the enormous differences. They are rooted fundamentally firstly in the position where capitalist structure stood in 1929 and then in 2007. The other difference is in the policy applied by capitalist governments that dominated over the world economy in 1929 and in 2007 are absolutely different.

The structure of world capitalist system was absolutely to what we know nowadays. The USA was one of the most important economies in the world, but they did not dominate over the global capitalist economy the way they do now. Great Britain dominated over capitalism for centuries, but at that moment their decadence was already clear and a battle began to settle who would occupy the throne of Great Britain: this was to be settled in the II World war.

That is to say that during the 1929 crisis, the structure of the world capitalist economy offered a panorama of various dominating imperialisms: Great Britain, the USA, Germany and France that contended for the dominance. In the current crisis, however, the structure of world capitalism is absolutely different and is determined by the undisputed predominance and hegemony of American imperialism.

The other substantial difference between 1929 and 2007 is the structure of monopolies, the companies that dominate and settle in the centre of capitalism. ¿What are monopolies? A group of companies that get together to dominate a branch of production, distribution, services of production in a country and act in agreement on prices, targets of production, distribution, services, etc, so as to eliminate competitors.

According to Lenin, *"... they reach an agreement on conditions of sales, terms of payment, etc; they share out the sales market. They determine the amount of product to produce. They determine the prices. They distribute the profits between the different companies, etc."* (4)

The surfacing of monopolies put an end to the stage of "free competition" in capitalism. Through these agreements the enterprises constitute a kind of league or union that allowed them to make headway in the combination of a branch of production in their country while trying to extend this domination to an international level.

These leagues or unions developed as from 1860, essentially in the USA under the names of trusts and in Germany as cartels. In the USA they achieved a central leadership of the magnates such as Mellon, Morgan, Rockefeller, etc.

According to Lenin, the emerging of monopolies went through three moments: *"...1) "1860-1880: the high pitch of the development of free competition. Monopolies are nothing but barely perceptible germs. 2) After the 1873 crisis, a long period of development of cartels, but these still constitute an exception are not solid yet; they still represent a passing phenomenon. 3) Boom in late XIX century and crisis on 1900-*

1903: cartels turn into one of the bases of the entire economic life. Capitalism has turned into imperialism" **(5)**

Monopolies constitute a Form of Accumulation that differs from what capitalism had seen so far. Form of Accumulation is constituted by the companies that use the capitalist class to accumulate capital over a determined period of time. Because there are many sectors of capitalist class, those sectors reflect different Forms of Accumulation that dominate, i.e.: different commercial, productive and financial that are active. But in a whole period of development of capitalism there is always on predominant Form of Accumulation around which the entire economy is structured. Then, we define a Regime of Accumulation a form of functioning of capitalism, around the predominant Form of Accumulation, during a certain time.

As to the monopolies, as we have already seen, even though they have been surfacing since 1860 they have never appeared as dominating Form of Accumulation till the early XX century. Their structure proved to be complex because even if they predominated one branch of production, they are combined enterprises that host several branches because of the domination they acquire over one of them.

This is how Lenin explains it, *"The so-called combination, i.e.: the converging of different branches of industry that by themselves represent either successive phases of the elaboration of some raw material... or else different branches where one acts as an auxiliary of another is an extremely important particularity of capitalism that has reached the peak of its development..."* **(6)**

But even if monopolies are combined enterprises we must never forget that the combination is in the service of the dominion of one branch of production. For example, let us have a look at the metallurgic branch, its cartelization is based on the unionised group of companies agrees on the distribution and advances towards the control of companies that will provide raw material, machinery and supplies, agrees on loans and credits and makes headway towards the control of banks.

That means that the cartel incorporates companies of different branches of production, but with the purpose of controlling a branch. That is why we define monopolies as groups of companies that reach agreements to dominate over a branch of production in a country.

In 1903, when these enterprises became the predominant Form of Accumulation, capitalist system – historically speaking – began its Highest Stage and final one, of decadence. Ever since XIV when

The End of the Corporations

capitalism began its ascent and the battle to displace feudalism and by 1903 it had been through two great stages: 1) primitive accumulation between XIV and XVII and 2) that of boom or apogee, about XVIII and XIX centuries.

Lenin defined that as from 1903," *a third stage had begun and it had 5 features: 1) "Monopolies arise and they settle in the centre of economy and play a decisive role in economic life; 2) Monopolies are the outcome of merging bank capital with industrial capital and this spawns a financial oligarchy; 3) The process of exporting capitals acquires exceptional importance; 4) Monopolies tend to turn international and share out the world among them; 5) The territorial division of the world among the major imperialist powers culminates and the domination of the monopolies and financial capital is established..."* (7)

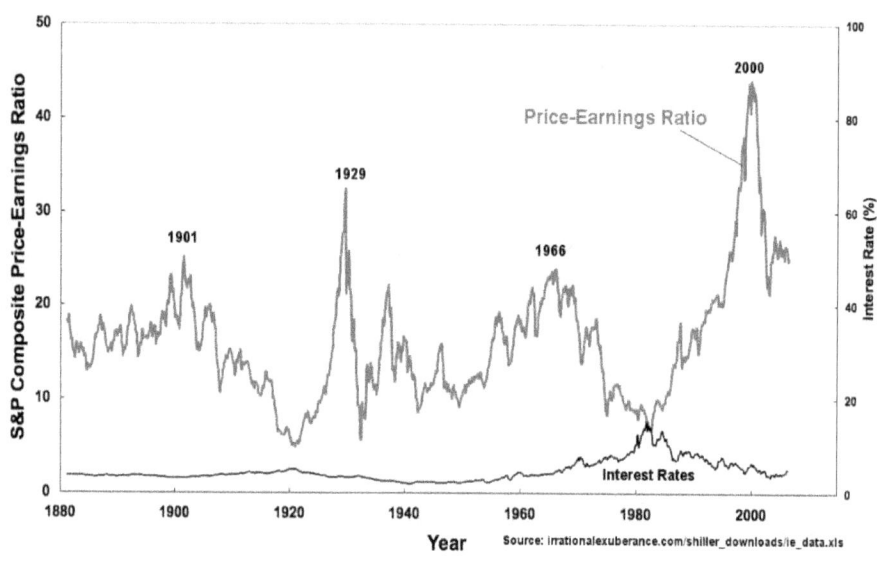

Ratio P/E in the index S&P500 since 1880 - The average PER (Price to Earnings Ratio) of compound shares S&P was 32.6 points in September 1929, a very similar average to the PER of August 2007, about 28.5 points.

Monopolies already tended to be international due to the existence of a capitalist world market, but the scope of its international domination over the branches of production, trade and finances, was still very limited in the early XX century was still very limited.

Some of them had subsidiaries in other countries – in the oil industry, fir example – and they tried to carry out operations for their world expansion. But their world domination had not yet reached the

The End of the Corporations

dimensions that – as we shall see – were reached by the multinationals during the ´post-war or the multinational corporations as from 1980 and 1990, which are superior monopolist forms.

Differences in policies of the capitalist administrations in the 1929 and in 2007

The policy of the Hoover republican administration in the USA in '29 was totally opposed to that of Bush-Obama in the 2007-2008. Hoover and other governments of capitalist powers did not implement bailouts; their policy was to "let the laws of the market work" and so let companies that had to fall, fall. During the first years after the '29 crisis the magnitude of fiscal deficits created to save banks and monopolies was not even similar to what is registered nowadays.

The fiscal deficit in the years '29 was about 2.5% of the GDP, while at present it is never under 20%. Hoover admitted serious problems with American economy but regarded the crisis as something transitory and that it was the local governments who were liable for carrying out the struggle against generalised unemployment and poverty. Capitalist governments refused to interfere with economy to solve the ´29 crisis because they feared this would be counterproductive policy.

In the early 30s, Hoover even dared to forecast that "recovery was round the corner" and he defended that American economy was to recover on its own and this led him to oppose state intervention firmly and he even criticised such European countries as Great Britain and France for adopting measures protecting the unemployed.

His popularity nosedived. Hoover began to implement reforms towards the end of his mandate, but he could not appear in public without getting booed.

Roosevelt and the Democrat Party had a sweeping victory in the presidential elections in November 1932 and the policy of the American government swerved 180°: he launched the policy of New Deal that consisted in stimulating public expenditure by investing in infrastructure, executed all kinds of projects like hydroelectric works roads, schools and in general every kind of public works.

Roosevelt's policy did not save economy from the crisis, but it was vital to contain poverty and unemployment through grants and public works. There is no doubt that leaders of capitalism have learned from 1929.When the current crisis began, the policy – as we have seen in chapter I was totally different: the governments of capitalist powers boosted bailouts and acted in a manner opposite to Hoover's trying to prevent the great companies from going bankrupt and economy from sliding into depression.

Solution to the '29 crisis: enormous destruction of productive forces in the II World War

New Deal did not pull American economy or the world out of the crisis. The contrary is true: between 1937 and 1938 economy suffered a serious relapse, *"Against all the prognoses and efforts to reactivate economy and control stock market, restrict great operations, etc, depression did not end. Instead, since August 1937 till March 1938, there was a 50% relapse on the stock market and unemployment totalled over 10 million..."* (8)

The Great Depression found no solutions in the measures of capitalist governments of those days; it was not the plans of Franklin Delano Roosevelt, or those of Edouard Daladier in France, Or Neville Chamberlain in England, or Hitler in Germany what pulled economy out of the crisis. According to Galvao: *"What put an end to the Great Depression, was not the return to the production for consumption but the resort to unleashing the means of destruction of capital in the II World War. Unemployment was no longer a problem when millions of workers were absorbed by the armed forces and war production."* (9)

The outbreak of the II World War in September 1939 was what began to reactivate economy in the main capitalist countries who invested enormous sums of money in military expenditure. Investments made by states oscillated between $ 260 and $ 339 billion of that time, almost $ 4 to $ 5 trillion by today's standards. The millionaire investments of capitalist governments were an enormous change in the flow of investments since the confection of the war budgets that implied enormous sum for the preparation of the conflict.

These budgets meant plans of adjustments that caused penuries and suffering for the masses because they consisted in cuts in social expenditures and increase of taxes. Just the same, it was all not sufficient for the resources of that day and mot of the countries had to go into heavy debt to afford the expenditure of war. The indebtedness forced governments to emit money without any gold reserve and this spawned strong inflation.

Since 1870, international trade had been functioning with gold standard, i.e.: the issue of gold to settle international transactions and debts as standard value, nations determined the parity of their currency with this standard value. But when countries at war were left with practically no more gold while all but the total amount of it was engaged in purchasing weapons and they began to replace these fixed rates by floating rates, i.e.: the price of the financial transactions and exchange rates were to be determined by the governments in a unilateral manner.

From what was happening in the powers that were getting ready for the war, neutral countries, and net exporters of weaponry or of raw materials and food had their harvest of gold in their reserve. For example, the American gold reserves that by 193 used to have 26% of world gold reserves soared up to 39% in 1918. The powers that were left without gold in their coffers began to use fiduciary money, printing money with no gold backing and this was what caused the great processes of hyperinflations of the nineties – for example Germany and Austria.

The lack of a stable system of payments caused the fall of world trade and pound sterling – which has so far been another reference currency – was being displaced by the dollar. At the same time, within the scope of industrial production, war needs definitely introduced mass production in series techniques as well as other numerous improvements in organisational techniques of industry. Also advertising developed and the fast expansion of advertising and propaganda cartel as means of communication.

Great amount of money was dedicated to research and development of all kinds of weaponry and as an outcome chemical industry made notable headway. The great demand of soldiers as well as their massive death during the war left the new industry in full expansion without labour force. This fact implied the need for women to join heavy industry; their numbers reached over 40% of the total composition of workforce and gave an extraordinary impulse to the movement for the claim for equal rights for women.

In this way, capitalism started on its way towards the solution of the crisis that had started in 1929 by the colossal development of destructive forces of mankind. II World War implied over 199 million of mobilised soldiers, equivalent to almost the entire population of the USA in those days, destruction of cities, infrastructure, concentration camps, the Holocaust, apart from the use – for the first time – of nuclear weapons in a military conflict. The final outcome was between 50 and 70 million casualties between the dead and the wounded.

After six years of war a significant part of Europe was devastates because combats were held on a territory much vaster than what was affected by the I World War. Due to air raid, cities were badly damaged and so were industrial areas that had been the main targets of these bomb raids. Berlin and Warsaw were reduced to heaps of rubble; London and Rotterdam were badly damaged, the economic structure of the continent that for centuries had been the centre of development of capitalism, was reduced to shambles with million of people living in extreme poverty.

In 1944 famine broke out because of the general devastation of farming and a wave of famine swept Holland and then the entire Europe, aggravated by the 1946-1947 relentless winter in the Northeast. After the war danger of starving was very real for millions of people. Scarcity of food was one of the most serious problems for millions of people and the situation became especially harassing in Germany, because between 1946 and 1947 the average daily consumption was of 1800 calories per person, not enough to keep good health on long term.

Supplies of coal diminished enormously. Hundreds of people froze to death in German homes. Railways that were among the main targets or air raids were destroyed and so were bridges and roads. Cargo boats had been sunk; small municipalities were practically isolated physically and economically due to lack of networks.

Due to stagnation of any growth of economies, high rates o unemployment and lack of food strikes and unrest accrued challenging capitalism. Two years after the war economies had not yet recovered pre-war levels and farming production stood at 83% of what it had been in 2038; industrial production reached 88% and exports not more than 59%

Plan Marshall, Keynesian regime and the "boom"

II World War marked the end of an economic period of capitalism characterized by crisis, stagnation and paralyses. But in 1945, after the war, capitalism resumed its march and entered the opposite period, that of great growth with high rates for nearly 30 years. It was known as the "post-war boom" How did capitalism manage to get out of the crisis of 1929 and from there to the boom? Three fundamental changes had been hatching in world capitalist economy and with the end of the II World War they became consolidated and produced the boom. The three changes are the following:

1) The USA imposed their hegemony and became dominant in World economy.

2) Keynesian regime of accumulation surfaced

3) The multinationals emerged as a form of accumulation superior to monopolies but adequate to the monopolist stage of capitalism,

1) Hegemony of the USA and domination of world economy

After the II World War, American imperialism imposed its global hegemony and this is the way Nahuel Moreno explained it: *"... All the old colonial imperialisms reach the end of the war completely destroyed... as from the post-war, the entire capitalist world, including imperialist countries, had to accept American leadership and domination... The logical anti-imperialist rubs cannot change this situation and American hegemony prevails over the capitalist world and its leadership."* (10)

The growth of American hegemony was a trend of economy and of the world political situation of capitalism that had been hatching for several decades. In 1926, Leon Trotsky had anticipated this tendency in the structure of the capitalist world system that was completely modified as since 1945: *"In these last years, the economic shaft of the world has shifted considerably. The relations between the USA and Europe have been radically modified... This evolution had been underway for a long time, there were symptoms indicating it, but not until very recently has it turned into an accomplished fact and now we are trying to work out the meaning of this formidable change in human economy and consequently in human culture... the USA are the owners of the capitalist world"* (11)

In 1945, in the midst of the ruins caused by the II World War, American economy constituted a third of all the exports happening in the world; Americans possessed two thirds of all the existing gold reserves and they produced 550% of all the goods in the world market of manufactured goods. The hegemony and the colossal development of productive forces in the USA was the lifebelt that capitalist economy found in the post-war and the tool for the reconstruction of capitalism.

2) Keynesian regime of accumulation emerges. The concepts of Pole of Accumulation and Axis of Accumulation

The emergence of the Keynesian regime was the other important change together with the hegemony of the USA. As we said, we define a regime of accumulation a form of functioning of capitalism, around the predominant Form of Accumulation, during a certain time. After the Plan Marshall, senile capitalism emerged from the II World War functioning in a very peculiar way, a phase with an uneven and combined development of world economy that we call Keynesian regime of accumulation.

This regime was a way of functioning of the capitalist system or economic formation historically given, also known as "welfare state". It consisted of high salaries, full employment, economic concessions for the toiling masses, social achievements and increase of social wages, plans of public works and a great process of industrialisation all this imitating aspects of the model imposed by Roosevelt in USA as a response to the 1929 crash. Keynesian regime began in the forties, developed in the fifties and sixties and was depleted in the 70´s.

We define Pole of Accumulation as the branch of production and technology, round which all economical regime structured, while we define as Axis of Accumulation, region and countries used by capitalism as a platform for development in a given period. From this point of view, Keynesian regime had the car industry and war industry as pole of accumulation. ¿How and why did the Keynesian emerge? In order to understand the political reasons that spawned the Keynesian regime we must go several years back and analyse the responses that capitalism posed to the '29 crisis.

From the political point of view, capitalism has had two answers to the '29 crisis, at that time the worst crisis of the capitalist system. In the USA the answer was the New Deal while in Germany it was the Nazi regime. Both of these regimes, even if diametrically opposed, had a common denominator: they sought for an answer to the global crisis. While New Deal sought a solution by means of agreements and manoeuvres against workers and their organisations, the Nazi regime sought the same by means of squashing of workers and their organisations, with concentration camps where the most aberrant methods of production in order to optimise the profits of the monopolies and the great companies.

The Nazi regime was due to the defeat of the proletarian revolution in Germany, while in the USA, the New Deal was a defensive regime for the bourgeoisie for the great companies could not defeat it. This is the way Leon Trotsky explained it: *"At present, there are two systems that compete in the world to save the capital...the Fascism and the New Deal. Fascism based its programme on the dissolution of workers' organisations, destruction of social reforms and the total annihilation of democratic rights... New Deal policy, which tries to save imperialist democracy... is only fully accessible to the really rich nations and from this point of view, it is an American policy par excellence."* **(12)**

Wall Street was another common denominator between both political regimes. The great corporations, monopolies and bakers of the USA boosted war industry in order to re-launch economy in Germany as well as in the USA and financed the arrival of Hitler to power. Wall Street financed the development of the industrial monopoly I.G. Farben, which was the basis of the power of the Nazi war machine. This is the way Anthony C. Sutton explains it: *"Without the support of the German industrial cartel, I. G. Farben, Hitler would have continued living as an obscure historic note… Without the capital supplied by Wall Street, there would have not been any I. G: Farben in the first place and almost certainly no Adolf Hitler… The industrial Farben cartel was created by three Wall Street Corporations: Dillon, Read & Co., Harris, Forbes & Co, and National City. The DuPont's, Standard Oil, International Harvester, General Motors and Ford – enterprises controlled by JP Morgan, had facilitated the rearmament of Germany… such enterprises as International Telephone and Telegraph (ITT), General Electric, International Business Machines (IBM), Alcoa and Dow Chemical were also implicated…"* (13)

In September 2004, Toby Rogers, journalist of The Guardian, wrote on the history of the Bush family, *"The grandfather of former president George Bush, senator Prescott Bush, was director and shareholder of companies that benefitted from their commercial relation with the financiers of the Nazi Germany… For decades of public life of the Bush family – American press made great efforts to skip a historic fact – that through the Union Banking Corporation (UBC), Prescott Bush and his brother-in-law, George Herbert Walker, together with the German entrepreneur Fritz Thyssen, financed Adolf Hitler before and during Second World War"* (14)

The Nazis and the Nazi regime were annihilated in the war by the allied armies as a result of a formidable mobilisation of European masses and so they vanished as a possible alternative for capitalism. Meanwhile, Keynesian regime developed in the USA taking advantage of the low salaries and the unemployment among the working class after the depression and got support from new technologies that made the development of mass production for mass consumption.

The impulse of war industry allowed for mass export of tanks, aeroplanes and weapon to allied states and so develops the "military industrial complex" and pole of accumulation pole of accumulation of the Keynesian regime, which was essentially American. But as from the year 1945 – 47, as America became hegemonic in world capitalist economy, this form of functioning of capitalism was internationally set up.

In order for America to impose Keynesian regime for the whole world, it was first necessary to establish international agreements with the retreating powers, such as England and fundamentally they had to agree with Stalin and the CPSU. It would have been impossible to for the USA to initiate a chain of investments that Plan Marshall implied without

The End of the Corporations

agreeing previously with Stalin, because during the war and towards the end of it great revolutionary processes swept across Europe firstly to defeat the Nazis liberate the countries from Nazi-fascism and then to face up against famine and generalised post-war poverty.

Such processes as the Maki resistance in France or the Partisanos of Italy and Yugoslavia would have made it possible for workers to seize power in France and Italy and the Red Army to take over in Berlin and liberate the East of Europe. Communist militants had been part of the leadership and they headed the resistance that made the defeat of the Nazis in most European countries possible. An order from Kremlin would have been enough for Europe to become socialist and that the main European economies like France, Germany and Italy would turn Workers' States, which would have changed the fate of mankind totally.

Source: GMO, Shiller

The evolution of the Standard & Poor's rate 500 since 1881 until the current crisis connected to the most important political and economic events 500 from 1881 up to the current crisis, linked to the most outstanding political and economic events in the history of capitalism. Source: GMO

But the government of the USSR in charge of Stalin and Stalinist bureaucracy, decided to agree with allied powers: the USA and Great Britain and initiate the capitalist reconstruction of Europe. This was one of the greatest treasons of world proletariat and international socialist revolution by Stalin and the bureaucracy that governed the USSR. Stalin agreed with Churchill, representative of the retiring old English imperialism and Roosevelt the president of the USA, representative of emerging imperialist power. This is how the "world order" was born out of the Yalta and Postdam agreements.

As Nahuel Moreno put it: *"... a front is established... between imperialism and Kremlin bureaucracy based on peaceful coexistence, nailed down in Yalta and Potsdam and the new world order: the UN, the sharing out of zones of influence. Even if the cold war with though rubs followed... generally they act in agreement with each other and defending this new world order... Stalin and Roosevelt divide the world into tow blocks controlled by American imperialism and Kremlin in order to halt, deviate, squash or control workers' world revolution."* (15)

After the International Yalta and Postdam agreements and as from the year 1947, "Plan Marshall" was launched according to which the USA invested millions of dollars, which allowed for the reconstruction of world economy taking advantage of the massive destruction of productive forces, the famine, brutal unemployment and the poor wages of European proletariat and toiling masses. Let us insist that the USA could implement Plan Marshall because after the II World War their economy represented a third part of all the world exports, had two thirds of gold reserves and produced half of all the manufactured good.

After the launching Plan Marshall, world capitalist economy experimented growth at historic rates for several decades. Possibilities for capitalist enterprises of achieving high rates of exploitation due to a brutal slide-down of standards of living, work and wages that became consolidated with the war among European toiling masses proved to be a magnet to attract investors and European capitalist governments used these "comparative advantages" to their own benefit ant attracted them.

The "German Miracle", for example, was the outcome of American investments that took advantage of the brutal reduction of living standards, achieve among others by Hitler and his concentration camps, apart from the division of Germany and its working class, the most powerful one in Europe and this facilitated the exploitation of German working class. The name of the plan passed on to history was the surname of the State Secretary of the USA, George Marshall who participated in the summit and he was the one who inspired the model, together with the English economist Lord Keynes.

American hegemony became clear in a manner in which the world trade was reestablished after the war under conditions imposed by

The End of the Corporations

Washington. In July 1944, a new international monetary system was established at the International Conference of Breton Woods and it determined agreements that were to replace the international monetary system of floating rates imposed after the Great Depression of the '30s for war expenditure.

The main goal of the new financial system was to return to fixed convertibility of currencies tied to the gold standard and Breton Woods decided that the dollar would be the pattern currency of the international monetary commercial and financial system, supported by the gold stored in the Federal Reserve of USA. Together with the dollar-gold parity, it was agreed that an International Monetary Fund (IMF), a World Bank (WB) and the International Bank of Reconstruction and Furtherance (IBRF) to regulate the newly created system.

The post war "boom"

Keynesian regime, as a regime of accumulation, allowed for the boom of world economy, with historic rates of growth that lasted for several decades. That was the economic base for the enormous social achievements attained by the masses in the USA, Europe, Japan and several underdeveloped countries. The boom granted stability to the political situation of imperialist countries, based essentially on important plans of public works for the reconstruction of Europe and Japan where the infrastructure had been badly damaged during the war.

The "boom" of world economy reached very important peaks of growth; in Great Britain at a rate of 17.5%, in the USA of 17.7 in 1950 and of 17.0 in 1969. In Japan, the peak of 36.5% was reached 1969 while in Germany and the remaining parts of Europe, economy reached 19% in 1968. **(16)** Toyotism and Taylorism became the base for the technologic pole to increase productivity of labour and commerce as well as international labour division was structured hinging round the axis of The USA– Europe.

The exploitation of the proletariats of both regions placed them in the centre of world and consolidated the Atlantic as the centre of world trade. As to the financial capital, one of the main features of the Keynesian regime was strong repression of speculative capital so in 1933, the Galss– Steagall Act was passed; in 1936 it was the Robinson-Patman and in 1937, the Miller-Tydings and they were combined with other previous, such as the Sherman anti-monopoly of 1890, and Clayton in 1914.

These laws sought to separate the deposit banks and the investment banks, to halt the great chains, unfair competition and to veto the participation of bankers in boards of firms. The anti-trust legislation of the Keynesian regime in the USA repressed speculative capitals that were placed in the London city. However, the great American firms could start monopolising the branches of production and trade because the monopolies of the remaining powers were shattered.

Now we have a general picture of the Keynesian regime. Its success was mainly due to super-exploitation of workers in the USA and Europe, the greatest proletariats, most concentrated and culturally most outstanding in the world, whose wages and standards of living were very much deteriorated by the crisis of the 30's and the war.

3) Multinationals became predominant Form of Accumulation

The third reason but from the economic point of view the most important one due to which capitalism could get out of the stagnation of the period 1929/1945 and leap into the post war boom was the emerging of the multinationals as predominant Form of Accumulation. This fact proved to be the qualitative change in the process of capitalist production, for it made an unprecedented accumulation of capitals and profits possible and caused enormous changes in the structure and functioning of capitalism ¿How come that the multinationals became the predominant Form of Accumulation?

The surfacing and development of monopolies since 1860 allowed for development and expansion of capitalism that lasted for several decades traversed by the crisis of 1873-96 even if these crises were part of the expansion and growth. By contrast, since 1907 the crisis of that years as well as that of 1914-18 and the beginning of the 1st World War, already expressed that capitalism had entered a downhill slope and stagnation that led to the crack of '29.

As Galbraith put it, the process of stagnation of capitalism happened as consequence of the erosion of monopolies as a form of accumulation. Why did the depletion of cartels and trusts happen? Because as they took over in economy, all the contradictions of capitalism became extremely sharper, firstly, because when concentration and centralisation of capitals in the different branches of production, the contradiction between the social character of production and the individual character of the appropriation of the wealth produced became sharper.

Socially produced wealth was getting more and more concentrated in fewer hands, the owners of monopolies, in a magnitude far above that of the industrial period when exploitation of child and female labour developed and ever increasing masses of workers were thrown into misery and poverty and crammed into great cities.

Monopolies sharpened this already existing social unevenness brutally, not only due to the extreme differentiation between the rich and the poor, but also because of the tensions and confrontations inside the capitalist class itself as an outcome of the fact that economic concentration implied also the bankruptcy and disappearing of minor sectors of capitalists in the hands of the more powerful trusts and cartels. Generalised poverty and the fall of the middle layer of the population aggravated by the monopolies caused consumption to dwindle and was a general brake on economy.

Secondly, monopolies sharpened the contradiction between the global character of production and the national states, because they started controlling branches of that production and trade within the national scope while at the same time they tended to develop internationally. As they began to dispute the world market, brutal struggles for markets cropped up among them and this was what constituted the base for both, the First and the Second World War. These contradictions showed the limitations of the cartels and the trusts to get as far as dominating world branches of production and trade.

The wars were the clashes and confrontations between the imperialist states to see which one of them would impose its own monopolies and, at the same time provides clear evidence that monopoly as a from of accumulation had entered the stage of its depletion. Capitalism needed a superior form of accumulation that would leap to the dominion of entire global branches of production and trade and this magnitude of centralisation and elimination of capitals and capitalists was only attainable by means of war.

The passage from predominance of monopolies to predominance of the modern multinationals

As we have seen, after the II World War all imperialisms emerged destroyed and it was on the USA, with its extraordinary development of productive forces, who could be up to the task of controlling world economy. This became concrete with the implementation of Plan Marshall that produced a change in capitalism: the modern multinationals displaced monopolies from the centre of world economy.

Plan Marshall, economic assistance for Europe from the USA was not disinterested: it was meant to extend their monopolies and finance their military bases abroad so as to consolidate their global dominance. American monopolies took advantage of the capitalist reconstruction of Europe to massively export their goods to European countries, boosting the economic reactivation as well as for their own implantation using Europe as the bridgehead for their world expansion.

It is no wonder that leading the post-war expansion there were the American enterprises: they had a good start with the unprecedented power of the home economy, their technological superiority and their enormous reserves of investment capital. By 1960, the USA had accumulated almost 50% of the direct foreign investments in the rest of the world. The Participation of England was 18% and Germany and Japan had barely 1.2% and 1.7%"... **(17)**

According to Noam Chomsky, Plan Marshall:*"created the framework for the investment of great amounts of American money in Europe,* **establishing the base for the modern multinationals.** *Some time later Reagan's Department of Commerce explained that Plan Marshall "prepared the scenario for private investment of great quantities in Europe from the USA" tracing the groundwork* **for the Transnational Corporation that increasingly govern world economy".** **(18)**

That is to say, with the contribution of American State to Europe, American monopolies became multinationals. A good example of this is Ford, the car producing monopoly of the USA, who created an organisation in the entire Europe as early as 1967. The mutation of monopolies into modern multinationals is the fundamental structural change within the productive scope of the international division of labour and trade that is developed in capitalism with the Keynesian regime.

So, the capitalist system adopted the physiognomy that we know today, as Nahuel Moreno pointed out, *"... The fact that I want to point out to is the emerging of the transnationals... With the exception of oil companies... that is to say, they are companies that have ten, twenty companies in different countries and all of them are coordinated working together."* **(19)**

Lenin had pointed out that the monopolies are national entities but that ever since early XX century, they tend to spread internationally Thirty years later and after the II World War, a great imperialist conflagration, the USA imposed their monopolies globally as part of the development of the Keynesian system. What difference is there between the multinationals and the monopolies? As we have seen, monopolies are the cartels and trusts, union or leagues of enterprises that control a branch of production in a country.

The End of the Corporations

Multinationals are not leagues of enterprises: they are a sole enterprise that controls a branch of production at a global scope; consequently, they are as superior form of accumulation that contains and engulfs monopolies. II World War allowed capitalism to pass from an inferior form of accumulation and concentration of capitals to a superior one, because monopolies such as General Electric, Ford, Coca Cola, etc, which – through a complex process of fusions and purchases of companies that lasted decades – has managed to dominate a branch of production in the USA **have now become a sole company on the global scope,** with very strongly centralised headquarters.

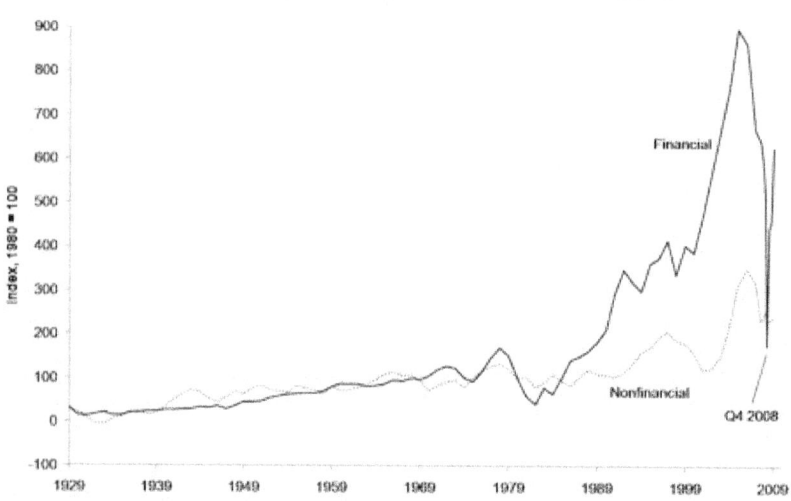

Figure 4.1: Real Corporate Profits, Financial vs. Nonfinancial Sectors

Source: Bureau of Economic Analysis, NIPA Tables 1.1.4, 6.16, calculation by the authors. Financial sector excludes Financial Reserve banks. Annual through 2007, quarterly Q1 2008-Q3 2009.

Fall of profit of corporations after the sub-prime Bubble, the fall reaches levels similar to 1929. Source NIPA

The board of directors of shareholders and their presence in the multinationals are no longer organisms that engage in complex negotiations inside the union of enterprises in order to agree about goals of production and commercialisation as in cartels and trusts. By the period from 1945 to 47, American multinationals are a sole command that imposes targets of production and commercialisation, aware of an immense, almost unlimited and unchallenged global market because the monopolies of the remaining imperialist countries a shattered after the II World War and are therefore in economic and financial disadvantage.

Secondly, in the years 1946/47, In the years 1946/47 the boards of directors of American multinationals imposed targets of production and commercialisation knowing they could rely on extremely high rates of exploitation due to the deteriorated standards of living in Europe and the USA.

Furthermore, they could rely on the Yalta and Postdam political agreements that warranted the investment and implantation because they acted as a political shield against revolts or revolutions that might have expropriated them or in some way hamper their interest in obtaining profit. The political and economic conditions of the 1945/46 conjuncture were very favourable for beginning to control the world market. The board of directors of this venture is a centralised command leading at the same time units of production and commercialisation of different countries where they have branches and can plan the development of the production counting with the international labour division inside the company.

They can produce different parts of goods and assemble them in different countries, calculating their benefits ahead of time in accordance with the conditions of exploitations that they obtain negotiating with different governments. That means, form the point of view of accumulation of capital and the supreme aim of capitalism that is profit, the multinationals is a qualitatively superior form of accumulation of capital, better than cartels and trusts, monopolies emerged in the XIX century.

In 1946/47 years, these new forms of accumulation came across enormous possibilities of super-exploiting workers in Europe and the USA with Yalta and Postdam agreements and with the investments by the American imperialist state spending money to facilitate the infrastructure, transport, highways, bridges, supplies, etc everything necessary for its development. What else can a capitalist ask for?

That is to say, it is the transformation of American monopolies into multinationals and the existence of these companies as the predominant Form of Accumulation what supplies us with the most important structural explanation of the changes that have been taking place after the II World War. The implantation of the hegemony, Keynesian regime and the multinationals are the three elements that explain the post war boom and the historic rates of growth achieved after 1945.

Multinationals exacerbated the fundamental contradictions of capitalism

But we must never forget two key elements in the passage from the predominance of the multinationals of monopolies to the predominance of multinationals. One is that the hegemony of the USA as well as the Keynesian regime and the multinationals are the outcome of the brutal destruction of productive forces implied in the II World War. That is to say, mankind had to pay a very high price for the outcome of the existence of private property of means of production in all this process of centralisation of capitals that the passage from the predominance of monopolies to the predominance of the multinationals meant. I meant millions o casualties, liquidation of infrastructure and annihilation of productive forces.

The second element is that the post-war boom has never meant that capitalism had managed to overcome the imperialist stage, that of decadence. To the contrary, it all happened within this stage that Lenin had taught about, and so the multinationals are a form of monopolist accumulation, as were the monopolies that had cropped up in the XIX century: they are Forms of Accumulation in the imperialist stage of capitalism. There is a fundamental importance in this if we are to understand why the post-war boom wound up by aggravating the crisis of capitalism.

The development of the predominance of the multinationals did not act solving the historic crisis of capitalist system; to the contrary, it opened the enormous crisis in capitalism in the late 60s. Let us see how this happened. With the reconstruction of Europe and the boom, multinationals as a form of accumulation became more and more general as empires previously destroyed in the war, such as England, Germany, Japan, France, etc. and developed their own multinationals.

First of all, multinationals aggravated the contradiction between the world character of production and national states. As Moreno put it: *"... **The transnational, more than anybody else before, responds to the law of monopoly, i.e.: it needs the national state.** There are semi-Marxist trends that say that they are great, because inevitably they will destroy national states... like this they will unite Europe and then Europe and the USA and then the USA and Japan and then we shall have the famous empire made out of transnationals ... **This is a lie, the transnational exacerbate the competition between them** and it turns increasingly more brutal....".* (20)

The other contradiction that the multinationals are making extremely acute is the one between the social character of production and the individual appropriation, because within the scope of concentrating wealth in few hands, multinationals have caused an unprecedented process of excessive accumulation of capitals. This is how Moreno explained it: *"The process of internationalisation of economy and the **centralization of American imperialism and the great international monopolies – the transnationals** – together with the speed of communications, allows a dazzling pace of obtaining surplus value, distribution of profit and accumulation on top of accumulation of capital. It is this very pace that accelerates the crisis of imperialist economy."* **(21)**

That is to say, because it is a superior form of accumulation, multinationals have achieved an unprecedented accumulation on top of accumulation of capital. But the accelerated process of over accumulation aggravated and exasperated the fall of the rate of profit. Who did this happen? That is how Moreno explains it: *"Every enormous increase of the mass of surplus value recovers the rate of profit and allows them to overcome the conjectural crisis. **But it prepares** another crisis greater than that one: when the capital accrues tremendously, there is super-accumulation of capital that seeks investments from which to obtain profit; as the mass surplus value remains unchanged and the capital has increased the rate of profit slides down abruptly originating a new conjectural crisis."* **(22)**

The enormous supra accumulation of capital that the multinationals implied, became active demolishing the rate of profit and forced the capitalists to seek higher and higher rates of exploitation in order to sustain the equivalent of the magnitude to the capitals accumulated by the capitalists with the multinationals. Since no higher rate of exploitation could be achieved, the enormous fortunes and the capital accumulated by capitalists with the multinationals acted demolishing the rate of profit and so aggravated the crisis of capitalism, because the very accumulated capital requires more and more exploitation to preserve the rate of profit. This caused the outburst of the chronic crisis of economy that developed with recessive peaks that began to come one after the other without capitalism succeeding at overcoming it.

As Moreno explained it: *"The final key to begin to understand all the phenomena that have been happening on the international arena since the late 60s, is the chronic crisis that has been going on since those days in world economy... it is constantly getting deeper and deeper and about every five years has been causing increasingly intense cyclical crises. The chronic crisis has been advancing from the peripheries towards the centre. This is a law that, to say the least of it, has been valid ever since 1966 – we believe that during the entire post-*

war... it has had three peaks or circumstantially acute crises. The first one since 1966-67, caused a fall of the rate of profit and American production... The second crisis happened between 1973 and 1975 and affecting the capitalist and imperialist countries as a whole... The third one starts in 1979 and also is extended to the entire world economy..." **(23)**

These recessive peaks happened because the fall of the rate of profit accrued fast and capitalism found it increasingly difficult to overcome the crises that stemmed out of them. Between 1970 and 1990, the rate of profit of the factories in the economies of G7 fell 40% with respect to the period of between 1950 and 70. By 1990, the rate of profit fell 27% compared to 1973 and nearly 45% compared to the highest level of 1955. **(24)** Contradictorily the recovery of the post-war world economy weakened American economy, "... it suffered a first period of stagnation in mid 50s. Between 61 and 66, the GDP increased an average 2.3% a year – very much under the averages of 6.1 between 1931 and 1950 or 5.2% between 1950 and 1955" **(25)**

With the multinationals, all the process of accumulation and surplus accumulation of capital and its speed have changed qualitatively due to the increase and speed of capital achieved. This accelerated the pace of the fall of the rates of profit and in this way also accelerated qualitatively the pace of the crisis of capitalism. This aggravation of the contradictions of capitalism started a dynamic that led the Keynesian regime to its final depletion. The depletion of the Keynesian regime led in its turn to the depletion of the multinationals as a form of accumulation.

From the point of view of the regime of accumulation, capitalism entered a transitional period that engulfs from 1966/67 up to the 80's, a decade in which new forms of accumulation crop up: the multinational corporations. At that time the Breton Woods commercial and exchange relations burst because in 1971, the gold reserves could barely reach a quarter of the official debts of the USA. The Nixon administration delivered a blow proclaiming free convertibility of dollar, signed the Smithsonian Accord according to which he devaluated the dollar to 7.89% in relation to gold thus cheapening the debts and good of the USA in order to strengthen the world market for American products.

In February '73, the dollar was devaluated a further 10%. Europe and Japan also abandoned the gold parity of their currencies and wrote a full stop to Breton Woods. The world returned to the floating rates and inflation began to accrue ushering in a long period of inflations that began to dawn and to sweep away the post-war agreements and the wages. World inflation aggravated with the oil crisis in '73-75 that pushed the prices of crude oil and raw materials of the whole world.

Post war: a grievous cycle of destruction of productive forces in the Third World

Faced with the crisis of Keynesian regime, capitalism needed high rates of exploitation to revert the crisis so they directed their capitals more and more aggressively towards the Third World, where the conditions of exploitation were beginning to outshine those of Europe and the USA. But in the post- II World War, great revolutionary processes, wars and convulsions began to accrue as an outcome of the crisis of the old colonial powers such as France, England, Japan or Germany who used to control that region but now emerged destroyed after the II World War, and this had weakened their colonial dominance.

That is what caused a spectacular process of national liberation and the emergence of new nations. Due to this enormous world revolutionary process – mainly focused in the underdeveloped countries – the newly emerging imperialism, the USA, began acting as a global gendarme and defender of capitalism as such aiming at defeating the uprisings and revolutionary processes that were happening in the backward countries.

From Algeria to Vietnam, from Korea to China, Latin America or Middle East, invasions of American armed forces and the armies of other imperialist countries aimed at defeating the revolutionary processes. This is the fundamental difference between the post war and the I World War and the II World War. While during the I and II World Wars, it was the different imperialist countries that fought each other, in this post-war it was imperialist countries clashing against nations, peoples and revolutionary processes in the III World Countries that challenged their dominance.

Moreno explained it like this, *"As from the post-war, the entire capitalist world, including the imperialist countries, had to admit American leadership and dominance... and the impossibility for the time being of new inter-imperialist wars... A stage of the character of wars is now closed and a new one is opened. The stage of inter-imperialist wars is over and the next stage of counterrevolutionary wars begins."* **(26)** From the economic point of view, the confrontations of imperialist armies against revolutionary processes stands for a spectacular development of destructive forces, in many aspects similar to that of the II World War.

Even though the revolutionary processes and the wars took place globally in the III World, there was a fundamental epicentre: the region of Asiatic South -East, where the greatest destruction of productive forces took place. As an outcome of this process a new axis of accumulation began in the Asiatic southeast and that was the key for the transition between Keynesian regime and globalisation. Axis of accumulation is the region and the different economies or countries that capitalism uses as platforms for their development during a determined period.

To illustrate the concept we may say that the axis of accumulations in the 1945/68 period was the duet the USA/Europe. The development of a new axis of accumulation in the Asiatic southeast was the outcome of a tremendous cycle of destruction of productive forces, which began with the atomic bomb in Hiroshima and Nagasaki and continued with the war in Korea between 1950 and 1953 with its toll of 779 000 fatal casualties, injured and mutilated in the American band and between 1 187 000 and 1.545 000 on the side North Korea, a total 2-5 million of civilians dead or wounded, 5 million left homeless and over 2 million refugees.

A new chapter began in the Asiatic southeast when the Japanese withdrew from Vietnam. After driving the Japanese troops out of the country, Vietnamese masses defeated French imperialism and declared the independence of Vietnam, whose war of liberation spread on to Laos, Cambodia and China. In order to halt the revolutionary process, the USA committed all kinds of historic horror and violations of human rights and yet they suffered a historic defeat.

The triumph of Vietnamese masses and the world was extraordinary, but the result of the destruction of productive forces that the Vietnam War implied was chilling. During that war 281,896 soldiers died and 300,000 were wounded on the American military side. As for Vietnamese masses, this was a real hecatomb: 5 million and a hundred thousand dead civilians. A million and a hundred thousand soldiers and guerrillas died in combat and at least 600 thousand were wounded. American Armed Forces dropped 7 million tons of bombs, among them a great amount of chemical weapons: Napalm, bacteriological defoliants, etc. – forbidden in the 1925 Geneva Protocol.

During the II World War, all the bands involved dropped a million two hundred thousand tons of bombs and explosives. Vietnam outdid them almost 6 times. The defoliant orange agent used in the bombardments by the USA until 1971 is still polluting the country up to our days. In the remaining parts of the region, imperialism kept on committing thorough destructions of productive forces. Such was the case of Indonesia with the Suharto coup carried out with the support of the CIA, the dictatorship committed massacres between the years 1965 to 1967 with 1.5 million of people killed.

In Cambodia, the Stalinist dictatorship of Pol-Pot between 1975 and 1979 exterminated 2 million people, almost a third of the population. In China, the failure of the economic plan known as the "Great Leap Forwards" caused the death of almost 32 million people during the famine and natural catastrophes; this spawned massive demonstrations and increasing displeasure among the masses.

Stalinist bureaucracy headed by Mao just barely managed to contain the great ascent of masses in the Cultural Revolution, but with the failure of the "Great Leap..." there was fear of a new outburst. In view of the defeat in Vietnam, the USA changed their policy in the Asiatic Southeast and relocated to the agreement with the Chinese bureaucracy taking advantage of the crisis of the Mao administration. The Stalinist Mao regime needed another plan and seeing the pressure of the masses and of the soviet bureaucracy threatening to intervene, made an agreement with the USA. China committed herself to stop the revolution in Vietnam in consideration of American investments to revitalise economy.

The agreement was punctiliously complied with as far even as invading Vietnam in 1979. Moreno says: *"Another colossal opportunity surfaced when, with the support of millions of Americans who demonstrated against the war, the Vietnamese toiling masses defeated American Armed Forces. Nothing would have been easier than to extend this triumph to Laos, Cambodia and the rest of the continent. But five years after, Maoist leadership attacked and invaded Vietnam... Vietnam, Laos and Cambodia suffer similar or worse penalties because of their betraying leaderships".* **(27)**

The End of the Corporations

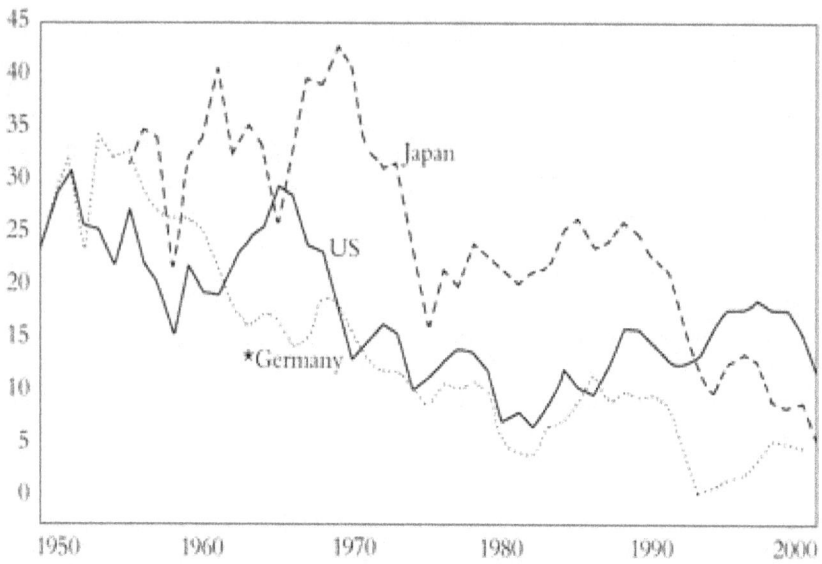

*Profit rate for Germany covers West Germany 1950-90 and Germany 1991-2000

The graph shows the falling tendency of the rates of profit of the main imperialist economies during the period 1950 /2000· Source: "The boom and the bubble" R. Brenner

In December 1971, after the Nixon-Mao summit and with the endorsement of the Chinese bureaucracy acting like the brake on the revolution in the Asiatic southeast, capitalism rushed to invest in the coastal provinces of China, where "special zones" cropped up in a slow process of penetration of the multinationals.

The arrival of the investments, the settling of enterprises and capital took advantage of the inexistence of a proletariat with tradition in the region, ages-old famine among peasants and the betrayal of the revolutionary process by Peking. This is also the way that the famous "Tigers" surfaced: Thailand, Malaysia, Singapore, Taiwan, and Hong Kong... all of them countries with dictatorial regimes that trample the most elementary democratic rights and squash every attempt at trade union organisation.

The "Tigers" of the Asiatic southeast acted as a magnet for investors because they offered a "paradise" for the voracity of the multinationals associated to native bourgeoisies. That is how the new "miracles" took place: the Japanese miracle and the miracle of the Tigers are products of brutish processes of destruction of productive forces in the region.

As soon as these processes were established, the axis of accumulation Japan – Asiatic southeast – the USA was constituted in transition of the Keynesian regime towards globalisation

Restoration of capitalism in the USSR, East of Europe, Cuba and China

The process of destruction of productive forces spread on to the Workers' States. Between 1940 and 1970, because of the defeat of the Nazis, the generalised process of the old imperialisms and the revolutionary processes in various regions of the Third World, capitalism was expropriated in the countries of Eastern Europe, China, Cuba, Vietnam, North Korea, etc. Twenty years later, as from the 70s, these countries began their way back to capitalism, and that mean the loss of important achievements brought about by the revolutions.

According to Martin Hernandez, *"the expropriation of the bourgeoisie, nationalisation of economy and centrally planned economy achieved what no capitalist underdeveloped country could ever achieve in the entire history. The USSR showed spectacular development within all the fields. The unprecedented development of their economy made it possible to eliminate famine, unemployment, illiteracy, deficient housing and it also made massive access of the population to science and culture so much so that the USSR took the lead in the space race... the China and Cuba cases also show spectacular results on the economic scope that, later on could also be observed within other areas"* **(28)**

The return of these countries to capitalism has not been the outcome of free choice by the masses; it was the produce of 70 years of policies of Stalinism made to repress violently workers and peoples. According to IWL-FI, *"... restoration of capitalism was not peaceful. It was one of the most violent events of the history of mankind... it was not something circumstantial; it was a historic process... There were several milestones: the civil war, the triumph of Stalinism and the Nazi invasion on the USSR, the cold war and the massacred against the uprisings in Eastern Europe..."* **(29)**

Between 1924 and 1953, the crimes committed by Stalin in the USSR caused the death of millions who died in the purges, famines, forced collectivisations and ethnic cleansings of Ukrainians, Chechens, etc. It has been estimated that in Yugoslavia 2 million died due to the vicious repression by the Tito administration between 1944 and 1977. The toiling masses of the socialist countries confronted the dictatorships of those days, but they were defeated.

This is the way Martin Hernandez explains it: *"...several political revolutions challenged the Stalinist dictatorships and could only be defeated by means of direct military interventions aided by the troops of the former USSR; so the Berlin workers of 1953, Hungarian workers' councils in 1956, the Czechoslovakian 1953 process and the multitudinous process of Solidarity in Poland in 1981.* **This is the way in which the conditions for "peaceful restoration" were prepared at the cost of forty or fifty million lives."** (30)

If the living standards were tough for the toiling masses under Stalinist regimes, the return of capitalism did nothing but to aggravate them. According to Martin Hernandez, *"Restoration of capitalism in the former workers' states does not prove ay superiority of capitalism but only its deep crisis... a catastrophic fall in economy and culture"... since the restoration of capitalism, birthrates are now negative due to the high rates of mortality caused by all kinds of diseases easily controlled in other countries."* (31)

Restoration of capitalism also meant serious development of destructive forces as the pinnacle of the 70 years of political betrayals of the "world official left" of Stalin, Mao, Khrushchev, Castro, Deng Xiaoping, Brezhnev and Gorbachov, and their policy of socialism "in only one country" and their systematic and permanent refusal to federate to build workers' states.

All their policy of dissolving the III International at request of capitalist powers as part of Yalta and Potsdam agreements made this vicious regression possible. The instauration of dictatorships of a sole party that committed massacres and persecutions, as well as the annihilation of oppositionists and of revolutionary Marxist wound up by crowning the policy of support from the left for the multinationals and a formidable tool to grant the capitalist system some more survival time.

The colossal development of arms industry and destruction of Nature

As we have seen with the two world wars and in this postwar, capitalism destroyed immense masses of capital and human lives. All the enormous process of destruction of productive forces left an outcome of poverty, misery, and child mortality rate for millions together with the deterioration of nature and environmental crisis. Destruction of nature is the produce of the policy violation of international covenants, environmental pollution, and depredation of seas, rivers and natural resources as well as the squandering of natural resources put into practice by imperialist governments all of which contribute towards increasingly visible and uncontrollable change of climate. They all affect the poor with greater force.

According to the Programme of United Nations for Development, *"... We must urgently give a decisive answer to the change of the problem of climate change. In 2007 global emissions of carbon dioxide ($CO2$) accrued again and reached 30 billion metric tons, which is equivalent to an increase of 32% with respect to the previous year and a 35% compared to 1990... The rate of deforestation shows signs of remission, but it is still alarmingly high and even if some success has been obtained in conservation... loss of biodiversity is still relentless..."* (32)

In our analysis of the development of forces destructive of mankind under capitalism, it is necessary to observe the expansion of arms industry. Military expenditure reached $ 1.4 billion and the expansion of the profits of arms consortiums in Europe and in the USA are the most irrefutable evidence of the increasingly close dependence of the economic development and with the development of war industry.

Wars, atomic bombs in Hiroshima and Nagasaki, massacres, torture and persecutions perpetrated by dictatorships and totalitarian governments that defend capitalism or invasions such as that of Vietnam and Iraq are an increasingly necessary resource to reactivate the economy in the G7 countries, above all in the USA and, at the same time, to avoid a global recession and also to emerge as the great capitalist super power after the II World War.

Military expenditure constituted an important contribution to the growth of their GDP, turning the American Military-Industrial Complex into a fundamental node for the development of their economy. The top five contractors are: Lockheed Martin, Boeing Northrop Grumman, Raytheon y General Dynamics, Honeywell, Halliburton y BAE Systems.

Thousands of smaller firms of defence and their subcontractors come hot on the heels of the big ones. Some of them, such as Lockheed Martin in Bethesda (Maryland) and Raytheon in Waltham in Massachusetts obtain nearly 100% of their business from contracts concerning defence.

Others, such as Honeywell in Morristown, New Jersey, have important sections in consumption of goods. Since March 2004, the contractors in defence of the USA have had some of the best budgets of the Pentagon, i.e.: since the beginning of the war against Iraq and have cashed in considerable increase in the total return to shareholders including from 68% (Northrop Grumman) up to 164% (General

Dynamics) from March 2003 till September '06. Military expenditures finance foundations that receive thousands of millions dollars, for example Bradley Foundation, John M. Olin Foundation, Scaife Foundation or Coors Foundation that act as permanent military lobby orienting American foreign policy towards war.

This bunch is to be found in American Enterprise Institute (AEI), Foundation Heritage, and the Institute of neo-conservatives from Washington for the Policy for Near East, the Centre of Policy for Security, Project for American New Age, etc. These political centres of lobbies of arms industry push the US Army on to adventures threatening peoples and democratic guarantees for the world population as a whole.

In 1991, after the fall of the Berlin Wall, the defence budget of the USA was 298 billion dollars. By 2006, this budget had increased to 447 billion dollars and this does not include the extra $ 100 billion spent on Iraq and Afghanistan wars.

In 2005 American military expenditure has been estimated at nearly 48% of the total military expenditure in the world while the population of the USA represents less than 5% of the world population and about 25% of the total world production. American military expenditure engulfs 21% of the total federal budget: in 2006 $2 144.3 million, equivalent of several countries put together. Such expenditure has been growing throughout time involving thousands of companies and millions of people.

In 2006, according to estimates by Rodrigue Tremblay, the Department of Defence of the USA employed 2 143 000 people, private contractors of the system of defence had 3 600 000 employees, a total of 5 743 000 jobs to which we must add some 25 million war veterans.
In short, in the USA some 30 million people – an amount equivalent to 20% of the Economically Active Population receive their income, directly or indirectly, from public military expenditure. **(33)**

According to Moreno: *"... During this post-war we have seen the colossal development of arms industry, i.e.: of the destructive forces of society and also the development of technology that has led to the impoverishment of man, to a crisis of mankind, increasing wars and a beginning of the destruction of Nature. The current development of capitalist economy... has an increasing tendency to the destruction of man and nature..."* **(34)**

The debate on the development of destructive forces and of technology

To avoid overwhelming our readers with data, in our analysis of the process of destruction of productive forces we have not mentioned the brutalities committed by imperialism in the Middle East. Above all in Palestine, in Africa and other regions and we have just mentioned a few in order to illustrate the concept.

But it is important to know what we are talking about when we mention the development of destructive forces so it is important to know the debate that Marxism and the left had been into during the post-war. In those days, defender of Capitalism and some Marxists, such as Ernest Mandel, asserted that the development of productive forces was the predominant element in the development of capitalism.

Nahuel Moreno refuted that hypothesis. He said, *"The inexistence in this post-war of a crisis like the one in 1929... the economic boom... during twenty years (since approximately 1950) plus a spectacular technological development, drove revisionists to pose **a new anti-Marxist economic conception...** that a new stage began, that it the neocapitalist or neoimperialist stage it is different from the imperialist stage defined by Lenin as the stage of total decadence and chronic crisis of capitalist economy."* **(35)**

The technological revolution, the economic boom, the expanding living standards of the masses in the First World and some other regions drove many economists and left sectors to formulate a theory of "neo-imperialism" where they asserted that productive forces were accruing. If the theory of "neo-imperialism" was true, then Marxism was wrong for it asserted that the fundamental feature of capitalism in the imperialist stage was not the development of productive forces.

¿Was Marxism wrong? According to the "neo-imperialist" trend, the great technological revolution that took place during the post-war was synonym of development of productive forces. Moreno explained the magnitude of this revolution: *"The greatest technologic revolution in the entire history of mankind was carried out under the dominance of imperialism... cybernetics, rocketry, atomic energy, petro chemistry, chemical fertilisers, scientific discoveries in all the branches... embodied in the most spectacular advances ever made by man: the beginning of the conquest of the cosmos, the universe..."* **(36)**

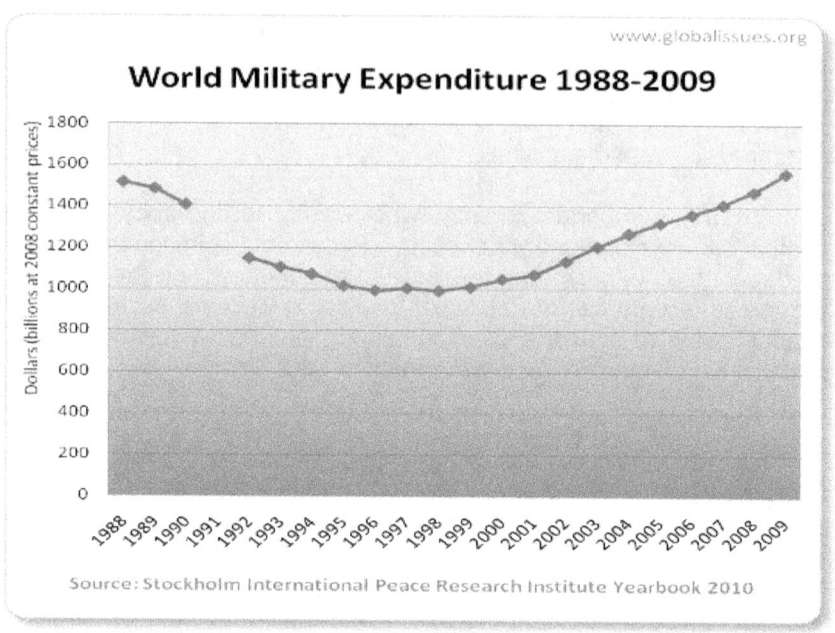

The chart shows worldwide military expenditure in billions of dollars. Source: Institute for Research for International Peace. - Stockholm (SIPRI) Yearbook 2008

But Moreno did not regard the great technological development is not a synonym of the development of productive forces, *"The assertion that in this allegedly new stage productive forces are undergoing a colossal development thanks to the enormous technological progress... is an anti-classist conception and anti-human... For us, the Marxists, the development of productive forces is a category formed by three elements. Man, technique and nature...* **And the main productive force is man:** *concretely, the working class, peasantry and all the workers... technical development is not development of productive forces unless it allows for the enrichment of man and nature, the same as science and education – are neutral phenomena that may become constructive or destructive depending on what classist use we give to them... and its utilisation depends on the class that can have it in their hands."*

Moreno said that the development of destructive forces was expressed in the growth of arms industry, *"***In this post-war we have witnessed colossal development of arms industry, i.e.: of the destructive forces of society*** as well as the technique that opened the path for impoverishment of man... crisis of mankind... increasing wars... beginning of the destruction of nature. The current development of capitalist economy increasingly tends to destroy man and nature."* **(37)**

Actually, during the post-war, there was a relative development of productive forces but within the framework of tremendous growth of destructive forces. As the processes of the development of productive and destructive forces were taking place simultaneously and contradictorily, it was not all about finding out whether one or the other existed; it was necessary to find out which one was the predominant process. The study of the Keynesian regime and of the development of capitalism has enabled us to verify that it was the development of destructive forces what prevailed.

With the depletion of Keynesian regime and the multinationals, a process of transition began during which the passage from the Keynesian regime to another, totally opposed to it, the globalisation, was prepared. And in the globalisation regime made another step forwards in the process of centralisation of capitals that gave room to a superior form of accumulation: multinational corporations.

The end of the Keynesian regime: what the Keynesian economists conceal

The growth attained by capitalism with the Keynesian regime has been clear: those who defend it and refer to themselves as "Keynesians" intend to prove that capitalism is capable of having a successful model that permits us to achieve economic improvements for the masses. These economists conceal the reasons for which in the years between 1945/68, capitalism produced the "boom".

When such "Keynesians" as Paul Krugman, Joseph Stiglitz and Nouriel Roubini assert that "Keynesian regime" can be re-created in dour days and claim in a loud voice for economic stimulus, public works, income tax, and claim that with these measures it is possible to overcome the serious crisis that started in 2007, they simply lie.

They conceal that the regime inspired by Lord Keynes was possible because cities, bridges, roads, counties, municipalities and factories had been destroyed. There was a precondition for the development of Keynesian regime: the destruction of thousands of buildings, deposits and transports. And what is more important, millions of human lives had been destroyed on battlefields, concentration camps and with atomic bombs. Through the war, capitalism confirmed its decadence, its cruelty and its capacity of inflicting great suffering to the masses.

With the I & II World wars, imperialism overcame the crisis due to the colossal development of destructive forces and the classical mechanism that Marx had called burning or annihilation of capital. The destruction of productive forces that preceded the Keynesian regime was a formidable business for the great enterprises and a colossal leap in the development of destructive forces with its top expression: war industry.

Since the beginning of the crisis of world economy, millions of people in the world and movements such as Occupy Wall Street, 15-O and The outraged of the world declared themselves against the multinationals. Many Keynesians approach these movements and declare their solidarity. Are the Keynesians for or against the multinationals? When Krugman, Roubini, Stiglitz or other Keynesians begin with their deceitful speeches against the multinationals, it may be a good idea to ask them a simple question: How did the multinationals emerge? The answer is simple: **from the Keynesian regime.**

Perhaps many believe those who defend the Keynesian system as a form of functioning of world capitalism. Perhaps they will believe when they are told that it actually allowed a relative development of productive forces. Those boom decades seemed to be contradicting the Marxist theses about capitalist economy being in the imperialist epoch, of decadence and predomination of financial capital.

And yet, the study of Keynesian regime confirms the decadence of capitalism because it proves that it was because of Keynesianism the, a much higher form of accumulation and concentration of capital than that of its predecessors, surfaced.

Keynesianism was an economic regime that, for a short time, did not need financial capital because it emerged and developed due to American investments in Europe. That means, it could rely on a first-rate investor: the imperialist state of the USA. Multinationals and Keynesianism, are complementary elements: the former is the form of accumulation of the Keynesian regime; the latter is the regime of accumulation of the multinationals. This criticism by the Keynesians are hypocritical and a negation of the entire history of capitalism, not of its ancient history but of its modern history.

Multinationals elevated the crisis of capitalism to such a high level that, in their attempt to solve it, capitalists were compelled to launch increasingly vicious attacks on the masses. This is how Moreno explained it. *"Only by achieving* **permanent and practically unlimited increase of exploitation** *can imperialism overcome the next momentary crises and the chronic crisis, for the increase of capital is constant and dazzling."* **(39)**

The contradictions of the Keynesian regime that evolved for the worse have been preparing conditions for the end of the "boom" and the transition towards a new world economic regime, totally opposed to Keynes's: globalization. What happened from that moment on was a difficult, traumatic and convulsive phase of transition from the Keynesian regime to globalisation, during which the modern multinationals and the governments of the G7 administrations made headway modifying the structure of world economy in order to try and solve the contradictions and crises of capitalism- This economic regime and its complex structure is what motivates the analysis of the next chapter.

Notes

(1), (2) & (3) John Kenneth Galbraith "The Great Crack" 1954

(4), (5), (6) & (7) Lenin. "Imperialism, Superior Phase of Capitalism" (1916)

(8) & (9) João Henrique Galvão (PSTU), Brazil "The historic meaning of the '29 Crisis" (Our highlights)

(10) João Henrique Galvão (PSTU), Brazil "The historic meaning of the '29 Crisis" (Our highlights)

(11) León Trotsky. Europe and America: The two poles of workers' movement and the accomplished types of reformism - 1926 New roles for America and Europe.

(12) León Trotsky. Fascism and the New Deal - Marxism and our epoch

(13) Antony C. Sutton "Wall Street and the ascent of Hitler"

(14) Toby Rogers. The Guardian September 2004

(15) Nahuel Moreno. Actualización del Programa de Transición. (1980) Thesis VII "Thirty years of great revolutionary triumphs

(16) Long waves, institutional changes, and historical trends. Minqi Li, Feng Xia, Andong Zhu.*Tsinghua University, Beijing, China*

(17) Peter Dicken "Las empress multinationals, los estates nation" Source: http://www.globalizacion.or/desarrollo

(18) Interviewing Noam Chomsky, http://www.ecaminos.org/leer.php/4920 (Our highlights)

(19) Nahuel Moreno. Escuela de cuadros Economía 1984.

(20) Nahuel Moreno. Escuela de cuadros Economía 1984.

(21), (22) & (23) Nahuel Moreno. Thesis on World Situation (Project by International Secretariat of the IWL, 20 de October de 1984) I. Chronic crisis of World Economy

The End of the Corporations

(24) & **(25)** Robert Brenner "Turbulence in World Economy" Chapter III The beginning of the Crisis and Chapter II The long upturn

(26) Nahuel Moreno. Actualización del Programa de Transición. Thesis VII - Thirty years of great revolutionary triumphs

(27) Nahuel Moreno. Thesis on the World Situation International Secretariat of the IWL-FI 20/10/ 84 International Secretariat of the IWL-FI, 20/10/84

(28), **(29)**, **(30)** & **(31)** Martín Hernández. "Restoration did not prove superiority of capitalism". Marxism Alive 16- 2007

(32) USAID Population Reference Bureau. Data Box of the World population 2009

(33) Rodrigue Tremblay, "The Five Pillars of the U.S. Military-Industrial Complex", September 25, 2006

(34), **(35)**, **(36)**, **(37)** & **(38)** Nahuel Moreno. Actualización del Programa de Transición. (1980) Tesis XIV

(39) Nahuel Moreno. Thesis on World Situation; International Secretariat of the IWL-FI – 20/10/ 84

The End of the Corporations

The End of the Corporations

A Marxist explanation to the capitalist world economic crisis

CHAPTER IV
Globalization

The End of the Corporations

CHAPTER IV: Globalization

"For the possessor of money capital, the process of production seems to be merely an unavoidable intermediate link, a necessary evil in order to obtain money. Consequently, all the nations with a capitalist mode of production are periodically grappled by a feverish attempt at making money without the participation of the process of production."

Karl Marx, Capital, Volume II (Quoted by Financial Times in October 2008)

Following the end of Keynesian regime and as from the Thatcher and Reagan administrations (1) a period of capitalism began during which a new regime, known as "neoliberalism", "globalization" or "New Economy", which we shall call globalisation, which is its best-known name. In this chapter we shall analyse this economic regime and the new predominant forms of accumulation that emerged with it: the multinational corporations that surfaced between the 80s and the year 2002/05 when their process of depletion began.

Globalization is a regime of accumulation that is diametrically opposed to Keynesianism. If in the Keynesian regime there were relative economic concessions for the toiling masses, globalisation meant a vicious economic, political and military counteroffensive against the toiling masses of the whole world in order to impose low wages, deregulation, privatisations and dismantlement of all the achievements of the toiling masses as well as re-colonization of the underdeveloped countries by the capitalist powers.

Globalization has been the outcome of a serious process of destruction of productive forces that took place during the post-war in the countries of the Third World and prepared the condition for the passage from an inferior centralisation of capitals – the multinationals to a superior one – multinational corporations. During, together with a process of concentration of capitals, a proneness to the concentration of the impoverished masses and the world proletariat, which was expressed in the surfacing of the megalopolises that we shell analyse more comprehensively in the last chapter of this book.

During various decades, there has been no steady economic "boom" as during the Keynesian regime. There has been some shifting from periods of economic growth and retreat. There has been great growth in the 90s, even if it took place in the midst of a general decreasing proneness and serious turbulences, maladjustments, and misbalance in the economy that were the outcome of spectacular accruing of financial and parasitic capital. The development of this ripe of capital boosted all the contradictions of capital to paroxysm.

During the "boom", between 1950 and 1973, economy grew at a rate of 4.9% a year. Between 1974 and 1979 this rate dwindled to 3-4% and in the 80's it lipped again to 3.3%, while in the 90's it fell to 2.3.Compared to the '73-'90 period, the growth in industry fell 33% in the G7. Comparing the '79 – '90 and '90 –'96, the US GDP fell 25%, and in G7 fell 45%. In the nineties, the GDP grew at a rate of 3.1% under the 4% of the 50´s and 60´s; of the 3.26 in the 70's and 3.2 of the 80's. **(2)**

As for the growth of productivity between '91 and 2001, the rate increased at 1.81 a year, better than the decade of the 80s but under the 1.94 of the 70's and very far from the 2.84 and the '60 and the 2.80 of the '50s **(3)** The rate of profit of the US for Dumenil and Levy in 1997 was half it worth in 1948 and between 60% and 70% of its worth for 1956-65. **(4)** Regarded as a whole this tendency shows that **globalisation is a regime that expresses the deepening of the general decadence of capitalism.**

The beginning of the globalization: Violent exploiting offensive in the 80's

Nahuel Moreno asserted, *"In the USA, imperialism has not managed to overcome its latest crisis. Since 1982, their production accrued. This was achieved because of the **super-exploitation of all the countries and peoples in the world, including the Americans, up to a degree unprecedented in the latest decades** ... Marxist who believe that American imperialism managed to overcome their crisis due* *to the colossal indebtedness of the Reagan administration of the Reagan administration can see only the outer aspect of the phenomena. Actually, Reagan obtained the loans and the capitals he needed because lately he had increased the exploitation of all the workers in the world. That is how he managed to push up the rate of profit – reflected in the rate of interest – and that attracted the capitals."* **(5)**

The eighties are a decade of violent attacks against the working class. Between 1973 and 1990s, American workers lost 12% of their real hourly wages in the private sector and 14% in the manufacturing sectors. In contrast, in the period 1890/1973 previous to globalisation, the rate of yearly growth of real wages over hour was of 2% and there was no decade when it was under 1.2%, but in the globalisation, these rates – for the first time in 80 years – became negative.

There was also the draining of wealth from the underdeveloped countries using the mechanism of the foreign debt, by means of which millions were transferred to the coffers of the multinationals. The economic offensive was accompanied by a political and military counteroffensive against revolutionary processes, such as the "contra" guerrilla in Nicaragua or the SDI (Strategic Defence Initiative), a missile shield in Europe aiming at the Kremlin. In spite of all the rubs and contradictions between the USSR and the USA, the world-wide anti-proletarian counteroffensive headed by Ronal Reagan (USA) and Margaret Thatcher (UK) was also accompanied by the USSR, the countries of Eastern Europe and China, due to the fact that Gorbachov and Deng Xiao Ping were also making headway in a tough anti-proletarian offensive.

The "Perestroika", Gorbachov's plan, opened the economy to the installation of multinationals and advanced in the dismantling of social achievements attained in those countries due to the revolutions that had expropriated capitalism. Neither Reagan, Thatcher, Nakasone, Gorbachov, achieved definitive historic political defeats over the masses, but they did carry out coups, manipulations and headway against workers' economic achievements and this caused enormous progress in social unevenness.

Capitalism achieved great economic growth in the 90s. But even in those phases when there was growth, the rates were far below the standards of the boom years and never reached the levels of Keynesian regimes. According to Brenner, "the rates registered during the economic cycle of the seventies and eighties... were... were below the long post-war expansion... during the nineties the behaviour of all the advances capitalist economies (G7)... was not any better than in the eighties and this in turn was worse than the previous decade and far below the fifties and sixties." (6)

In the globalisation, the pole of accumulation changed, the old industries that used to be the pole of the Keynesian regimen were displaced and a new pole of accumulation, hinging round the industry of telecommunication, informatics, biogenetics and pharmaceutical industry. If the car was the car was the base merchandise of Keynesian regime, the computer was the same for globalisation.

That is what Moreno pointed out to: *"...All the old industries and dominating monopolies are being displaced. The automobile, steel, coal, aviation, and domestic industries are at a dead end... I agree that Keynesian system is down and out... There are several other branches where capitalism is gambling now: informatics, space industry, genetic engineering, automation, etc. Some people say that all those problems will be solved as from 1890, when these branches begin to produce in huge quantities for an appetent market."* (7)

Changes in commerce with the Globalization

Where commerce is concerned, important changes took place compared to Keynesian regime; the peak moment was in 1995 when the World Trade Organisation (WTO) was created. This implied a set of regulations that favoured the multinational corporations, such as intellectual property, patents on technological breakthroughs, payments of royalties and technological breakthroughs. Establishment of grants and facilities of settling of corporations in countries, regions, municipalities and states where they can act on tax-free bases, with labour legislation more favourable for the search for profit.

The configuration of world trade was there to guarantee geographic areas and regions where the multinational corporations would be free to rule over the exchange as they please. In this way, they made headway in the consolidation of their profits, eliminating competition, colonising economies of underdeveloped countries and favouring the manipulation of prices thanks of monopolies in the productive branches exerted in areas of free trade. WTO allowed them to take advantage of the services of education and health placing them in the service of the great companies.

A change of historic nature is that after centuries when the Atlantic Ocean was the centre of world trade, the development of the accumulation axis of the Asiatic South-east, with the support from the economy of Japan, the emergence of the Tigers and the boom of China cause that as from mid-90s, the centre of world trade started to shift from the Atlantic Ocean to the Pacific Ocean.

Another among the most important changes in World Trade in globalisation is that since the 70s constant increase of prices and a permanent process of world inflation that affected raw material and oil, and this brought about the sky-high prices of food and rising dispossession of workers of their wages.

Another among the important changes that happened since the 70s is an endless process of world inflation that affected raw materials and oil; this in turn caused the price food to go up and caused more dispossessions of workers of their wages apart from worsening the living conditions of most of the world population. The increase of inflation was very important in the '70s, slightly smaller in the 80's and then it went up again in the 90s and the first decade of the XXI century.

The inflation has a double aspect: in the first place, it is a clear symptom of the serious crisis that capitalism has been suffering from ever since the two world wars that the post war boom and the superior monopolist forms of accumulation such as the multinationals simply kept on exacerbating. But on the other hand, it is a formidable tool of the capitalist state to push wages down and so facilitate the world exploitation that benefits multinational corporations.

Let us analyse this issue. In globalisation we have enormous masses of capital that began to turn massively to financial speculation with assets such as oil, food, currencies, companies, etc. This caused the proneness to systematic and permanent increase of prices which devastated the standards of living of most of the population of the world. Banks extracted small parts to offer workers and popular sectors at usury rates.

But these masses of capital are, above all, the base for enormous credits that allow the great entrepreneurs to develop all kinds of speculative manipulations. What do those masses of capital consist of? They consist of reserves in metals, dollars, titles and other currencies resulting from trade, industries, other counties suppliers of oil, gas, mining and agro-industrial surpluses. **And they come from the exploitation of workers and peoples of the whole world.**

This is the way Nahuel Moreno explained it: *"The explanation given by some Marxists saying that imperialist economy overcomes the crises merely creating purchasing power and by means of credit. If that were true, capitalism would develop easily and without crises creating purchasing power by means of loans. Actually,* **the money that is being** *lent comes from the exploitation of workers and looting on other countries."* (8) The enormous mass of capital constituted in globalisation is surplus value, that is to say: the unpaid labour of millions of workers in cities and in the countryside that are part of the toiling masses of the whole world.

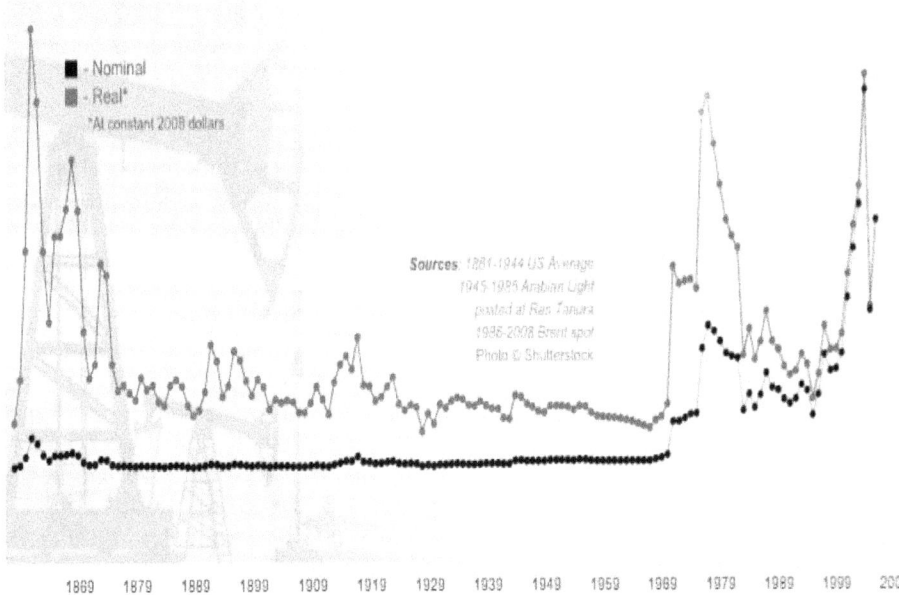

The table shows the evolution of the prices of oil in the 1860 – 2009- Prices remain relatively stable until the Smithsonian Agreements. From that moment on the tendency to increase is practically permanent. Source: Forbes

The phenomenon that Marxism defines as surplus value is labour and therefore a value that is in the goods that are being negotiated in the world trade, but which entrepreneurs never paid for, so they save it and it returns to them as profit. This surplus value is the inexhaustible source of capital that helps to establish the "global liquidity". Marx says, *"actually, profit is the form in which surplus value becomes manifest... In the surplus value the relation between capital and labour is exposed... i.e.: between capital and the surplus value such as it appears."* (9)

It is not only the surplus value that comes from direct exploitation of millions of workers what is to be found in this global liquidity; suction of indirect surplus value by means of the foreign debt and the uneven world trade with the underdeveloped countries is also there. Moreno says: *"Imperialism loots on underdeveloped countries subjecting them to an increasingly uneven exchange, extracting directly **great masses of***

surplus value from the investments of the monopolies that send the money back home and also through the mechanism of foreign debt." (10)

In globalisation, the exploiting offensive combined the direct exploitation that allow the obtainment of what Marxism calls absolute surplus value and the mechanisms of indirect exploitation that allow the obtainment of relative surplus value. The diverse mechanisms of direct exploitation are: extension of working time and of workday,

intensification of the pace of work or the "Sweat shops" in the Asiatic southeast and China, extension of overtime, migration of multinational corporations to zones of lesser trade union presence, attacks on covenants and achievements attained by workers, exploitation of immigrant workers, proletarianization of masses of peasants, etc.

All these mechanisms that allow for the extraction of absolute surplus value became widespread in the 80's with the Reagan and Thatcher administrations. They are of direct exploitation because they tend to augment the quantity and productivity in order to increase the surplus labour that employers do not pay for. This is what Moreno says about absolute surplus value: *"... Marx says that absolute surplus value is everything that exceeds the necessary value of labour force... everything that exceeds four hours is absolute surplus value and this is the base of capitalism that is to work more than what workers need..."* (11)

Inflation is also a mechanism of exploitation, only that it is indirect. It allows for what is known as "relative surplus value" to be obtained and is very effective at lowering the wages and salaries of workers and allows the great companies achieve broader margins of profit. Moreno analysed inflation and regarded it an essential element for the extraction of relative surplus value: *"What is inflation... We must stop here because it is a phenomenon of the phenomena in a vast majority of countries... Inflation is the relative (surplus value)... more sophisticated forms of exploitation have so far been... inflation is a constant dwindling of wages and salaries and of* **increasing the portion** *(in my opinion, relative)* **of surplus value."** (12)

Combining mechanisms of direct, and indirect extraction of surplus value, an enormous mass of capital that was massively transferred to financial speculation. This is the structural, deep reason for which a proneness to increasing prices systematically and permanently and this increasingly affected the standard of living of most of the world population.

The role of the American Federal Reserve

But what is more, inflation is the outcome of economic measures boosted by the G7 to consolidate the dominion of the multinationals over world economy as a whole and the measures taken by the administrations of capitalist powers to promote speculation with all kinds of assets and goods. For the achievement of this manipulation of the prices in world trade and in the exchange, central banks and – above all the Federal Reserve of the USA have a fundamental role, which as we shall see, allows us to corroborate that the endless increase of prices and of inflation are policies spurred and boosted from highest financial institutions of world economy.

Let us see the role played by Federal Reserve of the USA, known as the Fed. All the banks of the USA are by statute associated to the Fed including the private banks and Investment Banks, founded on 23rd December 1913. Because of this the Fed functions as a mixed ownership consortium for it combines public and private entities.

The fed has the function of issuing dollars, determine rates of interest, lend money to the State and regulate and control financial market by means of operation known as "Open Market". The structure of the Fed consists of a Board of Governors, Federal Committee of Open Market, 12 regional branches, and a network of associate private banks. Because the top 100 banks in the USA are in New York, this branch is factually the head of the Fed.

The Board of Governors is an independent agency and expresses the multinational corporations, above all the New York Fed, Its decision do not necessarily have to be approved by the President or any person of the executive or legislative branch of the government. The members of the Board and its President, who is the head of the Federal Reserve, are nominated by the President of the USA and that is how the current president, Ben Bernanke, was appointed by George Bush with the accord from the bosses of the Investment Banks. (13)

Up to the moment of the creation of the Fed, there was no steady trend upwards in the general level of prices. Inflation would happen during wars or catastrophes, but then prices would gradually decrease back to the previous levels... Since the foundation of the Fed, a steady trend upwards in the prices, cause precisely by the fact that the Fed is the only institution empowered to print dollars that circulate all over the world, That is how the Fed regulates the price of the money and is the entity that holds the control and the capacity to manipulate the price of dollar, issuing banknotes or omitting to issue, speculating with the

The End of the Corporations

payments of interests over the holdings of government securities or purchasing them.

When the Fed buys government securities, they make masses of dollars circulate, the price of which becomes cheaper and this leads to the downslide of the rate of interests. When the Fed sells public securities, they absorb money, produces draught of cash or liquidity on the market and this makes the dollar more expensive and pushes the rate of interest up. In both cases we have speculative manoeuvres to manipulate the price of the dollar and they may or may not have much to do with gold backing or the course of economy, but they do affect the prices of all the goods decisively and turns the dollar into the most important of them all.

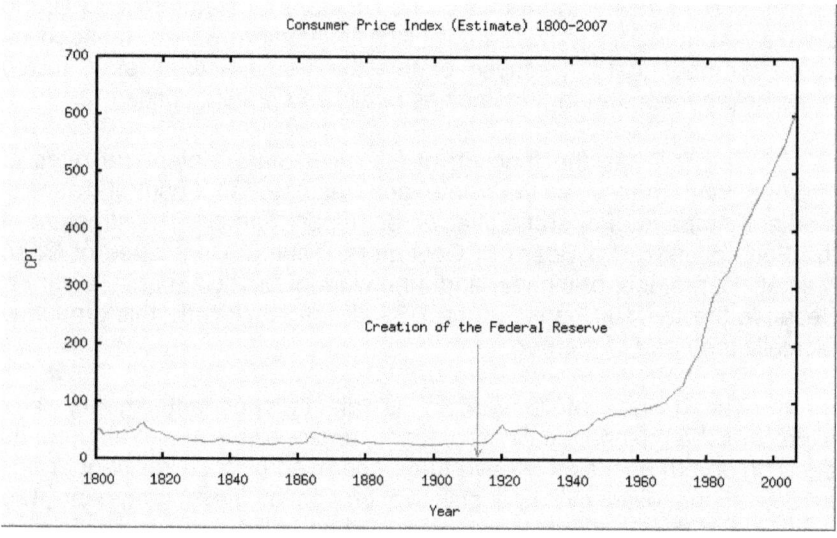

The consumer price index from year 1800 to 2000 in the USA – Inflation and increase of prices leap upwards the moment the Federal Reserve is created in the USA and another after the consolidation of the multinationals in the mid 40s and soars sky-high as from the 80s with the globalisation regime. Source: Wealthmonitor

Actually, the Fed is the Central Bank of the world with its own discretionary budget, its own Air Force of thousands of jets and freighters, vehicle fleets and managerial salaries of several hundred thousand dollars a year, In this way, it continues producing an impact with its decisions taken in consonance with the top notches in Washington and the bosses of multinational corporation, determining deeply the prices and the development of world economy

The origin of the unleashed speculation is to be explained by this role of the Fed and anyone who can presume that the emergence of investment funds and speculative panels of ever-increasing magnitude and the growth of informal speculative markets may be a construction outside the Fed and the Central Banks of the G7 banks have but a naïve vision of world economy.

The entire world financial speculation, titling and the venture capital are permanently boosted and encouraged by the Fed, the Bundesbank, the Bank of England and the central banks of the countries of G7 and the dominating classes, that pursue the mechanisms that will facilitate exploitation of workers and profits for Multinational Corporations.

According to Moreno, *"... the most important state intervention is to snatch a greater part of surplus value from the semi-colonial countries and the proletariat. And another thing: to organise the bourgeoisie, try to avoid a greater anarchy, but this is impossible, because the transnationals keep on fighting. That is to say there is the role of arbiter. **But the real role of the State is in foreign policy, to guarantee the exploitation of the colonial peoples, the defence of the transnationals...** the role of the state is fundamental, decisive...**essentially to increase the rate of surplus value"**.* (14)

The unbridled speculation causes real tragedy among the toiling masses in the world because markets speculate with all the goods assets that exist: currencies, oil, food, household items, energy, etc and that brings about a vicious attack on the living standards of those who find it increasingly difficult to purchase these goods. But speculation is boosted and sustained by the very central banks that sponsor investment funds and banks.

Twin deficits uphold world economy

The intervention of the Fed is the expression of the increasing intervention of the American State in world economy that led them to impose their hegemony. Because of this intervention, American fiscal deficit accrued geometrically until it reached those astronomic figures of today. In 1940, American fiscal deficit was $60 696 million, Today it is over $17 trillion. According to Moreno, *"The surplus accumulation of capital causes a great mass of it to fail to be transferred to production and become fictitious capital, usurious, of loans... American fiscal deficit is a spectacular example of this."* (15)

Fiscal deficit is added to the commercial deficit and that is what economists call "twin deficits". What role do these twin deficits play for the development of capitalism? Throughout decades, much of the discussion among economists centred on the meaning of both deficits and their implications in the global configuration of economy. The evolution of the "twin deficits" expresses that the gross of world trade is sustained by the USA **that imports high percentage of the products that are produced in the world.** The products come from the same American multinationals located in underdeveloped countries where they exploit cheap labour.

According to Alejandro Iturbe: *"During recent years, American economy was being built on the so-called "twin deficits" of the foreign trade balance and state budget.* ***The foreign trade deficit is the outcome of great increase of volume of imports of industrial consumer goods....*** *Almost a third of this deficit is spawned win the exchange with China."* **(16)** The USA absorbs much of the world industrial production and that is how they maintain the corporations. So the twin deficits act in a complementary manner, reaching the highest daily figures in history.

According to Iturbe, *"fiscal deficit is the combined result of several factors: reduction of taxes on great enterprises; increase of the expenditure in the military sector (including the wars in Iraq and Afghanistan) and, as we have already seen,* ***the financing of speculation through public debt...*** *In this way, from a $ 128 billion yearly surpluses in 2001, heritage of the Clinton era, they switched to a deficit of about $ 337 billion in 2006 (237 billion of "operative balance sheet" and about 200 billion additional for the wars)...* ***The sum total of both deficits meant that, in 2007, in order to function normally and not to get paralysed, American economy needed incomes from abroad for an average of $ 3000 million a day,*** *through the sale of treasury bonds, loans, direct investments, shipments of profits, royalties of the firms abroad, etc.* **(17)**

The best example of the complementary character of the twin deficits is China. China exports great part of its production to the USA, which produces a trade deficit between both countries in favour of China. But this is how the multinationals of the USA and the G7 located in China produce fat profits, firstly because of the cheap labour and then insuring the placement of their products in American market. The trade deficit with China is compensated for because the Chinese CP administration invests their surplus in bonds of American Treasury.

This allows for a major part of the capitals that *"exit"* from the USA to invest in China to return and provide the American Treasury with funds. According to Iturbe, *"...It is very interesting to analyse how this tandem USA-China has been functioning lately.* ***American bourgeoisie invested heavily in China, a country that sells their industrial products to the whole world (especially the USA itself). On the other***

hand, great part of the profit obtained return to the USA, mainly to buy U.S Treasuries. *In this way, a part of the state deficit is financed and the circuit is fed back."* **(18)**

The same mechanism is implemented by the USA in the remaining regions of the world to finance their multinationals, as Iturbe explained, *"That is to say, through the different mechanisms, American economy acts as a "vacuum cleaner" for a whole part of the surplus value extracted in other parts of the world"* **(19)** If both deficits – trade and fiscal – complement each other, one might as well ask, ¿what is their role in the configuration of trade and in the development of world economy?

A sector of economic analysts, point at American trade deficit as one of the elements of greater crisis in world economy. Is the American trade deficit an element of crisis of stability? This is how Moreno explains it: *"... I have my doubts as to the meaning of American fiscal deficit. Instead of being an element of crisis,* **could not it be an element of stronger stability?** *... I fear that that the interpretation of deficit as a serious symptom of crisis may be kind of vulgar Marxist reasoning. The trade deficit was the base the base of dominion of English imperialism for decades on end and maintained immense deficits..."* **(20)**

"The reason that has been studied endlessly by Marxism and that is that the deficit allowed them to exploit more than ever... It was their ship that transported the goods, their companies insured them, their enterprises that invested in almost all the countries on earth, their railways, and their borrowing operations filled their coffers with pounds sterling that far outweighed their trade deficit... **I may be wrong, but I am under the impression that if world economy has not yet burst it is due to American deficit".* **(21)**

Just as Moreno posed it, it is precisely the American deficit and the complementary character of the twin deficits what sustain the economy of most of the countries in the world, world trade, multinationals and, when all is said and done, capitalism. Those who see a signal of crisis in the American are merely ignoring facts of reality, which in this case, are conclusive. It was precisely in 1946, in the year when American deficit was the highest in relation to their GDP, when the USA rushed out to conquer the world.

It was in that year that American debt reached 108.6% and this was precisely what allowed them to rush out to conquer the world economy and the consolidation of their monopolies as the modern dominating multinationals. Daniel Munevar says:*"...the projected increase of the public debt during the forthcoming decade is an*

The End of the Corporations

unprecedented event in the post-war period in terms of speed of accumulation as well as of total amounts. Even so, the levels of expected indebtedness are – in relative terms -- far from the peak reached in 1946 of 108.6%. Therefore, it is noteworthy that this situation **did not represent a significant obstacle for the establishment of political, economic and military hegemony of the USA in the West."** (22)

Multinational corporations crop up

In the globalization regime, a new Accumulation Form became consolidated. These constitute a process of centralisation and accumulation of capitals that is superior to the modern multinationals of the post-war. In the post-war, the whole process of destruction of productive forces prepared the conditions to shift from an inferior centralisation of capitals – the multinationals – to another superior one: the multinational corporations that beat the modern multinationals while at the same time contain them.

Multinational corporations are enterprises that **control several braches of trade, industry and finances at a worldwide level.** If the main feature of the post-war modern multinationals was the control of **a branch** of global production, multinational corporations are a superior form because they **monopolise several branches simultaneously**, and this is what allows them to achieve greater accumulation of capital that what the post-war modern multinationals could ever accomplish.

The control over diverse branches of production, trade and finances that the multinational corporations achieved was the outcome of a convulsive process of mergers and acquisitions (M&A) that thrived increasingly as from the 80's. The colossal surplus accumulation of capital that is implied in this new For of Accumulation, caused a spectacular development of speculative and fictitious capital that participated in the M&A process.

This surplus accumulation is colossal, the greatest ever produced by capitalism and at present consists of nearly $ 700 billion in financial produce derived registered by the Basel Bank in mid 2008, but adding other speculative business it reaches a financial mass that may be crossing the line of $1 trillion. The process of centralization of capitals made gigantic headway during these last 20 years. By the year 2002, 300 transnationals out of 65 000 concentrated 30% of the world's GDP. 91% of the top 500 are American, Europe and Japan. (23)

"48% (239) of the top 500 firms are American... 31% (154) are in Western Europe and only 11% are Japanese. Third World nations: Asia, Africa and Latin America have only 4% (22)... the 5 firms that head the

list are all American: 8 out of the top ten are American and 64% (16) of the top 25 are also American, 28% (7), are European and 8% (2) Japanese... at the pinnacle of the global power, the American -European multinationals are unrivalled." **(24)**

The M&A are buying and selling enterprises, commercial movements that express deep clashes of sectors of imperialist bourgeoisie among each other with sectors of the bourgeoisie of the underdeveloped countries and workers and peoples of the world. The stronger sectors destroy the weaker ones in a tough and ruthless battle for the control of markets and capitals. Between the year 2000 and 2009, fictitious capital performed a monumental leap and grew from 10 times over from $ 95 billion to $1 trillion approximately equivalent to approximately 10 time the world GDP.

Fictitious capital is a concept used for the first time by Marx when he referred to securities lending the value of which is imaginary and illusory and only becomes concrete when swapped for money or property. The credit created by the banks is creation of fictitious capital because they make available money the do not have, *"... Not only most of the assets of the banks is fictitious, because it consists of titles and this kind of imaginary money... When this capital develops into interest-bearing capital and credit system, it seems that all the capital doubles and often trebles... most of this "money capital" is merely fictitious. All the deposits, except the reserve fund, are nothing but balances held by the baker, but they never exist in the deposit."* **(25)**

The exponential growth of fictitious capital implied in the multinational corporations caused capitals of diverse origins from tax havens and organised crime, rotate and circulate in an increasingly accelerated and convulsive manner causing great turbulence and maladjustments in economy.

The mega-mergers and M&A are neither natural nor spontaneous processes. Clinton passed the Leach-Bliley Gramm that derogated the Glass-Steagall and the antitrust legislation of the days of the great depression so as to facilitate the centralisation of capitals. The complex structure of the multinational corporations that emerge from the M&A process can be analysed in the case of several of them.

For example, let us see the JP Morgan Chase Investment Bank emerged in the year 2000 from the merger of two Groups: Morgan Bank and Chase Manhattan Bank, two traditional and aristocratic American Groups, include shares of 78 enterprises from 11 countries of the most diverse branches of production and trade. This structure of the Multinational Corporation that control several branches of the production, trade and finances simultaneously that we observed when analysing other corporations, such as Goldman Sachs, BNP Paribas, UBS, Barclays, Dexia, BofA, etc. that are Multinational Corporations because they control several world-wide branches simultaneously.

Banks of Investment are the heart of Multinational Corporations

The complex nature of multinational corporations can be explained by the location of the Banks of Investment that concentrate their activity on the control of the immense masses of capital that the M&A imply. Lenin anticipated the importance of banks in the process of concentration and centralisation of capitals saying, *"... taking a current account for various capitalists, apparently the bank is carrying out a purely technical operation...* **But when this operation accrues in gigantic proportions, it follows that a handful of monopolists subordinates commercial and industrial operations of the entire capitalist society..."** (26)

Investment banks should not be confused with commercial banks, because even if they are closely connected, they are absolutely different. While commercial banks are specialised in credit for enterprises and individuals for the purchase of all kinds of goods, investment banks are specialised in credit for the purchase and repurchase of an exclusive kind of goods: enterprises. Investment banks buy and sell of multinational and great enterprises by means of emission and creation of securities and assets such as the derivatives and so control the low of capitals, investments, collocation of shares and the M&A.

In globalization, the development of the multinational corporations placed the investment banks in the heart of the structure and since the multinational corporations are the predominating form of accumulation in capitalism, investment banks became the heart of the capitalist system. ¿How and where did the investment bank surface from? Let us have a bird's eye view at their history and development.

Since the development of monopolies, cartels and trusts in the second half of the XIX century, investment capitals as well as purchase and repurchase of enterprises were the dominion of rich individuals and families. The following oligarchies and families controlled the flows of capital, the Vanderbilt, Whitney, Carnegie, Rockefeller, Morgan and Mellon in the EE.UU, the Delessert and Pereire in France, the Mevissen, and Warburg or Siemens in Germany, the Rothschild in the entire Europe, and the Baring Brothers in England.

The End of the Corporations

These oligarchies made their fortunes by warmongering as with the War of secession in the USA, the Napoleonic wars in Europe or the Crimean War controlling the arms industry, steel industry and railways. Morgan Banks became the monopolist issuer of the war bonds for England and France and also invested in supplies for war equipment for both countries. In 1901 the American Steel Carnegie, the greatest steel enterprise in the Morgan group was the world's greatest and the Rockefeller controlled the oil industry with Standard Oil.

Financial oligarchies that controlled the most important cartels and trusts in Europe and the USA also boosted telegraphs and under their control developed the mining industry in order to possess precious metals, such as gold and silver to supply central banks of the most powerful capitalist states. Several banks were funded by these families to further investments such as Credit Mobilier, a bank that gathered capitals for the construction of the French railway but, at the same time, served credit to the Sate, founded societies of gas, Buses, Maritime Company the new trams in Paris. Mobilier also invested to build railways in Spain, Switzerland, Austria-Hungary and Russia. In 1853, the Darmstadt Bank was founded in Germany and the Austrian Kreditanstalt in 1855 – both following the Credit Mobilier model.

Such banks as the J.P Morgan or Goldman Sachs underwent important development in the USA. But in the midst of the Great Depression, the capital and investment banks suffered restrictions due to the crisis caused by the unbridled speculation they had spawned. The passage of the Glass-Steagall and other regulation of the thirties were repression against speculative capital. For example, J.P Morgan was compelled to opt for carrying out either activities of commercial banks or of banks of investment; they opted for the former because at that time it was regarded as more profitable.

Challenging this modification, many members of J.P Morgan decided to create a group that is now known as Morgan Stanley. After the II World War, this caused that during the Keynesian regime, investment banks had but marginal functioning. As late as the eighties, with the Reagan administration, they re-emerged and played a central role in great speculative manoeuvres, mergers and hostile purchases of companies, asset liquidations, bankruptcies, layoffs and scandals, massive layoffs and scandals. They were the central figures of the 20 crack and the financial scandal of RJR Nabisco in 1989.

Derivatives emerged from the investment banks

In the early nineties, investment banks began their way back to the centre of the scenario of world economy. Investment Banks

Shearson Lehman Hutton, KKR, Forstmann Little & Co., Morgan Stanley, Goldman Sachs, Merrill Lynch or Drexel Burnham Lambert were already active. But when with the Clinton administration, the entire legislation of the Great Depression was repealed, the M&A world process performed a great leap and increasingly complex speculative operations, such as the leveraged buy-out (LBO) or those of private equity.

They followed the tradition of commercial capital that says buy cheap sell expensive, for example, with the LBO heavily indebted great companies were bought anticipating a minimum capital and requesting loans what was called "leverage". Private Equity enjoyed its boom between 2003 and 2007 acting in a similar way only with companies out of the stock with the intention to restructure them in pursuit of profit. All those speculative manoeuvres use the derivatives, insurances on the future price of goods that "derive" from possible increases or slumps of the prices in the future. That is where their name comes from.

Derivatives are a special kind of fictitious capital spawned in the USA in 1993 as an outcome of studies of investment banks, above all of J.P Morgan and from there spread to the whole world and today, they constitute between 60 and 70% of the mass of 1 trillion of fictitious capital. They are extremely complex financial products, among which even more complex products, known as synthetic, developed and are documents of debts and options sold all in one "packet".

Euphemistically, they are known as "toxic assets" because they come from very different origins and of different degrees of reliability and contain bad debts that act as a veritable clockwork bomb. Investment banks develop a process of concentration of enormous masses of fictitious capital, of imaginary and illusive value that depreciate economy as a whole and, as far as they are not valorised, they prepare a serious crisis. Most of the M&A operations failed because they implied extraordinary levels of leverage and credits that left the corporations highly indebted in money and derivatives.

The entire M&A operation is a menace because the papers that are interchanged contain many debts and a sole declaration of default may cause generalised bankruptcy. At present an index, known as EBITDA (Earning Before Interest, Taxes, Depreciation and Amortization) is used to know the financial situation of the great companies. The EBITDA index of the companies that comprise the S&P500 top ten of the corporations shows that they emitted debt by billions between the years 2003-2007, but their profits dwindled after 2006 and those billions are pending payment.

PER (Price Earnings Ratio) is an important indicator used at the Stock Exchange and it is the number of times that yearly net profit is contained in the prices of a share. A high PER indicates the dimension of the speculative process, that leads the shares to a high price, several times the real price of the share and that does not reflect the real situation of the company. Taking the S&P of the stock exchange of New York in 1929, 1966, 1972 and 1987 an S&P a PER 20 times the value of the share was reached, and this was repeated in 2007, According to Moody's, out of the 20 greatest purchases carried out by Private Entity, only 4 have their companies is a stable situation, while all the remaining companies are on the verge of bankruptcy. **(27)**

Investments Banks boosted the hedge funds and the capitalist states did the same with sovereign investment funds. All those economic entities are integrated by rich speculators that cheat everybody with somebody else's money. The sovereign investment funds, for example, are state-owned financials of such countries as Norway, Abu Dhabi, Singapore, China ,etc that invest their trade surpluses and in some case they become more important than many of the top 50 banks in the world.

Among these entities the fictitious capital rotates as well as in the offshore centres or "tax havens", small countries where deposits pay no taxes, where enterprises can be founded that will not be compelled to publish their accounts or lists of directors and shareholders. This allows you to laundry capitals and get away with it and it attracts great wealth. In 1960 there were only 7 tax havens; now there are about 100. In the early XX century, they started on the Islands of Bermuda and in the 70s they thrived in Monaco, the islands of the Channel and later on in Ireland, Hungary, Rumania, Cyprus, Madeira, Singapore, Hong Kong, Finland and Gibraltar. By the late 1998, 60 jurisdictions grouped 4000 offshore banks with assets estimated at $ 5 trillion. **(28)**

Speculative bubbles and depletion of the globalization in the early XXI century

We have already seen how an enormous mass of capital that is the outcome of the exploitation of the masses of the world developed and how these masses of capital in the hands of Multinational Corporations and backed by the Fed are a structural component of the globalisation regime. We shall now see how these enormous masses of capital spawned the great speculative manoeuvres that became a characteristic feature of globalisation during the decades of the 80's, 90's, and the 00s and what relation there was between the latter and political and social events. And we shall also analyse the way this process led to the depletion of globalisation and of the multinational corporations in the first decade of the XXI, a process we can still witness today.

Top 10 Investment Banks

Rank	Bank Name	Founded	Revenue
1	JP Morgan Chase	2000	USD 97.03 billion
2	Bank of America Merrill Lynch	2009	USD 25.14 billion
3	Goldman Sachs	1869	USD 41.664 billion
4	Citigroup	1812	USD 70.17 billion
5	Morgan Stanley	1935	USD 32.03 billion
6	Deutsche Bank	1870	EUR 33.70 billion
7	Barclays	1690	EUR 24.691 billion
8	Credit Suisse	1856	CHF 23.97 billion
9	UBS	1854	CHF 25.443 billion
10	Wells Fargo	1852	USD 86.08 billion

Source: Finance. Maps of World

Let us begin in the late 70s. The increase of raw materials and, above all, of oil happened in the late'70s and provided oil countries and companies enormous profits. With the "oil up" and inflation of prices soaring sky-high after the Bretton Woods, the profit obtained by the great companies spawned to a mass of capital known as the petrodollars, The Reagan administration lured these petrodollars raising the rate of interest and the price of the dollar. With the "dollar up", the government of the USA sucked in capitals from all over the world who gambled buying gigantic masses of that banknote.

Entrepreneurs from all over the world, of every nationality, multinationals, great companies, municipalities and bankers bet on the dollar buying gigantic masses of it. The binomial "oil up" and "dollar up" created a spectacular worldwide bubble, an immense mass of capital that allowed Reagan to grant credits to the population enabling them to accede to the purchase of houses, cars, household appliances and university courses of studies.

This mass of credit and "easy money" that stimulated spectacular activity of the multinationals spurred one of the oldest frauds of capitalism: the repurchase of shares. According to Moyer and Mc Guigan: *"since the eighties, the repurchase of shares has become increasingly popular... during the time between 1983 and 1997..."* **(29)** Companies contracted credits to buy their own shares and the repurchase of share made the values of the companies go up but did not reflect the profits of the companies. Fraudulent operations became a general rule together with tax evasion and fake accounting, euphemistically called "creative accounting."

Savings and Loan entities settled in the centre of this speculative manoeuvre. "Reagan's bubble" recreated the atmosphere of speculation, cheap credit and false "sensation of wealth" typical of the 80's, New social sectors surfaced reflecting this phenomenon; the brokers and yuppies, lumpen sectors of the bourgeoisie dedicated to speculation. But the expensive dollar drove American industry to bankruptcy and their products became expensive compared to those of European and Japanese multinationals.

A crisis began in American economy that hit the Savings and Loans. In 1985, the Agreements at the Plaza were signed in New York between the USA, Europe and Japan in order to save the industry of the USA. Agreement was reached to push the price of the dollar down and of the yen and European currencies up, but in 1986, the crisis of American economy drove Savings and Loan to bankruptcy.

On 19 October 87, the crack known as "Black Monday" took place on Wall Street with the greatest slide-down in percentages in one day. This was the end of the "Reagan bubble", which caused such a serious crisis that led capitalist powers to seek an agreed mechanism of regulating banks, credits and transactions. We know the agreement published in Basil, Switzerland, under the name of Basil I by the Basil Committee that consisted of the authorities of central banks of Germany, Belgium, Canada, Spain, the USA, France, Italy, Japan, Luxemburg, Holland, the UK, Sweden and Switzerland. Basil I was all about a set of treatises in quest of impeding future bubbles and the crises that they might cause.

Basil I established recommendations to establish a minimum of capital that a bank must have in relation to the risks it was running and it became effective in more than 130 countries. But the mass of accumulated surplus capital continued accruing in spite of Basil I, it became colossal and adopted an increasing composition of fictitious capital for it was dedicated exclusively to speculative activity; this produced a serious development of dangerous bubbles and high destructive contents.

We call bubbles **the brutal and fast massive injection of capitals into a commodity that may be bonds of a country, currencies, industries or raw material.** These capitals multiply with the first successes, attract more capitals and spawn a ball that rises without a roof to be seen. At first sight of a slide down of the country, industry,

The End of the Corporations

region or raw material – panic ensues, capitals flee, the ball is deflated and all that remains is a trail of bankruptcies, poverty, paralysis and recession. The effects of the bubbles on any economy are similar to those of nuclear weapons: wherever they move nothing is left; only scorched earth. In the 90s, as an outcome of the increase of the rate of exploitation achieved by capitalism in underdeveloped countries and fundamentally China, the rate of profit grew and multinationals multiplied their capitals.

But if the growth of over-accumulated capitals was important, speculative activity accrued much more. As Brenner asserts, *"... between 1989 and 1997, the table of profits improved considerably for American companies... there was an increase of 82% and the rate of profit of the corporation increased 27.8%... However, such improvement in performance cannot justify the triplication of stock prices..."* (30)

In the 90's, as an outcome of the increase of the rate of exploitation achieved by capitalism in underdeveloped countries and fundamentally China, the rate of profit grew and multinationals multiplied their capitals. But if the growth of over-accumulated capitals was important, speculative activity accrued much more. As Brenner asserts, *"... between 1989 and 1997, the table of profits improved considerably for American companies... there was an increase of 82% and the rate of profit of the corporation increased 27.8%... However, such improvement in performance cannot justify the triplication of stock prices..."* (31)

It was in those days, and more precisely on 5th December 1996, that Alan Greenspan, at that time president of the Fed described this speculative explosion of capitalism saying that there was an "irrational exuberance" of the markets. That was the manner the he found to describe the serious imbalances that the overvalued financial assets were causing. Speculative bubbles kept on developing all through the nineties as a distinctive feature of globalisation. In 1989, the Japanese bubble developed, in the country that was at that time mentioned as the new world power, the way people now speak of China.

Let us see how this bubble developed. The '85 agreement at Plaza produced severe damage to Japanese economy. Structured round their exports to the USA, the expensive yen caused crisis in the Japanese industry and to the remaining countries of Asiatic southeast drowned Japan in cheaper goods, due to the depreciation of the yen. The flow of capitals to Tokyo did not take long before spawning a speculative bubble hinging round the sale of real estate. The value of Tokyo in 1989 was multiplied by 75, equivalent to 5 times the territory of the USA. A district of the capital (Chiyoda-ku) was worth more than Canada and the Imperial Palace in Tokyo was worth more than.

When the Tokyo real estate bubble burst and the Japanese bubble had lethal effect, Japanese economy collapsed and stayed that way for decades. In 1995, in order to save economy in Japan, the Plaza II agreements were signed; they pushed the yen down and the dollar up. Attacks against the prices of different foreign currencies and speculative movements of investors and speculators followed, for example, Soros against pound sterling in 1992 which brought the Bank of England to their knees.

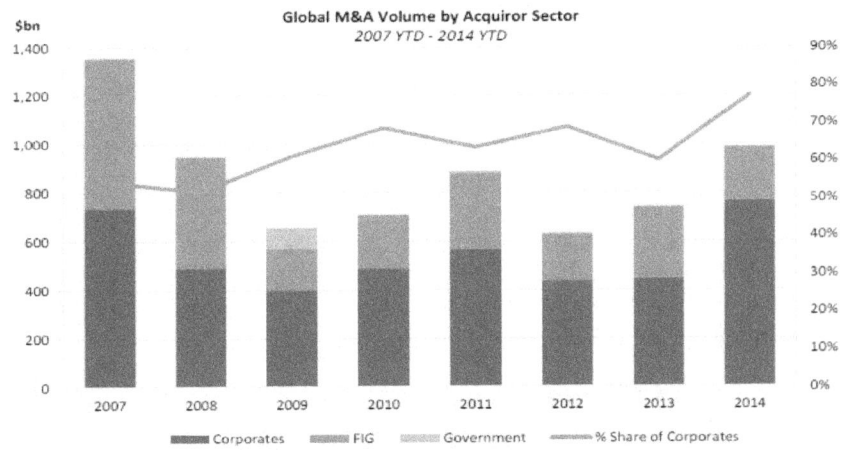

Global M&A 2007- 2014. After the Peak in 2007, the process of fusions and acquisitions fall abruptly and recover weakly after QE1 and QE2. Source: Dealogic

Then there was the Tequila effect in 1994 against the peso in Mexico, which caused the Central Bank to lose $4000 million and the collapse of their GDP in 95. As from 1997, overaccumulation of capital produced the fall of the rate of profit. New speculative bubbles surfaced with it; the one that produced the strongest repercussion on the development of globalisation was the one in the Southeast of Asia or "dragon effect" that hit the Tigers that had been up to that day the axis of world economy. Let us see how this happened.

The fall of the rate of profit since the years '96/'97 was a bad blow to world economy. *"...In 1995 the yields of these companies accrued 13%. In 1996 they reached 23.3%. But in 1995, this accruing of wealth dwindled to 7.8%"* **(32).** In turn, the fall of the rate of profit caused the fall of investment that had been on the upturn since 1992, *"... there were registers of a gigantic expansion on 17.3% in 1993, 16% in'94, and* up again 27.5% in 95. But then there was the descent by 0.7% in 96... **It was the reduction of these investments, spawned by the fall of the rate of profit,** what triggered off the process of crisis,,, driving the Asiatic southeast, Russia, Brazil, etc to a debacle." **(33)**

In 1997, the fall in investments produced 21.3% in Thailand, 43.4 in Malaysia and 22.9% in Indonesia. This combined with the Plaza II Agreements between the USA, Europe and Japan to push the yen down, which affected the industries of the multinationals of the Tigers oriented towards exports to Japan. According to Brenner, *"Ever since the 'inverse Plaza Agreement' in spring 1995, reached by the administrations of the 7G to impede the collapse of Japanese economy, the dollar was substantially boosted up against the Deutsche mark and the yen 29% and 50% respectively"* **(34)**

As the yen came down and the dollar went up the products of the Tigers became expensive, and that drove the Tigers' industry to bankruptcy. The pressure that the devaluation of the yen exerted on the economy of the Tigers forced their currencies to be devalued to avoid the bankruptcy of industrial groups. This unleashed a speculative attack on the currencies of Thailand in the first place, whose economy had been growing between 1985 and 1996 at 9% a year. The stock market collapsed 75%. Finance One, the biggest financial; the Thai "boom" came to an end and their GDP fell 7%.

The crisis spread to Indonesia that slid down 15%, to South Korea that fell 7% and the Philippines, whose growth was zero 1998. The consequences of the "dragon effect" were devastating; practically all the currencies were devaluated, stock exchanges and companies went down. The GDP tumbled down 31.7% in one year so millions of people landed below the poverty line. The countries most affected were Indonesia, South Korea and Thailand.

The IMF rushed in with bailouts for all those countries, and this also was good business and unleashed and M&A process for bankrupt companies, the Plaza II was a failure because it could not manage to recover Japan and it sank the Tigers that used to be the dynamic pole and a support for world economy. The "dragon effect" produced structural changes in capitalism; it liquidated the Tigers as a pole that had been the axis of world economy together with the USA in transition from Keynesian regime to globalization.

The blow received by world economy was so strong that it reduced the prices of oil, which affected the oil producing countries, especially Russia and in 1998, unleashed the speculative attack or "vodka effect on Russia". Then there was the attack on Brazil where the capital leakage was badly felt and $35 billion were lost; this led to stock market crash of Sao Paulo and the devaluation of the real. The "samba effect" was the prelude to "tango effect" of Argentina in 2001 and also forced the devaluation of the currency tied to the dollar 1 -1 and spawned the popular outburst that toppled the government.

The depletion of the Multinational Corporations

In 1999, the severity and continuity of the bubbles increasingly large and destructive led the powers to organise the Financial Stability Forum (FSF) consisting of Ministries of Finances, Central Banks and international financial organisms in order to promote international financial stability. The target of the FSF was to supervise and vigilance of economic institutions and economic transactions.

But this attempt was an absolute failure and the crisis spread from the peripheries to the centre and the following crises no longer developed in the underdeveloped countries but in the economy of American economy. In the late 90s and early XXI century three serious crises burst out and became combined: 1) that of the hedge fund Long-Term Capital Management (LTCM) under the influence of the vodka effect that made Wall Street shake; 2) the bankruptcy of the Enron Corporation or one of the most important energy companies in the world, and the 7th in the USA and 3) the crisis on the dot.com.

The outburst of the dot-com, initiated the crisis of the basic industrial branch in globalization: informatics. The rapid consumption of these products by millions of people produced a bubble surrounding their companies that led the NASDAQ index to 5000 in the year 2000. When the bubble burst, the NASDAQ fell to 3500, at 1300 in 2002. So 4854 companies disappeared in midst of scandals about fraud as was the case of World.com. The three crises combined started the world recession of 2000 – 2003.

This recession already expressed the process of depletion of multinational corporations and of globalisation as a form of accumulation. The enormous masses of fictitious capital had caused not only the fall of the rate of profit but also an accelerated process of devaluation of economy. Capitalist powers had to counter these trends and to overcome the crisis, but achieving this would have meant a new round of destruction of productive forces and burning of capitals much greater than what was done during and immediately after the II World war.

Between 1980 and 2000 with globalisation, the degree of destruction of productive forces was important. The Iraqi War had already taken place and the wars of Yugoslavia. Chechnya. Afghanistan,

Rwanda, the two wars in Congo and Bosnia and this taken into account together with the growth of poverty and extreme destitution, the increasing process of destruction of Nature and the development of arms industry had developed a process of great destruction of productive forces.

But this process of destruction of productive forces was not enough for capitalism to achieve a superior form of accumulation capable of overcoming multinational corporations. Let us remember that after the depletion of the cart4els and the trusts, capitalism developed a process of destruction of productive forces that opened the path for a superior form of accumulation: the multinationals.

During the post-war, the brutal destruction of productive forces in the underdeveloped countries allowed for a new and superior form of accumulation, multinational corporations, to emerge. But by year 2000, facing the depletion of the multinational corporations, capitalist powers had to develop a process of destruction of productive forces that would allow the passage to a superior Form of Accumulation.

The crisis was already there in the heart of world economy, American economy and the bursting of the "dotcom" bubble had started a serious recession. There was only one way of countering these tendencies: overwhelming the multinational corporations by means of a process of centralisation of capitals, with an enormous development of destructive forces.

The strategy of the Project for a New American Century (PNAC)

Bush launched the strategy known as Project for a New American Century (PNAC) after the attacks on the Twin Towers. 11th September 2001. This strategy consisted of a worldwide political, economic and military counteroffensive hinging round the slogan "war on terror" and defeat the "axis of evil". The PNAC strategy sought to overcome the serious crisis that opened in capitalism and draw economy out of the recession and for this purpose he established the development of a war of vast scope and long-winded in order to halt the revolutionary processes in the Middle East while disciplining the workers and the peoples of the world.

The PNAC also sought to maintain keep the military complex expenditures high while carrying out an important process of destruction of productive forces. It was impossible for the American State to carry out this strategy against the opposition of American people. That is why Bush took advantage of the impact of the terrorist attack on 11S to set up a deeply antidemocratic regime in the USA supported by the Patriot Act that sought to limit democratic liberties and the freedom of expression of the workers and the people of the USA and so to silence the voices of those who might choose to oppose this strategy.

The regime of the Patriot Act was a de facto reform of the Constitution, which placed the Executive Power, the army and security services in the centre of the political regime in the USA and so trying to wipe out historic democratic conquests of the American People. At the same time, a number of laws and decrees produced important cuts in the democratic liberties: attack on liberties, especially those of Muslim origin and the criminalisation of oppositionists.

The PNAC was a strategy meant to deliver a hard blow to the peoples of the world that might challenge the strength of capitalist powers and simultaneously sought to resume the offensive against the masses of the developed countries.

The campaign "Global War Over Terrorism" (GWOT), was boosted from the USA, but was adopted by all the capitalist governments and states in the world. The Political-military front that was articled round PNAC, expressed in the military coalition that carried out the invasion on Iraq in 2003, was one of the greatest in the history of capitalism within the economic scope. Bush sought to re-launch economy by copying Reagan with a bubble based on credits for mass consumption, this time hinging round housing.

Millions, lured by the ease with which these loans could be obtained, signed up and that was how the bubble of subprime mortgages soared. It began in 2002 and it burst 2007. All the financial structure signed up sub-prime papers that promised fabulous business and grew and grew for ever providing fabulous profits. The swelling of the wave of house purchasing pushed the industry of construction leaped and together with it, inflation began.

The prices of all the building materials soared and dragged all the prices behind it. To stop the rampant inflation wave, the Fed raised the rates of interest that rose from 1% to 5.75% in 3 years, but this rate hike made the credit granted to badly-off families too expensive for them to pay and aggravated the debts unpaid.

The End of the Corporations

Investment banks began to issue the MBS (Mortgage Backed Securities and the CDO (Collateralized Debt Obligation) papers that were to serve as insurance to cover any possible defaults. These documents were negotiated all round the world and became part of the coffers of the world financial system. Due to the gigantic magnitude of the credit bubble underway, the G7 states summoned the Basil II agreement in 2004, seeking to overcome the limitations of Basil I that ignored the essential aspect of credits: their quality and probability of loan default.

In 2004, in order to overcome these limitations, Basil II proposed a new set of recommendations that prove useless, because the Bush administration had already boosted an enormous bubble and pushed capitalism towards. The whole financial system was flooded with MBS and CDO, the value of which fell abruptly. By the year 2006, the USA Army and the Coalition for Freedom got militarily mired because of the heroic Iraqi resistance against the invasion. Simultaneously, the resistance of American people against the repression of the regime of the Patriot Act and the increasing unpopularity of the Iraq war plunged Bush into disrepute.

In this way, the two fundamental pillars of political, economic and military strategy of PNAC was suffering from increasing depletion and deterioration. The military defeat in Iraq meant the final blow for the PNAC strategy and opened a political crisis for the Bush administration. This political crisis combined within the economic scope with the disaster caused by the subprime bubble. The increase of the rates of interest that the Fed had boosted to stop the inflation made debtors unable to pay for the loans and so the bubble was pricked and banks were flooded with bad loans.

By 2006 about fifty financier businesses went bankrupt, there were millions of embargoes and investment banks together with the world financial system, faced the menace of bankruptcy. The Bush administration had managed to have a million, two hundred thousand Americans were cheated and far from fulfilling their dream of a house of their own, they were now being evicted from their homes. By 2007, the sub-prime burst and was global. If Reagan's bubble was the beginning of the globalisation, "bush bubble" was its end.

When the subprime bubble burst it revealed the depletion of the globalisation as a regime of accumulation and that of the multinational corporations as a form of accumulation. The military defeat of the USA impeded the burning of capitals and the process of destruction

The End of the Corporations

necessary to allow reaching a higher level of centralisation of capitals that manages to respond to the process of depletion of multinational corporations.

We are not saying that there was no destruction of productive forces; there was and the invasion turned Iraq, which used to be one of the most beautiful countries on earth, heritage of the emergence of humanity, into absolute rubble? If we add what happened in Afghanistan to this conflagration, the destruction is terrible but absolutely below the round of destruction carried out in the post-war.

A simple comparison will allow us appreciate the magnitude of this phenomenon: The Vietnam War, for example, in the post-war, lasted 11 years and was, as we have already seen, part of the greatest process of destruction of productive forces that stretched for decades in vast regions of the planet.

The Iraq war was solved in barely 3 years, to the detriment of the USA. The defeat of the PNAC had immediate effects on economy. Not only the crisis broke out in 2007, but because of this, also the process of centralisation of capitals fell. This can be verified in the data of the M&A process that suffered a hard blow with the crisis and fell 50% with respect to the levels previous to 2007.

The data of the M&A process prove that with the defeat of the PNAC the process of centralisation of capitals failed to make headway and suffered a severe setback. About 2010 when M&A reached $2.4 billion and thanks to the bailouts there was an increase of 23% with respect to 2009 and the strongest of all the period from 2008, for Thomson Reuters.

But all the data show that capitalism did not manage to return to the level of centralization of capitals that was necessary to overcome the depletion of multinational corporations, which as from 2007 – as we have seen in chapter 1 – began to queue to file bankruptcy.

The crisis made the M&A recede in relation to the levels from before 2007. Why – in the entire period that goes from the eighties up to now – has capitalism not managed to produce a process of destruction of productive forces similar to the levels attained in the post-war? Why have the powers failed to overcome the crisis caused by the depletion of the corporations? Why have they not achieved a superior form of

The End of the Corporations

accumulation of capital? We can find the explanation if we analyse some of the most outstanding political events in the XX century.

The fall of the Berlin Wall: A blow to globalisation

The fall of the Berlin Wall was a hard blow at capitalism and its globalisation. When the wall fell, the governments of the capitalist powers and the Stalinist regimes were working in partnership advancing with a brutal exploiting offensive and renewing together the Yalta and Postdam agreements.

But having toppled the pro-capitalist dictatorships in those countries, the popular mobilisation proceeded to hamper the joint plans of the powers. Without their Stalinist partners found it difficult to carry on with their plans against the masses of the most important economies. At the same time, the chain of popular uprisings grew and after the collapse of Stalinism in the countries of Eastern Europe, the collapse of the dictatorships in the USSR and in the republics in their orbit. The consequences for capitalism were important, because after the fall of the Berlin wall the circumstance that allowed the super-exploitation of European and German working class.

A fundamental condition that facilitated the exploitation of European and German workers during the post-war was to maintain the division by means of the Wall. Its collapse allowed a process of unification of the powerful European and German working class, one of the most highly qualified, concentrated, enjoying the greatest social achievements and the highest level of culture in the world.

At the same time, the oppressed nationalities that during the post-war had been violently shoved under imperialist domination began a process of liberation and this swept away the frontiers imposed by Yalta and Postdam. Because of Stalinist leaders who fell after 1989, imperialism had managed to survive the defeats in Vietnam, in China, in Korea and could continue with their systematic destruction of productive forces.

They had transformed these political defeats into even greater hardships for the masses which afforded great profits for the multinationals. But after the fall of the wall, these leaders of the "world official left", who had rendered great services to capitalism but now no longer had all this power.

The "world order" of the post-war fell and the "new world order" proved to be a terrible disorder for the capitalist powers. This is the way the IWL explains it, *"the bankruptcy of Stalinism in the 90s weakened the world order in two respects:* **the counterrevolutionary apparatuses that used to hold back and negotiate in the name of socialism...** *could no longer fulfil this task... there is a new world order established unilaterally on the institutions of imperialism and of the USA...* **It seems to be stronger than the previous one, but actually it is weaker...**" (35)

This explains why with globalisation, capitalism did not manage to match the economic successes of the Keynesian regime. The collapse of the Berlin Wall prevented a global GPA from cropping up like in Yalta and Postdam. These agreements that allowed for the post-war boom had been destroyed by the collapse of the Berlin Wall; together with them the economic and political order that had prevailed for the previous forty years collapsed.

The governments of the G7, analysts, and journalists of all kinds proclaimed that the fall of the wall was the triumph of capitalism and "the end of socialism". Many believed this story and most of the left succumbed to terrible confusion. We shall not go into debates that these events produced. We shall limit ourselves to verifying the impact that they had on economy. China is the best proof of the hard blow that the fall of Berlin Wall meant for capitalism and the course of globalisation.

The opposite event took place in China: the wall did not fall there. The Tienanmen demonstrations were ruthlessly repressed and defeated. As from that moment on China established itself as the "paradise" of the multinationals. Having repressed the demonstrations, China made headway in obtaining better rates of exploitation and all kinds of facilities for the multinationals take root.

If the fall of the CP dictatorships had complicated the plans of the capitalist powers in Europe, the triumph of the Chinese CP transformed that country to a bastion and a life buoy for capitalism. With the triumph of Chinese CP, capitalist powers obtained an immense market of millions of workers that Chinese dictatorship had disciplines to offer low wages, labour conditions of super-exploitation and that allowed – as we have seen – the growth of their economy in the 90s.

Salaries and labour conditions were very much deteriorated in the remaining countries of the former Stalinist orbit. Imperialism took advantage of these "comparative advantages" and this helped towards the growth of economy and granted the recovery of the rate of profit in the 90s that remained unshaken for most of the decade. Capitalism achieved a victory in China and had an economic mouthful of fresh air.

But with the fall of the Berlin Wall, their strategic plans suffered a tremendous blow, because it was the parties and their leaders, the ones who had rendered great service to capitalism by negotiating an agreement on the capitalist reconstruction of Europe who had fallen, those who had allowed the development of modern multinationals and halted revolutionary processes.

The collapse of the Yalta and Postdam that had made the boom possible was a strategic blow for capitalism. This is the central explanation of the reasons of which capitalist powers could not - in globalisation – develop a round of destruction of productive forces superior to that of the II World War or the post-war, which would have allowed them to overcome the depletion of the multinational corporations.

In this way, the fall of the Berlin Wall is the necessary prologue to the fall of Wall Street 20 years later. At the same time the fall of the Wall and the crisis of the Tigers modified the axles of the articulation of world economy. The economy of the Keynesian regime developed **round the USA- Europe axle** but the recovery of the proletariats and the masses of these countries during the post-war prevented capitalism from retrieving the high rates of exploitation that gave room for the boom.

That is why, the multinationals and the Keynesian regimes began to be depleted, the articulation axle shifted to **USA-Asiatic Southeast** (Japan and Tigers) in the transition from the Keynesian regime to globalisation. In globalisation, the axle of articulation of world economy shifted once more when the capitalist dictatorship of the Chinese CP was consolidated and economy was articulated hinging round the **USA/China** axle, the only place where a revolution headed by the masses against the pro-capitalist dictatorship of the CP has been – so far – defeated.

The course of globalization

So now we have seen the regime of globalisation, its complex structure, the emergence of an enormous mass of capital for financial speculation, the fictitious and parasitical character this capital consists of and rotates in economy.

We have also seen the emergence of multinational corporations, the role of Banks of Investment in the heart of its structure and of world economy. This structural picture allows us to understand how each of

The End of the Corporations

these constitutive elements of capitalism behaved since the beginning of the current crisis. We have also seen the tendencies that are developing since the beginning of the crisis. And we have analysed the current crisis comparing it to the '29 crisis so as to understand the similitude and the differences between both episodes that capitalism has had to face in the days of its decadence. However, the comprehension of the current crisis cannot be resolved by simply having an anecdotal look at it. Questions crop up one after the other: ¿Where is capitalism moving to? ¿Has globalisation finished?

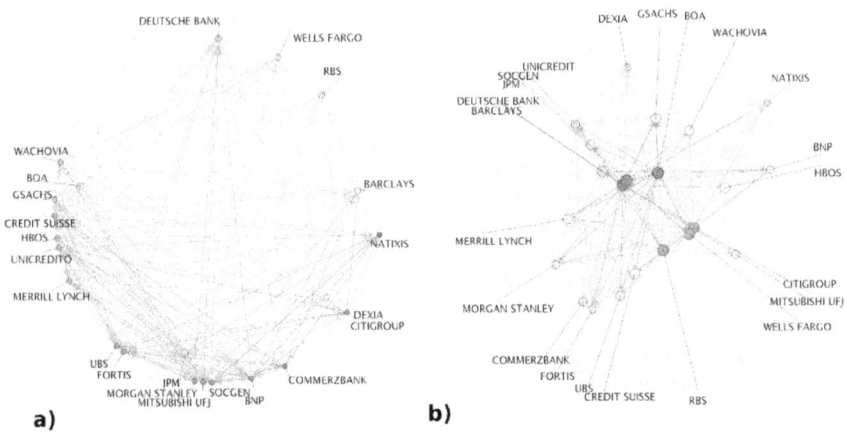

This chart shows the most important multinational corporations and their importance in the world economy. The lines show the deep interrelation of the Banks of investment and the nodes stand for the concentration of capital. Research offered by the scientific magazine Nature in June 2012. Source: Nature.com

The tendencies analysed as a whole in chapter II indicate that globalisation is coming to an end and capitalism must set up a new regime of accumulation as well as new form of accumulation that will prove superior to those of the worn out and a broken multinational corporations. Can this be done? What does it depend on? We began the answers to these questions by comparing this crisis to the one o '29 from a more historic point of view. But in order to answer them, not quite so circumstantial: ¿Has capitalism suffered this kind of crisis before in its history? ¿How has it solved it?

The analysis of the crises that capitalism has developed throughout its history has allowed us to understand the dynamics, the laws and the possible outcomes of the current crisis of capitalism. The role of the capital and its relations with the different modes of production developed in the previous centuries, the different manners that the

The End of the Corporations

capital developed in order to accumulate the capital and the successive crises of the process of accumulation are the items we shall present as from the next chapter.

Notes

(1) Ronald Reagan and Margaret Thatcher were the heads of the USA and of England respectively

(2) Robert Brenner: Turbulence in World economy

(3) The New Economy: What's New, What's Not. John B. Harms Tim Knapp

(4) Gerard Dumenil and Dominique Levy, "The Profit Rate: Where and How Much Did it Fall? Did it recover? (USA 1948-1097), 2005

(5) Nahuel Moreno. Tesis sobre la situación mundial- International Secretariat of the IWL-FI - 20/10/84

(6) Robert Brenner: Turbulence in World Economy

(7) Nahuel Moreno. "Opinión: La crisis ya empezó" International Courier 18, 1986

(8) Nahuel Moreno Tesis de la LIT sobre la situación mundial. 1985 (our highlighting)

(9) Marx: El Capital, Third Book, chapter II, Rate of profit, (our highlighting)

(10) Nahuel Moreno Tesis de la LIT sobre la situación mundial. 1985 (our highlighting)

(11) & (12) Nahuel Moreno. Economy School for Cadres. January '85 (our highlighting)

(13) *"Even if officially concealed, the problem of the private property of banks members of the Federal Reserve has been repeatedly challenged in Federal courts of justice as was the case of Lewis vs. the USA, decided by the 9th Circuit Court of Appeals that ruled that the Reserve Banks are independent corporations, of private property and locally controlled.."* Stephen Lendman Research Associate of the Centre for Research on Globalization

(14) Nahuel Moreno. Tesis sobre la situación mundial. LIT- CI (1984)

(15) Nahuel Moreno Tesis de la LIT sobre la situación mundial. 1985 (our highlighting)

(16), (17), (18) & (19) Alejandro Iturbe. El sistema financiero mundial y su crisis - Part 3 Marxism Alive 22, 2009

(20) y (21) Nahuel Moreno. Opinión. La crisis ya empezó. International Courier 18, 1986, page 8

(22) Daniel Munevar. www.cadtm.org

(23) UNCTAD, World Investment Report 2002, page 85. Sara Anderson y John Cavanagh, Top 200 - The Rise of Corporate Global Power, Institute for Policy Studies, Washington, 2000, page 3

(24) James Petras, "El mito de la tercera revolución científico-tecnológica en la era del imperio neo-mercantilista", en *La Página de Petras, www.rebelion.org*, 28 de July 2001.

(25) Karl Marx The Capital Book I Chapter XXIII General Law and Capitalist Accumulation

(26) V. I. Lenin: Imperialism, Highest Stage of Capitalism. Chapter II Banks and their new role (our highlighting)

(27) Moody's "$640 billion y 640 days later: how the companies that produced Private Equity during the recession in the USA

(28) U.S. International Banking Facilities (IBFs) Japanese Offshore Market (JOM) Bangkok International Banking Facilities (BIBFs)

(29) Charles Moyer, James Mc Guigan: Contemporary Financial Administration, page 505

(30) Robert Brenner "Turbulences in world economy"

(31) Robert Brenner "Turbulences in world economy"

(32) Jonas Portyguar y JR Soares: International Courier, February1999, number 76 "La crisis del neoliberalismo y del capitalismo globalizado pone al mundo al borde de una depresión".

(33) Jonas Portyguar y JR Soares: International Courier, February 1999, number 76 "La crisis del neoliberalismo y del capitalismo globalizado pone al mundo al borde de una depresión".

(34) Robert Brenner "Turbulences in world economy"

(35) IWL-FI "La situation in the world". Texts part of the "Theses on the world situation" VIII World Congress IWL-FI July 2006 Marxism Alive12 2005 (our highlighting)

The End of the Corporations

A Marxist explanation to the capitalist world economic crisis

CHAPTER V

Forms

The End of the Corporations

CHAPTER V: FORMS

"It is a well- known fact that conquest, enslavement, robbery and murder: to make it short, violence, play a protagonist role in real life history. But in the sweet political economy idyll has reined for ever... actually, the methods of original accumulation were everything but idyllic... they would resort to the power of the state, to organised and concentrated violence in society...".

Karl Marx. Capital, Book 1, Chapter XXIV

In the face of the magnitude of the historic character of the current crisis of capitalism, it may be well worth while to stop and ask ourselves: Has capitalism ever been through crises of similar importance? In what way have these crises been overcome? What political and social phenomena spawned the crisis? And the other way round: what political and social phenomena did the crises produce?

In order to answer these questions it is necessary to see the current crisis from a more historical perspective and to see how the different crises and analyse how the different crises developed within their different stages and how capitalism tended to solve the contradictions that were the produce of their own development.

In this chapter we shall publicise and develop the General Law of Forms of Capitalist Accumulation. This law enables us to analyse applying the Marxist laws of accumulation of capital, the different forms that throughout the history of capitalism, emerged to accumulate the capital and what are the forms of accumulation characteristic for each stage of capitalism.

Together with the above, we shall analyse the dynamics of the Forms of accumulation the characteristic of which is the succession of phases of development and depletion linked to periods of long expansion and stagnation live throughout the history of capitalist economy.

Finally we shall see the political-social mechanisms that explain the way in which the transition from a lower Form of Accumulation to an upper form through the development of capitalism.

General Law of the forms of Capitalist Accumulation

The Forms of Accumulation of Capital, and Predominant Forms.

Definition

The process through which capitalists accumulate means of production on one pole in order to accumulate capital and salaries workers on the other pole, in order to accumulate more capital.

As Marx explained, *"...the reproduction on a broader scope in order to accumulate more capital, i.e.: accumulation reproduces capitalist relationship on a broader scope: more capitalists or greater capitalists on this pole, more salaried workers on the other... Consequently, accumulation of capital is increase of proletariat... Every individual capital is a greater or lesser concentration of means of production with the corresponding command over a larger or smaller army of workers. Every accumulation becomes a means in the service of a new accumulation..."* (1)

The main target of capitalism is that capitalist accumulate capital and obtain profit. The necessary precondition in order to obtain this is that the means of production and exchange are to be private property, a target achieved by the capitalists by means of a historic process that placed productive, commercial firms under their control while expropriating the remaining social classes.

Therefore we can define Forms of Accumulation as such firms, property of the capitalist class, to accumulate capital at a determined period of time. Capitalists never used. Capitalists never used a sole form of accumulation.

There have always been different forms of accumulation i.e.: different commercial, productive and financial firms acted in order to accumulate capital and they, in turn, reflect the different sectors of capitalist class.

Capitalism finally imposed its rule as the dominating mode of production between the XVIII and XIX centuries, when bourgeoisie seized power in the most important countries and stamped out the remains of the feudal domination in the state.

In the historic periods, when capitalism was still an embryonic element and not the dominating mode of production, as well as in the days of predominance of capitalism different Forms of Capitalist Accumulation coexisted.

These Forms of Accumulation developed in an uneven and combined manner hinging round a predominant Form of Accumulation that was the driving and structuring engine of economy.

That is to say, when diverse Forms of Accumulation act simultaneously and at different levels of development, they hinge round the Predominant Form of accumulation and interplay with the Predominant Form of Accumulation that constitutes a Regime of Accumulation around the axis on which the entire development of capitalism is ordered. We call this Regime of Accumulation.

Together with the concept of Forms of Accumulation, the concepts of the Regime of Accumulation, Poles of Accumulation and Axis of Accumulation are parts of the General Law of Forms of Accumulation, whose respective definitions are to be found in Chapter III. The predominant Forms of Capitalist Accumulation have been as follows:

A- At and before the stage of the original accumulation (from X to XVIII century)

Pre-industrial forms of Productive accumulation	Forms of Financial Accumulation
Commercial Nations (from X to XV centuries)	Bankers and Usury (XIV to XVII centuries)
Factories (from XIV to XV ")	
Manufactures (from XVI to XVIII ")	
Business Enterprises (from XVII to XVIII ")	

B- The apogee of capitalism (from XVIII century to XIX)

Forms of Industrial Productive Accumulations	Forms of financial productive Accumulation
Industry (XVIII and XIX centuries)	Banks and Credit (XVIII and XIX centuries)

C- The stage of decadence of capitalism (XIX century up to XXI century)

Merger of the Productive and Financial Accumulations Forms

Monopolies	Late XIX and early XX centuries
Multinationals	XX century (between 1945 and 80's)
Multinational Corporations	Late XX century up to XXI

We shall now work out a historical analysis of the different Predominant Forms of Accumulation in the different stages of capitalism.

A) Forms of Accumulation specific to the stage of original accumulation

The first an embryonic Forms of Capitalist Accumulation began to surface between the X century and XIV century, even before the beginning of the capitalist mode of production, when the feudal mode of production still prevailed and it coexisted with the diverse modes of production and barbarian, Asiatic and even slave holder social formations.

The original or primeval stage of capitalism is the one when the bases for the development of capitalist production were historically established. In the early years of that stage, feudal relations of production existed in Europe and the vast majority of the population were owners of their own means of production and subsistence be that the small properties of the peasants or the great properties of the nobles.

During the stage of Primeval Accumulation, capitalists began to expropriate the nobles, the peasants and even sectors of capitalists. And were causing a cleavage between the producers and the means of production of which they were the owners. This spawned two phenomena: on the one hand, means of production became goods and capital the price of which was determined at the market. On the other hand the working class cropped up, that is to say the dispossessed workers, whose labour also is a commodity the price of which is determined at the market.

This is the way Marx explains it, *"therefore, the process that creates the relation of the capital can be nothing but the process of a split between the worker and the property of his labour conditions, a process that, on the other hand, transforms the means of production and social subsistence into capital and, on the other hand, transforms direct producers into salaried workers. The so-called original accumulation is more than just a historic process of split between the producer and the means of production. It looks like "original" because it configures the prehistory of capital and the mode of production that corresponds to it."* (2)

The stage of the capitalist primitive accumulation affected the great rural masses more than anybody else for they were evicted from the land while traditional forms and rights of access to means of production, to natural resources, to communal rights, to pasturelands, of open countryside and so on. Between the late XV century and early XVI century, feudal routines were dissolved in England due to violent eviction of peasants and the usurpation of communal lands by the noble lords who transformed them into pastures for cattle.

The second wave of expropriations was between the XVII and XVIII centuries when ecclesiastic possessions were expropriated and distributed out to the oligarchy and the peasants dwelling there were evicted. The process of the Primitive Capitalist Accumulation had some development also in the process of colonization of all the remaining nations and continents as an outcome of the geographic discoveries in the XV and XVI centuries. This process led to ruthless annihilation of pre-capitalist civilisations and modes of production in America, Asia, Africa and Oceania and this made the expropriation of millions indigenous peoples and peoples that lived in savagery, barbarism or Asian civilisations.

The following Forms of Accumulation of Capital developed between the X and the XVIII centuries:

1. **Trading Nations; Forms of Accumulation of the trading bourgeoisie**

Trading nations or maritime republics that cropped up between the X and the XIII centuries were Forms of Capitalist Accumulation whose goal was to accumulate capital practising trade based on the dominion over one or more maritime routes. These trading nations constituted an embryonic accumulation regime, with the maritime industry as the pole of accumulation. The Mediterranean was the axis of accumulation and was based on a number of cities located on what today is the territory of Italy: Amalfi, Pisa, Gaeta, Ancona, Bari, Ragusa, Noli, etc., and the powers of those days: Genoa and Venice.

Another regime of accumulation of the Trading Nations was located on the shores of the Baltic sea, with their axis including the cities of north of Germany and German trading communities round the Baltic Sea: Netherlands, Norway, Sweden, England, Poland, Russia, part of Finland and Denmark as well as regions where today Estonia and Latvia are to be found. This federation of cities constituted a great Nation known as Hanseatic League or Hansain the mid and late XII century and the early XIII with numerous cities in the north of Europe and surrounding the Baltic Sea: Lübeck in 1158, Rostock, Wismar, Stralsund, Greifswald, Stettin, Danzig, Ebbing, etc.

The name Trading Nations comes from the fact that they were enterprise-nations inasmuch as they enjoyed broad independence from the feudal authorities and an autochthonous. One or more families controlled the nation and this was what gave them the character of oligarchic republics where each one of them had its own currency, its own army, fleet, commercial colonies known as fundagos and "consuls of nations" who would watch over the commercial interests of their respective cities in the Mediterranean ports.

This is the way Engels explained it, *"The Venetians and the Genoese in the port of Alexandria or in Constantinople, each "nation" in his own fondango residence, inn, deposit, apart from headquarters constituted complete commercial associations"*. The trading nations begin their phase of emerging accompanying the expansion of European economy that was blooming in the midst of the apogee of the feudal mode of production in the X century.

The End of the Corporations

The great surpluses, the wealth of the nobles of Normandy, Burgundy, Castile, Aragon, Genoa, Venice, etc., allowed for an important commercial circulation over the Baltic Sea, as well as over the Mediterranean and the emergence of fairs. The most important of them was Champagne on the territory of what today is France, and they acted as a commercial land bridge between the two seas. The Hansa was selling ships and even reached the Mediterranean and Italy.

The Trading Nations emerged from the very bowels of the Feudal system and from previous social formations, such as primitive communism. This is how Frederic Engels explains it: *"the medieval merchant was in no way an individualist for he was essentially a member of some association as were all his contemporaries. In the countryside, the brand association predominated. Each peasant had his plot of land – originally of the same size... and consequently an equal share in the rights of the joint brand... And the same goes in no lesser degree for commercial associations that spawned the overseas trading... It is here that for the first time we come across profit and rate of profit... in the great commercial societies we can take it for granted that profit is distributed pro rata proportionately to the capital invested, exactly the same as the rights of the brand are distributed proportionately to the justified participation in the plot of land... Consequently, the rate of profit is the same for all."* (3)

Trading Nations also accumulated capital as an incipient proletariat began to develop and this is how Frederic Engels explains it: *"Navigation, on the scale at which Italian and Hanseatic maritime republics practised it, would have been impossible without the assistance of sailors, i.e.: salaried workers (whose wage relation) could be concealed under corporate forms with profit sharing) just as impossible as it would have been for galleys to function without salaried or slave oarsmen. In practically all the cases, the guilds of the mines that originally consisted of associate workers had already become stock companies for the exploitation of the enterprise by means of salaried workers. And in the textile industry, the merchant had already started putting the small weaving masters directly in his service, providing them with yarn and making them transform it into cloth in consideration of a fixed wage... Here we can see the early budding of capitalist formation of surplus value"* (4)

The Trading Nations began in the X century and achieve very high rates of profit. Just so as to be able to have a standard, let us compare the revenue of Genoa, which was one of the most important Trading Nations with France, the riches and most important monarchy in those days according to Perry Anderson, *"In 1293, the maritime taxes of the port of Genoa produced three times and a half more than all the royal revenues of French monarchy"* **(5)**

The accumulated capitals were so large that they allowed the emergence and establishment of gold standard for currencies, as Perry Anderson explains it, *"The maritime power of Genoa and Venice was what ensured a continuous trade surplus with Asia, a surplus that financed their return to gold... The return to gold currency in Europe in mid XIII century, with the simultaneous coinage (in 1252) of the januarius and the florin in Genoa and Florence was the resplendent symbol of commercial vitality of the cities."* **(6)**

The basis of economic expansion was the high rate of profit achieved by the Trading Nations and this is how Frederic Engels explains it, *"This original rate of profit was necessarily very high...the business was monopolist trade with monopolist profit."* **(7)** The Trading Nations began an upward process to the apogee that included the XII and XIII centuries and produced an outstanding economic expansion in the embryonic regimes of accumulation that settled in the Mediterranean, the North Sea and the Baltic and was fed back with the economic apogee and the economic expansion of the feudal mode of production predominant in Europe with which they developed and combined.

The capitalists of the Trading Nations arrived at all kinds of agreements and associations of a corporative character in order to obtain jurisdictional, fiscal and customs privileges and at the same time mastery of various personal domains was achieved. During the upwards phase of Trading Nations, new exchange operations and accounting emerged, scientific discoveries were made and technologies cropped up to ensure commercial routes and to protect investments.

Seaworthy helmsmen were trained and lighthouses were built, compass was perfected and so were mathematics, astronomy, cartography and geography: all that in the service of navigational industry. Cities in danger of being raided by pirates organised their defence autonomously creating powerful navies to create bases, call ports and commercial establishments that influenced the political life tremendously. That is why, in the XI century Trading Nations took up the offensive and fought important wars against the Byzantine and Islamic maritime power and thus competed for the control of commerce with Asia, Africa and Mediterranean routes.

The Crusades allowed them to destroy the power of Islam in the Mediterranean and the Norman invasion of England put an end to the Viking incursions into the North Sea. The emerging of the rate of profit of the Trading Nations gave continuity to the equalization process of the different rates of profit a process that preceded the fall of the rate of profit and Frederic Engels explains it like that: *"The equalization of these different corporative rates of profit was established by the inverse process, by competition. At the beginning, the different rates of profit (were equalised) for the different markets of the same nation... Next it was the turn for a gradual to equalize the rates of profit in the different nations that exported equal or similar good to the same markets, so quite often this or that nation would be squashed and would exit."* (8)

The excessive accumulation of capitals that occurred after the equalization of the rates of profit caused the rate of profit in the Trading Nations to slide down and this process was combined and re-fed with the general crisis of the feudal mode of production in the XIV century. The crisis of feudalism caused the collapse of consumption, ports were paralysed, the price of goods fell abruptly and bankruptcies became widespread. This spawned a real political, economic and social cataclysm known as the "crisis of XIV century" when nearly 40% of the population of Europe died.

That was the beginning of the depletion of the Trading Nations and a violent process of centralisation of capitals that led to wars for the domination over maritime routes. The depletion of Trading Nations as a Form of Accumulation, combined with the terminal crisis of the feudal mode of production caused an extremely violent process of destruction of productive forces and centralisation of capitals, the Hundred Years' War. Together with famine and plagues, wars annihilated nations, cities entire regions. With millions dead, the Hundred Years' War was an immense process of destruction of productive forces when capitalism was officially born.

Actually, the Hundred Years' War a number of wars between nations that controlled European economy in those days and acted as the hinge between the feudal mode of production and the capitalist mode of production that emerged and started it stage of Original Accumulation. At the same time there were enormous peasant insurrections and of the workers of craft guilds in Florence or of the weavers in Ghent.

In the XV century, geographic discoveries accelerated the decadence of the Trading Nations, according to what Frederic Engels explained, *"This process was constantly interrupted by political events while the entire Levantine commerce decayed due to the Mongolian and Turkish invasions and the great geographic-commercial discoveries carried out since 1492 did nothing but to accelerate this decadence and, later on, make it definitive."* (9)

The End of the Corporations

The Trading Nations kept on with their decadence after the geographic discoveries in the XV and XVI centuries that became possible because of the technological development and the accumulation of capital achieved during the cycle of apogee and created means for their financing. But the geographic discoveries and the process of colonisation of Africa, Asia, America and Oceania were already stemming out of the beginnings of capitalist mode of production and its stage of primitive accumulation. As these continents were being colonised and that capitalist mode of production needed a longer period to surface and be consolidated, during the first centuries capitalists often implemented capitalist Forms of Accumulation and capitalist regimes, seeking support in non-capitalist relations of production.

2. Goldsmiths and Silversmiths and the early Bankers. Form of Accumulation of Financial Bourgeoisie

Together with the Commercial Nations, another Form of Accumulation emerged: financial industry based on the first bankers and usurers. The great accumulation of capital that Trading Nations achieved, allowed for the increase of the numbers of capitalists dedicated to the industry linked to development and circulation of money, its transport, storing, insurance and loans.

Because there was the danger of robbery, the practice of placing precious bullions and coins under the custody of goldsmiths, used to work with precious metals, receive and keep gold and silver coins for capitalists who had to store the profit obtained.

As this practice became more necessary, goldsmiths started charging commissions and so they were turning into bankers as they discovered when they discovered that it was not necessary to keep all the coins deposited in their vaults, so they made them circulate as loans and diverse payments while they extended receipts of deposits for the capitalists who deposited their coins and metals.

The capitalist who made their deposits started using the receipts they had received from the goldsmiths to make their payments. The goldsmiths extended receipts of deposits for a higher value than that of the coins that were in their custody and in this way, the value of the money or reserve that the goldsmiths had at hand to face withdrawals in gold and silver coins represented merely a fraction of the total value or the receipts extend by them.

That is how the concept of banks of fractional reserve; goldsmiths and silversmiths were no longer mere guardians; they became bankers. The activity of the banks became primarily manifest in all those place where different kinds of currency circulated and this spawned moneychangers. The first banks cropped up in 1155 and were mainly devoted to traffic but they also accepted deposits and, by XIII century southern cities in Italy, like Siena and Florence, had built rudimentary banking centres.

In the XII century, pooled funds began to crop up as great masses of capital deposited by various capitalists who would get organised together and began to grant government borrowing to Italian cities. In Italy, these government borrowings were known as Monti, which means pool or common fund, and Bank among the Germanic peoples, which was later Italianized as Banco and the accumulation of public loans was called either Monte or Banco, which originated the use of this words for entities that accumulated capitals as deposits.

Bankers had connections with the Trading Nations and when smaller enterprises began to mushroom in which capitalists combined commerce with the administration of money, currencies and investments. The Fugger, the Welser, the Vöhlin, the Höchstetter, the Hirschvogel, etc. are the great families of Berman bankers who, together with the Italians dominated the circulation of goods and money in those centuries in European economy, just as the Rostchild would do in the XIX century.

The bankers of Genoa, Florence, Venice, the Hansa as well as those from Castile, Aragon and Portugal financed the ventures of geographic discoveries of XVI and XVII centuries. These discoveries were in quest not only of new routes of navigation abut also of colonisation of new ports, exploitation of new labour and extraction of precious metals to feed the accumulation of capitals.

That so as to build up enough accumulation of capitals so as to finance and form the basis of money in metal as well as trust funds, indispensable accumulation to back necessary investments that allowed them to launch the capitalist mode of production.

This is the way Frederick Engels explained it, *"But also closer partnerships associations, with more determined targets as the Genoa Manoa that controlled the mines of alum in Phocaea in Asia Minor or on the Chios Island in XIV and XV centuries or the great commercial society of Ravensburg that since the late XIV century did business with Italy and Spain, funding branches there and the German society of the Fugger, the Welser, the Vöhlin, the Höchstetter, etc. from Augsburg, or the Hirschvogel of Nuremberg and others who, with a capital of 66000 ducats and three ships who, with a capital participated in a Portuguese expedition to India between 1550-1506 and made net profit 150% according to some and 175% according to others."* **(10)**

Transition from Trading Nations to Factories

The first form of predominant capitalist accumulation, the Trading Nations, began to emerging in X Century, and your development was possible when the allied trading powers launched numerous armed expeditions against the Muslim, the oriental Christians, Russian and Byzantine, the movement of the Cathars in the south of France and the Jews. It is estimated that the diverse slaughters and wars carried out by the crusaders caused five million deaths throughout three centuries.

The process of destruction of productive forces unleashed by the struggle against the Byzantines and the Muslim allowed them to become dominant in the Mediterranean and to reach the peak of the boom phase and to control commercial exchange in the Mediterranean and with the East. During the IV Crusade (1202-1204) Venice and Genoa took over the commercially most important maritime towns of the Byzantine Empire and became the riches states in Europe.

When the phase of depletion of Trading Nations began, a violent process of destruction of productive forces broke out with the wars of Pisa and Genoa in 1284, the wars of Saint Sabas in 1252 between Genoa and Venice, the war of Chioggia in 1372, the wars with the Kingdom of Hungary in 1352 apart from the wars against the Germanic Empire and the wars against the Popedom among others, while 1362 wars of the Hansa broke out against Denmark.

But the most important process of destruction of productive forces took place during the Hundred Years War, between the mid XIV century and mid XV, a period that was the hinge between the feudal mode of production and the capitalist one. The vicious destruction of productive forces that constituted the crisis of the XIV gave room for headway in these forms of accumulation and the process of centralisation of capitals and caused the transition of the Trading Nations to a superior for of Accumulation i.e.: Factories.

The destruction of productive forces in the Hundred Years' War was centred geographically round France that was the most important economy in those days and the bastion of feudalism. The destruction of productive forces in the Hundred Years' War was geographically centred on France that was the most important economy of those days and a bastion of feudalism.

Ravaged villages, millions on the death toll, the development of technology in the industry to serve wars caused serious alterations in the

The End of the Corporations

prices at the market of products suffering unprecedented pressures of supply and demand. At the same time millions of peasants fought wars for their freedom and this allowed for the emerging of the first salaried workers, even if in incipient numbers.

In some cases, feudal lords had to yield to the pressures of their serfs in quest of their deliverance from serfdom but in other cases the insurrections were annihilated so the Hundred Years War implied a struggle between sectors of the dominating classes for control over the emerging industrial zones of greater economic importance such as Guyenne and Gascony.

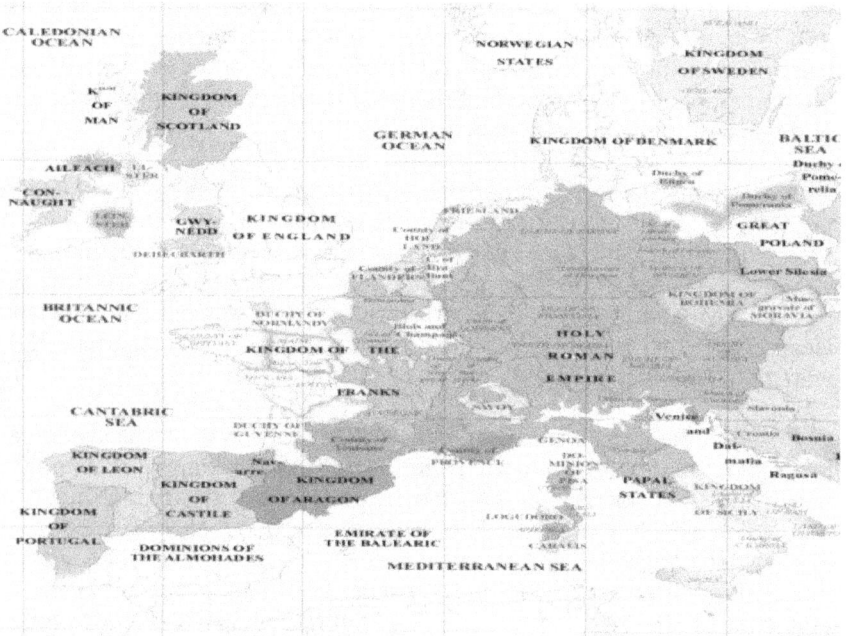

The map shows the XIV century Europe: the kingdoms, duchies and counties protagonists of the Hundred Years' War. Source: Euratlas

Other wars developed similarly, among them the civil war in Normandy, The War of the Roses in England, the War between England and France, the war between France and Bourgogne, the struggle for the control over Flanders and the Netherlands, civil war in Brittany and civil wars in Castile and Aragon. In all the nations of those days, in duchies and kingdoms where wars occurred, alliances changed constantly as well as the sectors of classes whether nobles or capitalists aligned in different manners. With the development of war industry great fortunes of bankers and capitalists also cropped up financing war industry and military technology.

After the Hundred Years' war, an important part of the nobility disappeared important centralisation of capitals occurred and bourgeoisie continued its ascent so the ascent of the world of cities based on trade, and the centres of power began to shift towards new burghs or cities where the new Forms of Accumulation, Factories, settled. During the decline of the Trading Nations, Portugal and the Kingdoms of Aragon and Castile developed enormous commercial activity with the geographic discoveries of XV century and this transformed them into powers even if as the last glow of the decaying Mediterranean capitalism.

3. Factories, Form of Accumulation of the merchants, entrepreneurs and contractors

Factories are a Form of Accumulation that emerged in the XVI when capitalist merchants began to hire salaried workers in the cities as well as in the countryside. Merchant developed these ventures and became contractors since they found it cheaper to produce commodities in ports than to transport them one port to another and this allowed them to achieve important savings and profits far better than what they used to obtain with simple commercial activity.

According to Engels, *"... there already was a rate of profit of commercial capital. What could then urge the merchants to take over the accumulative function of contractors? Only one simple thing: greater profit..."* (11) Factories were based on manual work and simple cooperation, where each worker complied with a determined task without all the workers who acted on the goods grouping in the same workshop.

It is the capitalist himself who takes the goods from one place to another, for different workers to give them a different touch. In these techniques of industrial branches, such as textiles, goldsmithing or metallurgy productivity of labour was achieved as from the simple cooperation and manual work following the tradition of craftsmanship.

These Forms of Accumulation had their pole of accumulation in textile industry and mining and constituted a regime of accumulation in which the emerging industries as factories combined production and distribution with Trading Nations. The axis of accumulation was the tripod constituted by Normandy, England and the Netherlands on the Channel and the North Sea. It was precisely this geographic zone, together with France, what constituted the epicentre of the violent process of destruction of productive forces that the Hundred Years' War implied when the dominating classes disputed the control over these incipient new industries.

The Hundred Years' War expressed the emerging of a dynamic regime of accumulation as an alternative to the decadence of the regime of capitalist accumulation established in the Mediterranean. This is how Moreno explained it: *"there is an extraordinary development of Mediterranean capitalism the decadence of which had already begun by the time America is discovered. Its discovery does nothing but to accelerate its decadence and the development of the new north-western capitalism that had already emerged and shifting towards the Mediterranean before the discovery of our continent. Mediterranean capitalism, impregnated with aristocratism and feudal forms, has a commercial character, usurious and international in opposition to the northeast of Europe that was manufacturing and national."* **(12)**

Factories are Forms of Accumulation where salaried labour was exploited to produce commodities and so be able to compete better with the other markets. Factories and the grouping of salaried workers is a process of exploiting salaries labour something that allowed the merchants-entrepreneurs to push the prices down so as to compete better with the other merchants who tended to adopt that form of production so as not to lose the contest for markets. Factories and the grouping of salaried workers is a process that went along 3 paths that spawned different ventures: a) privatised craftsmen's guilds, b) domiciled rural labour and c) privatized mining concessions. Let us analyse these three entrepreneur variants:

a) **Privatised craftsmen's guilds**

One of the slopes that spawned the factories was the process of privatisation of craftsmen's guilds, industries that existed in feudalism and produced small-scale for small communities, following strict norms of production determining common targets that started turning property of capitalists.

Those craftsmen guilds had a pretty rigid internal organisation on three levels: masters, journeymen and apprentices-servants. Only masters were entitled to vote statutes by which the guild is to be ruled and to appoint the prosecutors and bosses. Journeymen were entitled to living quarters, food and a salary but the apprentices-servants had very low wages and remained in that state for a lifetime.

At first, equality and solidarity were the main traits of the guilds. Conditions of contracts and of work would vary from one guild to another and as time went by, the merchant would proceed as intermediary in the

The End of the Corporations

activities of the exchange of goods. Later on, regular purchase of good from the small producers became habitual and the merchant would provide small producers with raw material and would lend them money and so the small producers would fall under the economic power of the merchant.

Simultaneously a process of social differentiation began inside the workshops that were dominated by the masters, who were beginning to turn into owners. This accelerated the process of drifting apart of the masters and the apprentices while the former began speed up the appropriation process until they turned the guilds into companies of their property. In turn capitalist societies emerged between commercial capitalists and craftsmen masters or the masters were expropriated by means of usury.

Regardless the manner, the guilds gradually became factories for they became enterprises with one or more capitalists as owners. In several cases, the power of the privatised guilds spread as far as control of municipal governments and in industries connected to exports, the master could much faster become capitalist and owner of the enterprise.

That is how the mediaeval craftsmanship workshops gradually disappeared and were replaced by new privatised workshops out of which the new capitalists or entrepreneurs were emerging. That is how Reyna Pastor de Togneri explains it: *"handicraft corporations fall into a period of stagnation that was to last until the XVII and XVIII centuries when they vanish because they could not face up to developing capitalist forms. Organised in such a way as to increasingly benefit the masters, they will as often as not spawn new entrepreneurs."* **(13)**

b) **Rural domiciled labour**

Rural domiciled labour is an enterprise that crops up because capitalist merchants would hire peasant labour to produce their goods. The merchant takes goods and raw material to peasant families' homes and the latter will do different kinds of work such as weaving, yarning, dyeing, Peasant families combine the work they do for the capitalist and their own tasks in the fields until one by one, they fall under the control of the capitalist either out of need or because they become indebted to him.

That is how Reyna Pastor de Togneri explains it, *"distributed the premium among the peasants" and so acquired part of their workforce... the entrepreneurs controlled the diverse processes of production and took the yarn to the fuller mills, to the dyer's, etc. Due to this system, the peasant gradually turns into an industrial home worker who produces for the market and sells part of his workforce to the entrepreneur."* **(14)**

This kind of Factories cropped up due to the changes that took place in textile industry. For centuries, industry was based on luxurious drapery consumed by the oligarchies of Burgundy, Florence, Venice, the Papacy and Genoa, etc. But as from the beginning of the crisis of XIV, this luxurious drapery was in crisis due to the paralysis of commerce, the fall of the living standards and the decadence of nobility. Luxurious drapery included the complex technique of producing silk brought through Islam and stolen by the Crusaders.

Textile industry based on luxurious drapery was relegated to the background by the cheaper woollen drapery consumed by the popular classes and by the bourgeoisie supplied by the wool of sheep from England and Castile something that combined with the use of windmills in Flanders and Castile and of watermills in England, taking advantage of the enormous waterfalls in those regions; that boosted the textile industry.

According to Reyna Pastor de Togneri, rural domiciled labour was the most important enterprise of the Factories: *"the importance of rural domiciled industries constituted the transitional form accrued as time went by; because of the number of employed workers, because of the amount of the production and because of the geographic area it occupies, this activity was doomed to accelerate the original accumulation of capital in the hands of merchants and bankers and also to be the one that would begin the transformations among the peasants... for it drove them away form the land, deprived them of their means of production and forced them to do routine work for long workdays and gradually turned them into salaried workers."* (15)

England, the place where nobility emerged much weaker after the Hundred Years' War, where textile industry had great headway because of sheep rearing as well as because of the climate with great waterfalls that allowed for the building of mills more fitted to drapery production, was the epicentre of rural domiciled labour. That was where ventures flourished that began to proletarianize masses of peasants and the merchants as well as the commercial capitalists could grab hold of the craftsmanship workshops much faster.

c) Privatisation of mining concessions

Following a process similar to the one that the craftsmanship guilds had been through, mining concessions were appropriated by capitalists, masters' turned-entrepreneurs, merchants trafficking metals and coins and purchasers of tin. Mining concessions were communities that signed up contracts with feudal authorities, charged a reward for the

The End of the Corporations

exploitation of mines and exploitation of metals and, the same as the craftsmen's guilds; they had rules that imposed equality of the members.

But, as Perry Anderson explains, mining was struck by a serious crisis in the XIV century: *"extraction of silver to which the entire urban and monetary sectors of feudal economy was connected ceased to be practicable or cost effective in the main mining zones of Central Europe because there was no way of opening deeper pits or of refining the more impure minerals... scarcity of metals caused repeated cases of debasement of the currency in one country after the other and consequently inflation rampant."* (16)

The crisis of mining exploitation together with the need for commerce to establish currencies led to increasing need of the capitalist merchants to take over mining industries and even to expand them to newly discovered and colonised territories as in the case of America, where the instauration of the system of Mita (1) implied enslaving tribes so far living in primitive communism.

The appropriation of mining concessions, the same as the appropriation of the craftsmen's workshops by capitalist or process of their privatisation, was part of the stage of the primitive capitalist accumulation or process of privatisations for it was part of the expropriation that capitalists were carrying out on the remaining social classes. In this way, the development of various industrial branches and allowed for an incipient process of development of the working class for workshops and mining settlements mushroomed and where labour force salaried.

Conclusions on Factories

Factories started emerging in the later part of the XIV. They reached their pinnacle in late XV; this gave room for expansion of economy until early XVI. Privatised craftsmen's guilds as well as the domiciled rural labour and the privatised mining concessions combined at that time with the budding Forms of Accumulation such as Trading Nations, banks and usury apart from the decaying feudal production.

Factories means headway in the centralisation and accumulation of capital and this was expressed in the importance of cities such as Flanders in textile and mining industries. But in the early ~~XVI century, factories began t~~heir phase of depletion, economy once

---

(1) Mita was a compulsory public service agrarian, mining, domestic service, etc. Native inhabitants, especially in the Andean region were assigned to the premises where they worked in semi enslaved condition.

The End of the Corporations

more became stagnant and a new violent process of destruction of productive forces occurred with the strongest points in the 80 Years' War with epicentre in Flanders and the Dutch States in mid XVI.

However, the depletion of the Factories expressed not only the contradictions coming from the capitalist development, such as the levelling and falling profit rate as happened with the Trading Nations. The depletion of Factories combined economic elements with political elements as their development has been seriously limited by the existence of nobility in power, unlike the case of Trading Nations that thrived in cities, where the bourgeoisie were in power.

Factories are enterprises the development of which challenged the social structure of feudalism, clashed against it and drowned in it. Bourgeoisie had to charge against the institutions that supported the feudal order and against the Catholic Church in order to be able to pass to a Superior Form of Accumulation. Wars combined the struggle for the centralisation of capitals and the struggle for power in the nations that nobility controlled and this gave Factory an unstable and transitional character.

Factories were not a solid Form of Accumulation as the Trading Nations were; they were rather transitional between the medieval cottage industries that by mid XVI century were developing a crisis and the capitalist manufacturing that emerge by mid XVI century. According to Alberto J. Plá, *"the qualitative leap from craftsmanship to manufacture is not simple and has an intermediate stage: that of domiciled work. But the process is slow and actually it develops by successive stages. For long periods of time, old and new forms of production coexist."* (17)

For nearly two centuries, Factories as industrial ventures that begin to have bourgeois owners at the steering wheel were a fundamental component of European economy and even if they were transitional enterprises, they were vital for the development of the mode of capitalist production during the stage of primitive accumulation.

Transition from Factories to Manufactures

During the Hundred Years' Wars important changes in military industry took place: feudal knights were overridden and first professional armies appeared not joined by pact of allegiance with their lords but paid by kings and bankers and the development of new military technology. The army and the king constituted the pillar of a new regime in a feudal state. Absolute monarchy and the challenge of economic,

The End of the Corporations

social and political power of the nobles allowed for slow headway towards benefitting the bourgeoisie that the kings encouraged.

Even if most of the population was still peasant, the economic impulse and the news no longer came from the castle or the monastery but from the cities, epicentre of the development of Factories. When they started the phase of depletion, a violent process of destruction of productive forces began that allowed for a new centralisation of capitals and development of manufactures.

This violent development of productive forces had its epicentre in the 80 Years' War, a complex of wars centred round the struggles of the protestant princes of Germany and the Netherlands that reflected the ascent of the bourgeoisie against the nobles of France and Spain, the strongest power in Europe in those days dominated by the nobles of Habsburg.

The movement of the Lutheran Reform led the process of confiscations of lands that used to belong to the Church and that was vital for the development of the textile industry. All the plot of the 80 Years' War was a set of eight different wars that took place between 1562 and 1648 and included wars of Catholics and Calvinists when the Seventeen Provinces of the Netherlands fought against their sovereign, the king of Spain, Carlos V. Those 17 provinces sought their independence from Carlos V and Spain.

The rebellion of the monarchs of the Protestants was headed by Martin Luther and Calvin, but the process of destruction of the productive forces was very violent. The nobility repressed the Protestants brutally: they were persecuted and executed with great cruelty. Among those executed there were the top leader of this radical reform, Thomas Müntzer and the Spaniard Miguel Servet.

After 80 years of vicious confrontations, destruction of cities and towns and millions mortal victims, the war ended with the triumph of Holland and gave room to the centralisation of capitals and that was where the United Provinces came from and achieved their independence and the bourgeoisie began their ascent and imposed a state that was modern for those days and had a Parliament with chosen representatives in all the provinces.

In the XVII century, the United Provinces, part of what today we call Holland and Belgium, emerged triumphant and prevailed as a world power and that turned them into one of the world centres of development of manufacturing industry together with their powerful navy and merchant fleet. This zone of Europe lived an important economic

The End of the Corporations

and cultural ascent as the produce of their development and expansion of Manufactures, Forms of Accumulation that were the outcome of thriving industrial development that Flanders and geographic areas comprised in the Netherlands have been enjoying since the Middle Ages, but they could clear the path as a result of the violent process of destruction of productive forces that the 80 Years' War implied.

Another process of destruction of productive forces that cleared the path of Factories towards Manufactures as predominant Form of Accumulation was the annihilation of popular insurrections taking place between XIV and XV centuries due to the generalised economic a political crisis of the governments that launched vicious measures against the masses.

The most terrible measures were the Labour Laws that were passed in practically the entire Europe limiting the increases of wages and generalised taxes that triggered of revolts like one in maritime Flanders (1323-1327) and urban Flanders (1338-1380), the French "Jacquerie" (1358), and the revolution of the Ciompi in Florence (1378).

Continued with the insurrection of English Tylerists or the Peasants' Revolt (1381), the insurrection of Ghent (1372 - 1382), Hussite insurrection in the Kingdom of Hungary-Bohemia (1408 -1415), the Calabrian Insurrection (1469 -1475) and the remensa movement in Spain (1462 -1484), just top mention a few. All these insurrections and revolutions were defeated.

Only the beginning of the revolutionary process that allowed for the development of the Helvetic Confederation (1290-1351) could break away from this general logic of defeat. All this enormous process was simultaneous to the beginning of expropriation and genocide of millions of the native tribes, who lived in primitive communism or in Asiatic societies in America, Asia, Oceania and Africa.

4. Manufacturing – Form of accumulation of the manufacturing bourgeoisie

Manufacturing surfaces in the XVI century as the Form of Accumulation in which the capitalist groups workers in a workshop or establishment and manual work is based on the division of labour between salaried labour which exceeds simple cooperation that belongs to Factories. Each one of these workers specialises in one or two determined operations; this accrues the productivity of labour, exploitation of workers and produces cheaper commodities, which allows greater accumulation of capital and profits.

In manufacturing, the division of labour makes a worker achieve greater expertise, but he is no longer the producer of an accomplished commodity and so his dependence on the capitalist acquires a new and steadier character. According to Marx: *"it consists in gathering workers belonging to different and independent crafts, who have to work on a product until its definite end working under the orders of a single capitalist... And as for the characteristic form... it prevails during the manufacturing period proper, which in very general lines lasts from mid XVI until the last third of XVIII."* **(18)**

There are two kinds of manufacture: the heterogeneous and the organic. We have the heterogeneous variety when we have a commodity consisting of a number of partial products that can be produced, independently and even in different workshops, and then be assembled and combined; that is the case of clocks, for example. In contrast to that, workers of different specialities are concentrated and they carry out the entire process of production up to the end and so create a determined type of commodity.

Organic manufacture allows the articles to go through a series of processes, through a number of specialised workers and that the diverse phases of the process of production that used to be successive will now become simultaneous.

This allowed for more goods to be finished at the same time and created the premises for great industrial production, contributed for the subsequent division of labour and created the premises for the great industrial production, up to a great extent it simplified many operations, perfected the tools and prepared the means to pass on to machine production.

Manufacture favoured concentration of means of production in the hands of capitalists and meant ruin for most of the craftsmen. But even though labour division in manufacturing made capitalist production of good accrue and that social work performance should grow visibly, Manufacturing did not engulf the entire social production.

The contrary is true. An immense number of small industrial enterprises still coexisted and that was the characteristic feature of the manufacturing period of capitalism that many Manufacturers combined their production with Factories as did the domiciled rural labour and the lingering medieval craftsmen's workshops.

The End of the Corporations

The role of the State in the development of Manufacturing

State had an important role in the development of Manufacturing as can be seen in the example of France, where home market and exporting goods for markets that was known as mercantilism was the policy of Minister Colbert and Luis XIV in France. This was due to the fact that the emergence of broader home markets and a colossal growth of overseas markets produced by geographic discoveries caused extraordinary increase of the demand for goods that the development of production in those days could not satisfy.

Manufacture went hand-in-hand with the development of absolutist regimes in the feudal state, increasingly based on the bureaucratic state machinery, the army and the whole crowd of officials hinging round centralised and increasingly absolute power of the king. The development of the new Forms of Accumulation required from these more and more antidemocratic, brutally repressing not only of the conquered civilisations but also of the small production and the new exploited of Europe.

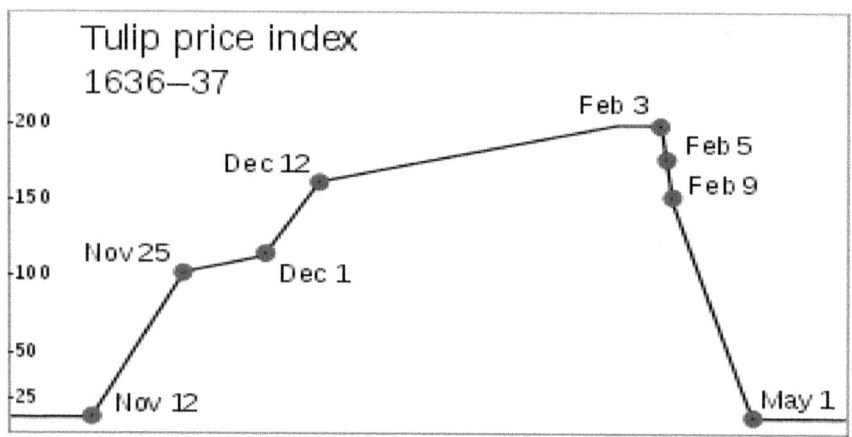

The graph shows the bubble of tulips in Holland in 1637. Source: Based on data by Earl A. Thompson

Viciously repressive institutions such as the Inquisition, witch hunts, liquidation and persecution of oppositionists, accusing of heresy any scientist or person who would reject the idea of God or of the divine authority of the King, even if these absolutist regimes conflicted with the bourgeoisie that had to impose their own state and institutions that would allow the development of their economic interests.

The European countries that best developed Manufacturing were England, France, Netherlands and Switzerland. In the colonies, the states established mining and industrial manufactures. As in the case of the mitas, the missions and the Encomienda (2), they were based on salaried work and slavery of the tribes and still living in primitive communism. There were also great extensions of land where tribes captured in Africa did the work and so Manufacturing was developed in the Indies.

At that time, the process of destruction of productive forces that led to manufacture consisted in veritable genocide. There is no agreement among researchers as to the numbers of Indians killed in America between the XVI and XVIII centuries but the toll can be considered as between 50 and 90 million. The system of enterprises known as encomiendas in Spain, where the Indian was supposed to be receiving a salary for his work consisted of a brutal process of exploitation tat wound up by enslaving most of the Indians who worked there.

Neither do researcher reach any agreement regarding the numbers of men and women captured to be sold as slaves by the XVII century in the phase of depletion of the Manufacturing, but the estimates hesitate at about 60 million Indians enslaved and distributed in 24 million in America, 12 million in Asia and 7 million in Europe while about 17 million perished during the voyages.

This was the fate of the tribes of primitive communist tribes annihilated by the armies and navies of European states and monarchies. In Europe, the consolidation of absolutist states was based on the development of mercenary armies with great activity during the 80 Years' War between Spain and Holland, consisting of impoverished and displaced poor noblemen, together with dispossessed peasants and craftsmen who found a job in the army.

The hedging in of lands have been accelerating the expropriation of the peasants and caused a spectacular increase of the numbers of poor and tramps. The great capitalist magnates invested great amounts of money in financing wars, invasions and the development of military technology to broaden markets. The developments of Manufactures allowed to a colossal process of extraction of metals coming from the American continent.

---

(2) Encomienda existed when the crown assigned a certain number of aborigines to a Spanish subject known as encomendero, in consideration of services rendered

Phases of emerging, rise and depletion of the Manufactures

The phase of emerging of Manufactures, allowed for the application of intensive labour in the mines on the American continent and this allowed for a constant flow of precious metals and an increase of money reserves in Europe, which multiplied by four between the XVI and XVII. The silver extracted from the American continent between 1530 and 1650 reached 11 600 tons, that means, an annual average of 96 500 kg a year and as for gold, the amount extracted during XVI century was 153 561 kg, very important amount by XVI century standards.

This produced an increase of the amount of money in circulation for bankers used these reserves to develop emission of securities, papers and every kind of fictitious capital. With the boom phase of Manufactures, economy began to expand and European population accrued, overcoming the serious demographic crisis that had begun after the Hundred Years' Wars when Europe suffered such diminishing of population that the cost of labour and salaries soared because there was no available labour.

The boom of Manufacturing has also allowed an agrarian expansion and recovery of mining activity. The slow recovery of population increased nearing XVII in 2/3, boosted the demand for food and all kinds of goods. A regime of accumulation was established with a pole of accumulation in the textile and mining industries. After the 80 Years' War when Holland defeated Spain, the regime of accumulation of the Manufacture established the axis of accumulation in Holland and England.

By the XVII century, Manufacturing began the stage of depletion and this became manifest in the serious crises that crisis that erupted in all the economies as an outcome of the levelling and then the fall of the profit rate in Manufacturing, according to Engels, *"... it always allows the manufacturer to produce at a lower cost than his outfashioned competitor, the craftsman... the same process is repeated: the surplus value he grabbed allows the manufacturing capitalist to sell not so expensive as his competitors until the generalisation of the new mode of production that spawns a new levelling."* (19)

The depletion of Manufacturing as a Form of Accumulation caused a violent process of destruction of productive forces in the European countries as well as in the colonies. In Europe, the war between Holland and England broke out and that defined the predominance of England over Holland. This war was combined with the genocide in Africa, with the War of the Baltic and the civil war in England that culminated with the English Revolution led by Oliver Cromwell. With the bourgeoisie in power, England led the transition from a depleted Form of Accumulation, Manufacturing, to a superior one, Industry.

Manufacturing allowed great extraction of precious metals developed by Spain and, at the same time, it relied on this fabulous accumulation of capital for expansion in England and Holland. This is how Moreno explained it, *"... It today, knowing everything that we already know, we had to write a course on Marxist political economy, it would be quite a bit more complex, richer... I would begin by saying that the process of original accumulation was a process not essentially English even if its centre was in England... The base of English original accumulation was not given by the proletariat but by raiding Spanish galleons. A great raid that fixed it all... they re-founded English capitalism with all this fabulous mass of surplus value that came from Latin America from the non-proletarian exploitation, from the Indians and the slaves."* (20)

The great mass of accumulated capital as precious material originated the great inflation of XVI century. It was studied by Hamilton and caused a great debate among economists and historians. It was called the "revolution of the prices" and was an inflationary process that took place in Europe in the XVI century, a process during which prices grew six-fold in 100 years. The XVI century was the outcome of 2 simultaneous processes: on the one hand, a fabulous mass of capital accumulated one of the most important in the history of capitalism.

This mass of capitals that accumulated consisted of the precious materials coming from America and the fictitious capital that rotated at terrific speed developed by the bankers in order to finance wars fleets, armies and the economic activity in general. But while this process was developing swiftly, the transition of Factories to Manufacturing was still in its infancy. i.e.: industrial production was still very poor and so was the development of the proletariat.

In the XVI century, the increase in the prices expressed an aspect of the Law of Value because the heaps of over-accumulated money needed valorising by means of human labour in the capitalist sense of the word. As manufacturing thrived, inflation of the prices began to dwindle following the accruing of salaried labour in Europe combined with the brutal exploitation of human labour accomplished by the manufacturing firms established on colonised continents where, even if there was salaried work, exploitation was based up to a great extent on slave labour. But this unevenness between the strong accumulation of capital based on exploitation of precious materials and the weakness of industrial development also caused the emergence of speculative bubbles in capitalism, ancestors of the speculative bubbles we can see today.

The surplus accumulation of fictitious capital was, in its turn, the base for inflation. States had to get deeply indebted in order to boost the armies and enterprises intended to consolidate Manufacturing. This need for the states and firms to obtain loans, led bankers to issue securities and debt papers that would finance the plans for commercial expansion. This impulse of papers, titles and loans of every kind boosted inflation by the state or "inflation of Benefits", as Hamilton called it. Speculative bubbles like the one in Spain in 1557 and the one Tulip in Holland in 1634.

The "inflation of benefits" allowed for wages to be pushed down for they were quite high due to the lack of population after the War of the Hundred Years, but now wages grew no more for labour was abundant as the population accrued. IN this way, ensuring the general dwindling wages, capitalists could exploit human labour with the development of Manufacturing.

That is to say, the great inflation of the XVI is very similar to the great inflation developed before and during the globalisation regime between the XX and XXI centuries only expressing two diametrically opposed stage of capitalism. If the "great inflation of the XVII century" was part of the stage of birth of capitalism and expressed the first steps along the path of valorisation of capital developing production, the "great inflation of the XXI century" expresses its decadence and the increasing incapacity of capitalism to valorise capital by developing production.

5. Commercial Ventures – Colonising Bourgeoisie's Form of Accumulation

Commercial ventures are a Form of Accumulation constituted by societies of investors that achieve profit based on control of trade and exploitation of labour in the discovered colonies. From this point of view they are a more developed version of Trading Nations, but in this case, the Commercial ventures acted as a veritable state and government, carried out investments, developed manufacture and exploited local labour force and this allowed them to obtain enormous profit.

These ventures were: The British Company of the East Indies, founded in 1600, The Dutch Company of the West Indies of 1602, The Danish Company of Eastern Indies of 1664, The Swedish Company of Eastern Indies, founded in 1731 and the Oostende Company. They were all founded by influential businessmen who would obtain the Royal

The End of the Corporations

Charter and exclusive permits to engage in trade with colonies for long periods of time.

The Commercial Ventures and Manufacturing developed in a joint and combined manner between XVI and XV centuries. As soon as the companies arrived at these colonies, they built the first manufacturing ventures. For example, The British Company of Eastern Indies had 23 factories in India and their profit was so great that they had to bribe kings and officials to prevent other ventures from landing and so be able to control the monopoly of economic activity in the zone. Great profits caused such great surplus accumulation of capital that in 1730, they spawned a speculative bubble of the South Sea Company in England.

These Companies were commercial ventures but they were also entitled to coin money, legislate, choose rulers and form armies of their own. For example, in 1670, King Charles II entitled the British Company of Eastern Indies to captain armies and form alliances, declare war or establish peace and exercise jurisdiction both civil and military within their operational territory.

In 1689, the Company was practically a state inside India that administered Bombay, Madras and Bengal and possessed powerful military force. After the triumph over France, the British Company of Eastern Indies consolidated the monopoly of trade in India and went as far as controlling a fifth part of world's population while the Dutch Company of Eastern Indies engulfed the entire Indonesian archipelago.

These forms of accumulation began in the early XVII century and by the end of the century the Commercial Ventures had started their process of depletion caused not only by the fall of the rate of profit but also and fundamentally due to the process of rebellion of the peoples against the imperial and colonialist oppression that put an end to the exploitation of the Companies. In India there was a massive revolt and popular revolution that in 1857 was called The Sepoy Mutiny and led to the dissolution of the most important of all those undertakings: The East Indies Company.

Transition from Manufacturing to Industry

When manufacturing was depleted, a violent process of destruction of productive forces through a complex of wars that included the War of the Thirty Years that occurred between 1618 and 1648 and the French-Spanish between 1635 and 1659, the wars between England and Holland between 1649 and 1660 and the Civil War in England, the latter actually was a deep revolutionary process in which bourgeoisie seized power in England and imposed a parliamentary political regime following the Dutch model.

The centre of all the conflagrations was the battle for the control of the manufacturing industry in Europe with epicentre in Holland-England and the manufacture established in the colonies. But there were also the wars fought by the Trading Ventures and the Anglo-Dutch Wars as well as the civil wars in England that were also part of the process of expropriating pre-capitalist social classes that was so characteristic of the process of Original Accumulation of capitalism.

The process of expropriation engulfed the primitive tribes from the colonies living in original communism or Asiatic societies apart from the expropriation of peasants, sectors of nobility and even other sectors of bourgeoisie in continental Europe as well as in Wales, Scotland and Ireland. The War of the Thirty Years was fought between 1618 and 1648, mainly in the Germanic Holy Roman Empire, i.e.: what today is German territory in which most of the European powers of those days took part in order to grab hold of German and Italian enterprises developed by the Hansa and Italy an the flourishing industries of both regions, apart from a serious clash between the nobility and the bourgeoisie in ascent and both continued their struggle for power.

Mercenaries were employed as a general rule in this war and the devastation of entire territories that were depleted by armies in need of supplies. The constant episodes of famine and epidemics decimated the civilian population of the German states and – up to a lesser degree – of the Netherlands and of Italy and led many of the implied powers to ruin. During those years the population of the Holy Empire was reduced in 30%.

In Brandenburg it was reduced by 50% and in some other regions to two thirds. Masculine population of Germany was reduced to half. In the Czech countries a third part of the population perished during the war as an outcome of famine, diseases and massive expulsion of Protestant Czechs. During that war, the Swedish armies alone destroyed 2000 castles, 18 000 villages, 15000 towns in Germany.

The wars between England and Holland In the years between 1652 and 1666 involved all the economic powers of those days, such as France, Sweden, Spain, etc and ended in the defeat and decline of the predominance of Holland. The development of these wars allowed for a superior centralisation of capitals and for world supremacy of England that carried out the most important industrial revolution.

Both, England and Holland were commercial power with enormous fleets that dominated world commerce. But even if capitalism was going through the final stage of the original accumulation and the commercial capital still prevailed, it was these territories that were in the vanguard of the development of manufacturing and later on of Industry as Forms of accumulation that inaugurate the industrial state and the apogee of capitalism.

Based on the fabulous capital achieved through colonial exploitation and domination of the seas, Holland but above all England, could boost and finance the scientific discoveries to incorporate technology and new machines that gradually started displacing Manufacturing and initiated Industry. The booming development of industry was to drive England to displace Holland as a world power but at the cost of a brutal confrontation between the two powers and this implied enormous development of destructive forces.

The first Anglo-Dutch war took place between 1652 and 1654; the second was between 1665 and 1667 and ended with Dutch victories in the battle of the Four Days and Medway and the Third Anglo Dutch war between 1672 and 1674 and a front in which England joined France against Holland. The civil wars in England developed between 1642 and 1689. The first civil war in the years 1642-1645 was a confrontation between the parliament and the royalty where Parliament won and eliminated the Court from the Star Chamber and executed William Laud, Archbishop of Canterbury and Count Strafford, an important ally of the king.

During the second English civil war between 1648 and 1649, Cromwell repressed the rebellion in Wales and defeated the Scots in Preston, defeated the royalists, executed King Charles I and proclaimed English Republic. With the third English civil war, between 1649 and 1651 annihilated the royalists in Ireland and Scotland and controlled England. At the same time, wars between companies broke out, for example: the English with the Dutch and Portuguese in the zone of the Indic Ocean after which the British Company of the Western Indies consolidated the monopoly of trade in the zone.

B) Forms of Accumulation specific to the Stage of the Apogee of Capitalism

Insofar as that the capitalist mode of production became dominant and definitely displaced the feudal mode of production and also insofar as the bourgeoisie was conquering the power of the state we entered the stage of the apogee of capitalist mode of production that engulfs the XVIII and XIX centuries up to early XX century. This stage began after the triumph of 3 great revolutions: the 1648 English revolution led by Oliver Cromwell, the 1776 American Revolution and the 1789 French Revolution.

Capitalism boosted the production, trade and finances sweeping away all the previous social formations and pre-capitalist modes of production and reached its zenith of its development as an economic, political and social system. At this stage of the apogee of capitalism, the predominant Forms of Accumulation are: industry in the scope of production and the Credit Banks in the scope of finances; we shall now analyze that now.

1. Industry: Form of Accumulation of Industrial Bourgeoisie

Industry is the Form of Accumulation emerged in the XVIII, when the capitalist incorporates machines to the factory where he groups workers. Labour division combined with machines that replaced manual labour gave room for series production. Increased productivity of labour and the exploitation of labourer and consequently industry implied a leap in the process of accumulation of capital and profit. The modern salaried proletariat surface in industry and the capitalist mode of production is consolidated with its two fundamental social classes: the proletariat and the bourgeoisie.

This process began in 1735, when John Wyatt announced his spinning machine that revolutionised the textile industry. But the introduction of machines also allowed a revolution in the production and trade because it revolutionised transport and communications.

In the early days of industry, the most important technological innovations were the steam machined and what was known as Spinning Jenny, related to textile industry, but hot on their heels there came other machines and technologies and were a permanent improvement of the process of production. We include all farming and countryside production as well as all the production at sea, such a fishing and raw materials are included here.

Even if they move in different conditions, such as the outcome of the land revenue in the case of the countryside, as industry developed, the process of expropriation of small owners and as machinery was introduced in the countryside revolutioning the entire production the entire production was finally absorbed by industry and became just another variant of the industrial Forms of Accumulation. That is how the landownership became consolidated.

In 1713, after the wars of the XVII century, the Utrecht Treaty consolidated the domination of England that became the axis of the accumulation and new industries cropped up, such as chemistry, electricity or car industry together with the development of new forms of energy such as gas or oil. Industry spread on to other countries such as Germany, Russia, the USA, Japan, the Netherlands and a so far unprecedented scientific revolution accrued.

The phase of the emergence of industry coincided with the apogee of the capitalist mode of production and this allowed for a steady expansion of economy. But the revolutionary character in the production means that industry also developed all the contradictions of capitalism much more intensively. But we shall analyse this in chapter 6.

During the industrial boom, the levelling of the interest rate only that now this process developed much faster. This is how Engels explained it, *"...industry, that due to the endless revolution in the production increasingly reduces the costs of production of goods... on the other hand it levels the rate of profit of the different branches of commercial and industrial business reducing it to a sole general rate of profit and, due to this levelling, makes sure that industry maintains a position of strength that corresponds to it by eliminating all the obstacles that up to that moment prevented the transfer of capitals from one branch to the other."* (21)

In the early XIX century, industries began to enter their phase of depletion, and this unleashed a new and violent wave of wars and revolutions. Industry produced a rapid development that collided with internal customs and social formations inherited from feudalism and that is why the revolutions and civil wars that pushed bourgeoisie to power were followed by new revolutions and civil wars in which bourgeoisie eliminated internal customs, broadened the home market, imposed national frontiers and so the modern states emerged.

With the 1848 revolutions, modern capitalist national states emerged. These wars and revolutions were in 1848 in France, Italy, Germany, in the Austro-Hungarian Empire and the American civil war o 1862. All this process of destruction of productive forces cleared the path for a higher Form of Accumulation: monopolies, the outcome of the fact that these wars and revolutions of 1848 as well as American civil war allowed the development of the countries, national unity and home market.

With the emergence of countries and home market Forms of Accumulation that allowed the dominion of a branch of production within the scope of a country, monopolies, trusts and cartels to control and this spawned the entrance of capitalism into its highest and final stage of decadence, the imperialist stage.

2. Banks and Credit – Form of Accumulation of Financial Bourgeoisie

During the days of apogee of capitalism Banks and Credit developed as a Form of Accumulation of financial capital and these institutions comprise the modern banking system. Even though both had antecedents with the first Banks in Genoa and Venice with the development of the Trading Nations, are the real expression of the capitalist mode of production and turned the old demands of the bourgeoisie against usury and merchants who monopolised financial capital during the entire period of primitive accumulation.

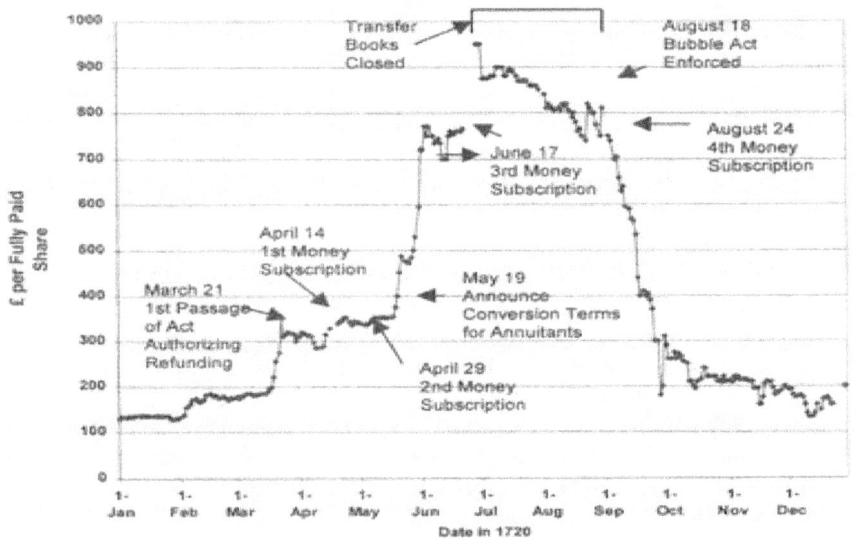

Figure 17.1
Daily South Sea Share Prices, 1720. Data courtesy of Larry Neal.

The bubble of the South Sea Company in 1729 in England - Source: Unleashing Financial

Credit was born by reaction against usury, a Form of Accumulation that, together with the banks expressed the beginning of the consolidation of the mode of capitalist production. According to Marx, *"The development of the credit is carried out as a reaction against usury... I mean precisely the subordination of the capital that produces interest to the conditions and needs of capitalist production. According to Marx, "The development of credit occurs by reaction against usury... It* means precisely subordination of interest-producing capital to the conditions and needs of capitalist mode of production... it is the starting point of the modern credit system. Credit associations, constituted in Venice and Genoa in the XII and XIV centuries, were spawned by the need of overseas trade and the wholesale trade based on it, of getting rid of the domination of the methods of aged methods of usury and monopolisers of the trade of money"* (22)

It was precisely the dominating class of financial tycoons get busy founding banks that emit debt bonds and distribute credit while being part of the State that emerges from the functioning of the Banks and boosts their functioning. This class is born inextricably linked to the State and the state to this class of capitalists, just as Marx explained, *"Even though banks as such, founded in these republics are regarded at the same time as establishments of public credit that anticipated money for the State on taxes to be collected, we must never forget that these associations the notables of the above mentioned states that the merchants who constituted these associations were at the same time the notables of the afore mentioned states and had the same interest in liberating their state from usury as in getting rid of it themselves and at the same time to assert and reinforce the submission they had with respect to the State"* (23)

This is the way Karl Marx explains it, *"this violent attack against usury, this demand of submitting the interest producing capital to industrial capital is nothing but the harbinger of the organic creations that, in the modern banking system, establish the conditions of capitalist production: on the one hand, banks deprive usury capital of its monopoly by concentrating all the idle - dead-like - reserves and launching them on to financial market and, on the other hand, limit the monopoly of precious metals and crating credit money"* (24)

In 1694, six years after the revolution headed by Oliver Cromwell, Bank of England became the first officially acknowledged bank. Just as Bank of France, Bank of England did not start as a state-owned bank or as a crown enterprise; it was a private bank, controlled by the Rotschild clan, the European banking dynasty that managed the finances of England, France, Germany, Austria and Italy, together with associates Khun, Loeb, Lehman, Warburg, etc. The Bank of England was nationalised in 1946, after the end of World War II, at the beginning of the Keynesian regime; the same as Bank of France.

If the industrial production revolutionised all the aspects of production and achieved an all but unprecedented mass of goods but at the same time, credit soon developed tendencies to concentration and centralisation of capitals and left thousands smaller capitals in ruins. And this allowed great capitals to expropriate lesser capitals and allowed centralisation of capitals.

Credit was born as a rejection of usury, a Form of Accumulation that, together with a Charles Marx explained the role of credit, *"It does not only turn into a new and powerful weapon in the competitive struggle. By means of invisible threads, it draws money resources that, in larger or smaller masses, are dispersed all over the surface of society towards the hands of individual or associated capitalists. It is specific machinery for the concentration of capitals... credit.... A new and terrible weapon in the competitive struggle and finally becomes immense social mechanism for centralising capitals ... just as capitalist production and accumulation develop, so do competition and credit, the two most powerful tools of centralisation."* (25)

The increasing centralization of capital that credit and Banks boosted the base of the formation of monopolies, carters and trusts that cleared the path for the stage of decadence of capitalism: the imperialist stage, when financial capital began to prevail over the industrial stage.

This is the way Frederic Engels explained it: *"...these changes tend to concentrate all stock speculators, all the industrial and farming production, commerce as a whole as well as the means of communication and organisms of exchange so that the Stock Exchange becomes the most eminent representative of the capitalist production itself. In 1865 the Stock Exchange was still a second rate element in capitalist system... things are different today. Even since the 1866 crisis accumulation has been increasingly gaining speed..."*

"... There is still progressive transformation in industry in stock companies. All the branches, one after the other, yield to this fate... mining, steel and iron industry, chemical industry and textile industry... the same goes for commerce... the same within the farming scope. Banks increasingly turn into mortgage creditors. If this goes on, is possible to predict that all English and French lands will fall into the hands of the Stock Exchange. Finally, all the investments abroad are made as share..." (26)

C- Forms of Accumulation specific to the stage of Decadence of Capitalism

Fusion of Forms of productive and financial Accumulation

The Forms of Accumulation corresponding to the imperialist stage or the stage of decadence of capitalism are Monopolies, Multinationals and finally Multinational Corporations. You will find our analysis corresponding to these Forms of Accumulation in chapters III and IV, together with the analysis of the political- social mechanisms that allowed for the passage from one Form of Accumulation to the other.

General Conclusions

The mechanism by means of which the passage from one Form of Accumulation to another, superior Form of Accumulation is through a violent process of destruction of productive forces. Marx worked out the laws of accumulation of capital that explain how this process develops from the economic point of view; what still remained how this was done in combination with the political and social factors. The process of destruction of productive forces required for the centralisation and accumulation of capital implied permanent destruction and liquidation of social classes and sectors of classes through wars and revolutions.

In this way, the laws that explain the passage from one Form of Accumulation to a superior one link the laws of Marxist economics to historical materialism. The mechanism of annihilation and burning of capitals that capitalism developed to solve their crises and make headway in the forms of accumulation and centralisation of capitals is explained fundamentally by the role of private property and social classes.

Property of means of production and exchange spawns bourgeoisie as a dominating class with the different sectors of the bourgeois class who are in permanent dispute over capitals and profits. Behind the trading nations, factories, industries, manufactures, monopolies and multinationals there is the social class that owns these different means of production and different sectors of this dominant class.

It is the struggle in defence private property, interests and profits what explains the reason for which capitalism evolves in different Forms of Accumulation. The different Forms of Accumulation are surpassed and transformed; for example, monopolies still exist but are surpassed and contained in the multinationals. The whole process of evolution of the forms of accumulation was gradually deposited on one another as we can see in geological layers.

In the development of this mechanism we can observe behind each violent process of destruction of productive forces there have always been a new centralization of capitals that permitted a superior Form of Accumulation and a period of long expansion of capitalist economy. With the depletion, the period of expansion comes to an end and a long period of stagnation of economy and that inevitably leads to a new process of destruction of productive forces.

Periods of long expansion or of long stagnation have lasted for different amount of time. Sometimes they lasted for barely a decade and on other occasion they lasted for 60 or 70 years and sometimes even more than that. But these periods can be explained by the phenomenon of the emergence of a new Form of Accumulation and its rise, and that is what explains the long periods of expansion of capitalist economy.

On the contrary, the depletion of the Forms of Accumulation is what explains the long periods of stagnation. Two types of crises combine permanently and dialectically: the small crises, chronic, systematic, part of a regular development of capitalism with the larger crises, as we shall see in the following chapter- This happens due to the fact that regular crises happen always either in the framework of a period of stagnation or in a period of expansion. These periods are determined by the rise or stagnation of the predominant Forms of Accumulation.

The General Law of the Forms of Accumulation allows us understand more fully the development of the crisis of capitalism and allows us to overcome the old schemas such as the old opinion that capitalism in its apogee kept on developing productive forces for a long time and then, during its decadence, only developed destructive forces. With the General Law of the Forms of Accumulation, this scheme is definitely overcome.

Additionally, such old theories as the Theory of the Long Waves that explains the inevitability of crisis by means of economic cycles with consecutive upwards and downwards periods connected to the surfacing of new technologies and braches of production are now swept away. It is now clear that capitalism has alternated between the development of productive forces and destructive forces in all its phases and that the engine economy and of overcoming one Form of Accumulation to go to the next is the development of the destructive forces and of the war.

Nahuel Moreno anticipated some of these conclusions in his last courses of economy and he evidenced doubts as to the progressive character of capitalism, as to whether throughout its history, capitalism evolved in a contradictory manner with the development of productive forces. This is the way he expressed it: *"I have my doubts... if capitalism has not always been a contradictory phenomenon that developed technology and annihilated nature and man and whether it is not a permanent law of capitalism... These are my personal doubts... I am terribly worried about the numbers of Indians and the numbers of African Negroes massacred by capitalism in the XVI century and XVII century; I mean... some of the estimates are lurid. Almost 90% of the native population was annihilated in 50 years... So I do not know if it is not that capitalism has a permanently pernicious face against the development of productive forces... From the very beginning, it was very progressive from the point of view of technology in the period of great technical development, but objectively it has been leading to barbarism. That is to say, what we are witnessing now is not the consequence of a great wonder that changed and became bad; it was evil from the very beginning and now it is becoming more and more evil..."*

"My doubt is whether it all began with imperialism... or whether it began when capitalism arrived... for it is the first system of production that does not work for consumption that from the word go is such an irrational thing that it goes against productive forces from the very beginning. Technically, it is the one that most develops precisely because it does not produce for consumption. But at the same time it is the one that most destroys nature, it obliterates everything from the beginning. And today it is the monstrosity of a law that has been permanent." **(27)**

Notes

(1) & (2) Karl Marx: The Capital, First Book, chapter XXIII. The General Law of Capitalist Accumulation

(3) & (4) Frederic Engels: Supplement and Complement for Book III of Capital

(5) & (6) Perry Anderson: Transitions from Antiquity to Feudalism; Second Part 4 Feudal dynamics

(8), (9), (10) & (11) Frederic Engels. Supplement and Complement of Book III of the Capital

(12) Nahuel Moreno – Cuatro Tesis sobre la colonización española y portuguesa

(13), (14) & (15) Reyna Pastor de Togneri: Historia del Movimiento Obrero. Capítulo I Artesanos y Campesinos en crisis

(16) Perry Anderson: Transitions from Antiquity to Feudalism; Second Part 4 Feudal dynamics

(17) Alberto J. Plá - Historia del Movimiento Obrero. Introducción

(18) Karl Marx. The Capital, First Book, chapter 12; Division of labour and manufacturing

(19) Frederic Engels: Supplement and Complements to Book III of the Capital

(20) Nahuel Moreno: School of Economy 1984

(21) Frederic Engels; Supplement and Complement to Book III of the Capital

(22), (23) & (24) Karl Marx, The Capital; Third Book, chapter 36, Notes on the pre-capitalist period

(25) Karl Marx, The Capital, First Book, chapter XXIII, General Law of Capitalist Accumulation

(26) Frederic Engels, Supplement and Complement to Book III of The Capital

(27) Nahuel Moreno: School of Economy 1984

The End of the Corporations

The End of the Corporations

An explanation from left to the capitalist world economic crisis

CHAPTER VI

Accumulation

The End of the Corporations

CHAPTER VI: Accumulation

The rate of profit constitutes an incentive for the capitalist production (the exclusive goal of which is the valorisation of capital), its slide-down dampens the pace of formation of new independent capitals, and so it emerges as a factor that is dangerous for the development of capitalist production, boosts surplus production, speculation, crises, existence of surplus capital together with surplus population."

Karl Marx, Capital, Book III, Chapter XV

If globalisation is reaching its end, capitalism needs to establish a new Regime of Accumulation as well as new Forms of Accumulation that can outstrip the depleted and broken Multinational Corporations. Accumulation or process of amplified capitalist reproduction, as we have seen, accumulates means of production in a magnitude unprecedented in history of mankind and that is what explains the magnitude of the current capitalist crisis.

For a better analysis of this accumulation, this chapter is divided into two parts. In the first part we shall see how capitalism has created a greater accumulation of proletarian masses and of unemployed who produce a colossal amount of wealth such as has also never been seen. In Part II we shall see the other pole and how this mass of wealth has been transformed by capitalism into capital, how the deepest laws of economy function in this process of transforming wealth into capital, and what movements were spawned by the process of accumulation in combination with the different types of capital.

We shall see the course followed by those types of capital that act at the beginning divergently and separated only to converge later on and finally to merge. And we shall see how, as the different types of capital were combining, they developed the most important contradictions and movements of capitalism.

We shall then analyse the link-up that exists between the Accumulation and the Marxist Theory of Crisis, and this will ultimately allow us to make the diagnosis of the current crisis of capitalism that we call Qualitative Perturbation of the Process of Amplified Reproduction or of the Process of Capitalist Accumulation.

Part I – Accumulation of the toiling masses and the emergence of the megalopolis

The accumulation of the toiling masses and of the unemployed is the absolute Law of Accumulation. According to Marx, *"The proportional magnitude of the industrial reserve, therefore, accrues on a par with the power of the wealth. But the greater this industrial reserve army in comparison to the active proletarian army, the greater the mass consolidated surplus population or the layers of workers whose poverty is inversely proportional to the torture of their labour. Lastly, the greater the layers of workers consisting of sickly and needy people and the industrial reserve army, the greater the official pauperism will be. This is the general, absolute law of capitalist accumulation."* (1)

Today there is a mass of surplus population of workers, poor and sickly and unemployed that Marx is talking about unprecedented in the history of capitalism. In the 2009 UN report we can read as follows, "In 2008, the world has reached an invisible but transcendental landmark: for the first time more than half human population, 3.3 billion people, live in urban zones. This amount is foreseen to reach nearly 5 billion". (2) This urban surplus population has been spawned by the Multinational Corporations.

These Forms of Accumulation have spawned revolutionary changes in the demographic structure of social classes, geographic location, the composition of the above mentioned, the displacement of workers and migrations that have an enormous impact on the political and social situation in the world. That is to say, parallel to the development of multinational corporations and of the process of concentration of branches of production, trade and wealth as their property the process of concentration of population in cities has also occurred. Firstly, the great urban concentrations mushroomed – such as Mexico DF, Sao Paulo, New York, Bombay, New Delhi, Tokyo, etc. defined as megalopolis that emerged as an outcome of enormous migrations to the interior of countries.

Migration movements are silent movements, permanent with successive waves, veritable demographic revolutions that produce a deep impact on the social structure of all the countries in the world, shaping all social classes but fundamentally the working class. These demographic changes produced the enormous development, growth and extension of the world working class through the proletarianization and urbanisation of enormous masses of peasants and popular sectors in the world.

Growth of the world population and development of migrations

World population just about reached 7 billion between 2011 and 2012 and the UN foresees a world population over 11 billion. The fastest growing regions are Africa, Latin America and the Caribbean; their population will increase almost 50% and, within this ensemble of countries, the poorest will double the size of their population by 2050: it will reach 2 billion.

China alone, with her 1.3 billion inhabitants and India, with 1.1 billion represent almost 40% of the world population and the estimates of the Census Bureau of India indicate that in under two decades, India may surpass China in the amount of inhabitants. After the two World Wars, the genocides, the massacres and massive destruction of productive forces carried out by the capitalist powers caused the enormous migrations to become a global phenomenon.

The Population Division of the United Nations has estimated that the stock of migrants accrued at a rate of 1.9% year, a rate that is above the total growth of the world population, i.e.: 1.8 a year during the same period of time. According to Jose Moreno Pau, *"... imperialist looting drives workers of the colonies and semi-colonies to seek the lifeline in the metropolis... the need of cheap labour in the metropolis spawns the migration movement. We are witnessing an inverse phenomenon to what happened in the XIX and early XX centuries, when some 55 million Europeans migrated to other continents, mainly America..."* (3)

These migration flows are going in two directions: on the one hand there is the migration from the underdeveloped countries to the advanced ones and on the other hand, from rural areas to towns. In both cases, the world figures of migrants are growing and are heading for the same destination: the cities that increasingly combine different races, cultures, languages and habits and also combine and change the class composition and above all, of the working class that incorporates the migrant proletariat as one of their most militant components.

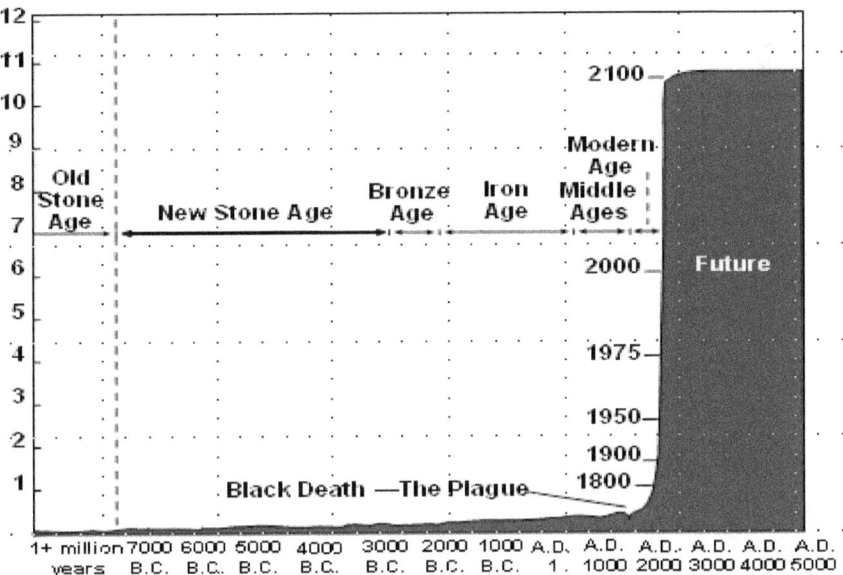

World Evolution Population in History. Since the beginning of capitalism, the upward curve soars and multiplies by ten. Source: Population Reference Bureau and United Nations, World Population Projections to 2100 (1998)

Migrations into the G7 are divided as follows: 50% goes to the USA, 40% to the EU, 5% to Canada and only about 3% to Japan. The migration that reaches EU comes from Middle East, North Africa and East Europe apart from other regions. EU harbours approximately 80% of the Arab/Muslim migration that reaches western societies. Migration waves head for the developed countries that are geographically nearest. Europe is 78% of migration from Eastern Europe, 79% of migration from the Middle East and 93% of North Africa.

The USA is the chosen destination of 98% of immigrants from Central America and Mexico. At the other end of the world, the migrating population in Japan comes almost exclusively from East Asia. In the case of the USA, this phenomenon is modifying the social structure and the people who define themselves as Hispanic, Latinos or Chicanos are turning into the first minority surpassing the Afro-Americans for the first time in the history of the USA. After the II World War, with the surfacing of the modern multinationals in the midst of the capitalist reconstruction of Europe, capitalist states and governments boosted and led this internal migration from rural to urban areas so as to supply the new emerging industries with labour; this allowed for the reconstruction and reconstitution of the powerful European proletariat.

According to Jose Moreno Pau, *"... We must remember that the industrial reconstruction of the main European imperialist powers after the II World War, could be achieved not only because of Plan Marshall but also due to the displacement of millions of workers from south of Europe, Turkey and North Africa towards industrial zones..."* **(4)**

Nowadays, most of in immigrant to Europe live in Germany, France, Spain, UK and Italy. Turks are the most numerous group of immigrants in Europe, with considerable presence in Germany, Denmark and Netherlands. But the disastrous condition in which immigrants to Europe live is the same as that of their peers in the USA, Japan and the remaining imperialist countries.

This is the way Jose Moreno Pau explains it, *"... once more, immigrant workers have become the most exploited sector, doing the least qualified and toughest jobs (building, agriculture, industry, cleaning, domestic service...). These are the sectors with the highest rates of outsourcing and precariousness. That is why immigrant workers are most frequently affected by occupational accidents..."* **(5)** With globalisation, migration of qualified labour from underdeveloped countries also accrues and is used to develop areas and sectors that suffer from labour shortages, such as industries of production and use of information, communication and high technology.

This importing of "gray matter" and personal or professional qualifications in accordance with the governments that have established the "green cards" or special permits has been going on since the 80s. According to José Moreno Pau, *"... on the other hand, they also import qualified labour that has lately joined the army of grantees of scholarships and researchers who work for the multinationals for very poor salaries and minimal sanitary rights. This is part of the brain drain that implies impoverishment of their countries of origin, where people see how the investment in education is lost. The migrating labour reaches the cities when the migrants are old enough to work so the host countries have saved years of health care and education expenses..."* **(6)**

To make it short, imperialist countries develop and boost migration as part of the world plans to make headway in the exploitation of workers. According to José Moreno Pau, *"...imperialist countries of the EU used immigrant labour to divide the working class and keep their salaries increasingly low and increasing their working hours. They substitute social services for the sick and old and small children with domestic work... the contributions of immigrants to the percentage of the population in the developed countries... represent between 10% and 20% of the population of the central European countries..."* (7)

In Africa, migrations have several components, migration to oil producing countries, from the poorer countries to the more developed ones and movements of refugees spawned by wars it is the region with the greatest number of refugees, the total number shifter from 3 million in 1985 to 6.8 million in 1995. In Asia and the Pacific, Japan, Malaysia, Korea and Taiwan joined Hong Kong and Singapore as labour-importing importing with a policy of annihilation and systematic cuts to the immigrants' rights meant to facilitate their exploitation and use as cheap labour, cannon fodder for imperialist armies.

With increasingly harsh migration laws, the situation of immigrant workers is getting worse as days go by. This is the way Jose Moreno Pau explained it, *"... they suffer from exploitation, division into those with papers and the paperless; those nationalised and those that have not been nationalised and lastly, division by nationalities is still boosted. Imperialist governments offer immigrants the possibility of joining invading armies, such as the USA to Afghanistan in exchange for papers and permit to live in the country with their families. But even then immigrants as such suffer from racism and xenophobia, formation of ghettoes and clandestine conditions..."* (8)

And yet, for decades now immigrants have been central to increasingly important struggles to defend their rights to residence and labour rights. Particularly the struggles carried out during the early years of the first decade of the XXI century against the anti-migration laws in France and in the USA which placed them in the political centre of the world. Specifically, between 2005 and 2006, some of the most outstanding battles for the immigrants' rights of these last decades were fought. In November 2005, thousands of young French youths staged a revolt that lasted for over a fortnight the main feature of which was the burning of thousands of cars in the in the suburbs of Paris where over half the population under 15 comes from Africa.

A few months later, in March 2006, the same youths were on the move again together with thousands of young French and challenging the legislation of the Chirac-Villepin administration and the "First Job Contract" (CPE), that spurred the young student workers because it was an attempt at liquidating the aspects that were most favourable for working youth by introducing precariousness at jobs and making it possible for employers to take on young people and to dismiss them without any reason within two years.

A year later, in 2006, the struggle against the HR4437 Act and the legislation that slashed down the rights of the immigrants, fundamentally the Latinos. This attack had been preceded by brutal discrimination and persecution of Muslim immigrants after the 11S events. The entire process of the immigrant struggle was crowned with a huge national demonstration on the On May 1st 2006, when millions moved in all the American cities to struggle against the greed of the great corporations, above all in the construction meat and service industry that pretended grievous cuts in the rights of the Latinos in order to ensure cheap labour available when workers have no rights and are compelled to give their work for small coins.

That is why, between 2005 and 2006, the struggle of immigrant minorities for their rights in France and the USA, echoed all round the world and placed the immigrant in the centre of the scene with all their mobilisations against the policy and laws of exploitation of this sector of the working class by the G7 administrations in the service of the interests of the great corporations and multinationals and in this way they turn the migrating proletariat into the most belligerent sectors within the world working class due to the fact that they are among the most exploited and oppressed ones. The great Latino mobilisation precipitated the crisis of the sub-prime, because the expansion of the business of real estate sales has always been based on the exploitation of immigrant labour force in the building industry, meaning in this case the Latino workforce.

The concentration and the growth of the working class spawned the megalopolis

The great urban concentrations that emerge from the migrations are the megalopolis. These conglomerates were inexistent 60 years ago, but because half mankind is migrating from the countryside to cities and from underdeveloped economies to more developed ones, they are now growing convulsively and dramatically. The term megalopolis was first introduced in the 60's, by the French geographer, Jean Gottmann, more precisely in his book "Megalopolis, The Urbanized North-eastern Seaboard of the United States".

In this book, Gottmann referred to an urban system to a population of 10 million inhabitants or more, the nucleus of great cities, amplified by satellite cities, creating a megalopolis. These enormous urban concentrations are in the centre of the political situation because it is there that the fundamental political processes of the mass movement, mobilisations, insurrections and most important revolutions occur.

But also as we shall now see, because these megalopolis, are enormous workers' concentrations. Not only vast sectors of mass movement concentrate with their ensuing social groups and sectors of class such as the unemployed, the lumpens, and the marginal, and sectors of the poor and rich middle class and a powerful proletariat that, as we shall see, engulfs now the five continents and through its mobilisations gives a specific tinge to the fundamental worldwide political processes.

The worldwide urbanisation underway and the demographic transformations show the degree of the development reached by the working class due to globalisation. As Chris Harman explains in his excellent piece of work *"The workers of the world"* and gives the following figures, *"... **the working class (exists) as never before as a class in itself...with a nucleus of some 2 billion people,"** around which there is another 2 billion whose lives are "subject to the same logic as the nucleus... by mid 90's 2.4 billion people participate in this global workforce, About a fifth part of that, 379 million people work in industry, 800 million in service and 1 billion in agriculture".* **(9)**

And he goes on, *"...**capitalism has created a world working class in the last century and half.** Industry and salaried labour exist today in practically the entire globe. Industrial working class is present in the whole world. But the uneven and combined development of the system implies that it is very unevenly distributed among the different regions. A good guesstimate would be that 40% of the nearly 270 million industrial workers are in the OECD countries; in China, Latin America and the former USSR, about 15% in each country, in Asia about 10% and about 5% in Africa..."* **(10)**

The installation of the multinationals in China and India, which caused the accruing of proletariat in those countries, did not prevent the growth of proletariat in the developed countries as Harman pointed out, *"...in 1998 the number of industrial workers was about 20% higher than in 1997 and nearly 50% above what it had been in 1950..."* **(11)** In the remaining countries of the First World it grows unevenly: in Japan labour force grew to more than double between 1950 and 1971 and then grew 13% in 1998. In Great Britain it slid a third and in France more than a fourth, but on the whole in 1998, there were 112 million industrial workers in the G7 countries, a growth of 25 million in quantity of industrial workers in the most developed industrial countries.

The weight of the working class in the most industrial countries is determining in the most important country in the world, the USA. According to Harman, *"... As a whole there is at least 42 million "Service workers" in manual occupations or routine white collar workers in the*

USA. If we add the 33 million workers in traditional manual industries, we shall see that about three quarters of American population are workers." (12)

Baldoz Koeber and Kraft assert, "... *Right now there are more Americans employed in the production of cars, buses and car parts than in any other moment since the Vietnam War...*" (13) According to the data of the World Bank, the total of workers within the world scope is growing faster than ever before in history, the world labour force accrued from 1.8 billion in 1980 to 3.1 billion in 2008, i.e.: an increase of 1.2 billion workers in the last 30 years. The world proletariat accrues in great proportions. In China alone there are 18 million internal migrants a year that find jobs in industry.

Within the world scope, according to the above data, at least a fifth of the total increase of the 1.2 billion between 1980 and 2008 are industrial workers and this means that the industrial proletariat grows and spreads all over the world. Globally, the working class has now a more complex structure, with diverse layers due to the changes produce.

This is the way Roberto Antunes explains it, "*...our first challenge is to try and understand what proletariat stands for today in the most ample sense of the world, without thinking of workers or "proletarians of the world" as exclusively the industrial proletariat... it comprises all the salaries workers, men and women who live by selling their labour power and who do not possess the means so production... the working class today engulfs all the social labour, all the collective work and sells their labour force in consideration of a salary*" (14)

Antunes analyses the diverse layers of the world working class, "*... the working class also includes the ample span of service sector employees who do not directly create value... also the rural proletariat that sells their labour force to the capital, the season labourer of the agro-industrial regions... the precarious proletariat... working part-time, whose main feature is season labour as is the case of the Mc Donald's employee, in services... according to the ILO data today there are more than a thousand million working men and women who are precarious of underemployed... o unemployed.* (15)

One of the most spectacular examples of growth and strength of the world working class is precisely China. In 1986, 30 million peasants migrated to cities; by 1988 the figure stood at 50 million; in 1989, between 60 and 80 million and in 2003 migration reached the peak of 98 million. In 2001, industrial proletariat was more than 160 million workers, a figure higher than the number of industrial workers in the OECD (131 million), in India (25 million) and in Indonesia (13 million).

But if we add the remaining sectors that compose the working class (agricultural proletariat and proletariat of services) in China, to the forces of industrial proletariat we shall realise that the greatest proletariat in the world has surfaced in China, consisting of hundreds of millions of workers. The same phenomenon happened in India and in all the other countries of Asiatic Southeast, above all the "Tigers" that were the dynamic pole of world economy in the transition from Keynesianism to globalisation.

50 years ago, there were no powerful proletariats as those that are there now. If we take into consideration the existence of these hundreds of millions of proletarians that did not exist 50 years ago, the development of the working class in the remaining colonial countries and the fact that G7 countries the working class has accrued, we may than see that **in the globalization, the working class has reached a magnitude and weight more important than in the rest of the history of capitalism.**

The Theoreticians of the "End of the working class"

During the last 15 years, above all in the nineties, numerous authors spoke of the end of the working class. Many essays with pseudo-scientific pretences presented the reality of capitalism as the beginning of a new era, where technology would make the working class disappear or at least would diminish its social importance substantially and its specific political weight. Books like Jeremy Rifkin's "The End of Work", where the decline of the power of global labour was announced, mushroomed.

This budding of pseudo- scientific literature that announced "The End of the working class" pretended to show an idyllic and angelical capitalism, where technical headway would make producing conditions change so much that they would belie Marx's theses that capitalism, by means of accumulation, a great working class and masses of unemployed population. The "post working class" literature flourished on a par with "post-Marxist", "post socialist", "post-ideologies", etc, that was so characteristic for the years that followed the fall of the Berlin wall.

In the chapter "Requiem for the Working Class" of the book by Rifkin, we could read things such as, "In many communities, the dimly-lit factories of the second industrial era had already disappeared. Environment is no longer polluted by industrial fumes, oil, machines and workers are no longer covered by grease and filth. The whistles of the kilns and the endless jingling of gigantic machines is, at present, merely a memory of the past".

Evidently, Rifkin spoke of a dreamland that does not exist, very far away from the reality of capitalism that can be observed in the workers' concentrations in China, India and the terrible working condition that most of the world's population suffers from. But the quackeries about the "new capitalism" that leaves the planet with fewer and fewer workers working conditions of maximum beauty collide with reality that moves in the opposite direction.

There is not a single fact of reality that proves that the working class has receded: the contrary is true: its sociological importance is enormous and keeps on increasing. Of course there is nothing to prove that capitalism has lost its tremendously exploiting character or that it holds for most of the world's workers conditions increasingly outrageous. Throughout chapter II we analysed the terrible conditions of poverty and exploitation to which corporations and capitalist governments submit the toiling masses of the world at present.

Other authors have developed the thesis about the loss of political importance of the working class. Tony Negri - in his books, Empire (2000) and Crowd (2005), and John Holloway in 2001 in "Change the World Without Taking Power ", were among the representatives of this trend of opinion that upheld the working class had lost its political import and that the confrontation with capitalism would be carried out by other social sectors. Out of this thesis another one I derived: that "new revolutions made by a "crowd" without the class contents having any weight at all.

These theoreticians of the self-managing and autonomous "new revolution" were a version of Rifkin's vision of capitalism but "from the left". This vision culminates with an embellishment of capital but from a different angle: capitalism can be changed from inside, the crowds, organised in "Networks" and "nodes", will make all the changes without having to seize the existing power.

Consequently, there is no need for the working class as social agent to fight for an alternative power because capitalism will be modified from inside by the action of the crowd". The emergence of such movements as the outraged in Europe and "Occupy Wall Street in the USA seemed to bear out all those theoreticians of the "new revolution" but the truth is that Holloway as well as Negri and Rifkin are being flatly contradicted by reality. The new movements that are surfacing are children of the capitalist crisis that started in 2007.

Young activists and leaders who are boosting them regard the concentrated power of the multinational corporations that is far from the naive and innocent look bestowed by the Negri's and Holloway's who thought capitalism was something easily demountable from inside. The wave of general strikes in Europe and in the world, the resurfacing of the trade union movement in the USA, show that the working class with all its strength and plenitude has begun to challenge the brutality of capitalist powers that try to destroy their way of living. Far from the "idyllic" world that Rifkin painted, reality tears down all their chatter.

The movements of the young and of the outraged and the proletarian strikes will keep on converging while they begin to build a world movement for struggle against capitalism. And in this struggle we shall see not only the greatest crisis in the history of capitalism but also the way this crisis mobilises the largest and most important working class in the history of capitalism. This crisis has done nothing but to make us resume with renewed force Marx's ideas. And the return of Marxism will put an end to all that petty bourgeoisie chitter-chatter and illusionism of all those who formulated the existence of a "new capitalism" that can be reformed by means of "networks" and "nodes".

PART II Accumulation of Capital and the movements of the different types of capital

As from now on, we shall analyse this other pole of accumulation, the accumulation of capital, its movements and contradiction that this process has spawned. These enormous masses of workers, toiling masses of all categories have produced masses of value expressed in wealth, in a magnitude historic for capitalism. This historic magnitude of wealth is the continuation of accumulation that has been going on for centuries, out of which, due to private property, capitalists grab hold of in order to obtain more profit and capital.

In this section we shall begin to analyse step by step the movements and the Marxist laws of economy that explain how the contradictions of capitalist system are linked until the current crisis is reached and its diagnosis. We shall keep on showing this linking briefly and schematically so as to facilitate the comprehension, making it clear that it is not precisely this way that things happen in real life.

In real life each one of these steps and layovers that we shall analyse occur simultaneously, in combinations, convulsively and not necessarily in the same order in which we present them here. We are going to start by analysing how the wealth that capitalist society accumulates today. Who produced all this immense and infinite quantity of wealth? How can its value be measured?

Defenders of capitalism assert that it is the capital that spawns value and this is what is governments and agents of capitalism teach and reproduce even at schools and universities. But the interests and aspirations of the champions of capitalism run into real trouble when it is all about the Law of Value. What does this Law consist of?

Let us see how Karl Marx explains this Law of Value: *"The wealth of societies in which the capitalist mode of production predominates is presented as an "enormous wealth of goods". Well then, if we set aside the use value of the main body of the goods, only one property will remain: that **of being the product of labour**... This product is no longer a table, a house or thread or any other useful thing... it has been totally reduced to undifferentiated **human labour...**"* (16)

According to the Law of Value it is labour what produces value, wealth and goods: *"... the Law of Value dominates over economic processes in the regime of capitalist economy. In very general terms it has the following contents: the value of the goods is the specific and historic form with which the productive power of labour is imposed... What are goods? The objective form of social labour spent on the production of it. And how do we measure the magnitude of the value? By the magnitude of labour contained. Labour is the substance and immanent measure of values?"* (17)

What do we understand by labour? According to Nahuel Moreno, *"... **Labour is physiological truth,** it is essential expenditure of human brain, muscles, nerves and senses. **That is to say, it is abstract work.** All use value is the product of a human expense of energy, regardless the historic epoch it may be ..."* (18) Moreno explains that Marx's formulation that the value of merchandise is determined by three elements: abstract work contained in it, the time during which social character it occurs and the social character, that is to say, that it is produced by millions of workers in different branches of production.

According to Moreno, these three elements are the **determinations or determinants of value**: *"... That means that every time an object is produced, (the worker) works, that is to say, he spends human energy, **he transfers human energy to the object,** two: he transfers it **during a certain time** and three, he does it in society ... "* (19)

That is, it is human labour was allows for wealth to be produced, which in capitalism becomes merchandise. But these goods have no value in themselves; it is labour what bestowed value on them, a process that has been taking place not only in capitalism but also in all the previous societies. According to Moreno, *"... the exchange of goods* *transforms what at any epoch of makind are the three properties or features of every human production into social property of the objects. But characteristic of human social production, **not of the objects...**"* (20)

However, even if the Law of Value acts in all societies that have ever existed, whether primitive communism, Asiatic mode of production, slavery or feudalism, after discovering that this law is fully valid for all societies, Marx concentrates on the analysis of the Law of Value in determined society, capitalism. The law of Value then assumes a class character, that is to say, it explains the product of the exploitation of human labour of a determined class, the working class, committed by a determined class. Bourgeoisie at a determined time: capitalism.

This labour and value, becomes manifest in capitalism in a different manner than in societies previous to capitalism: it is expressed in merchandise. And consequently, these goods are the expression of the class character of the Value Law in a capitalist society. This is how Nahuel Moreno explains it, *"... in my opinion, value has a lot to do with class value. That is to say, it is the bourgeoisie who want us to believe that goods have value... that capital it worth."* (21)

That is to say, goods have no value. That is to say, commodities have no value, it the work contained in them what gives them value. But even not having any value, goods are the expression of the value created through the exploitation of human labour, committed by the bourgeoisie in the capitalist mode of production. In this way, it is with goods, and especially one of them: money that the class character of the Law of Value is expressed in capitalist society. So let us see how money develops in capitalism.

Money and prices stem out of value

Objectification of human labour contained in the commodities is expressed when their exchange takes place, i.e.; when trading, as a social process that allows the exchange of commodities, according to Max, "they can only interrelate their goods as values and therefore only as commodities when relating them antithetically **with any other commodity."** (22) But in order to develop, trade requires an element, a commodity that will act as a general equivalent allowing this exchange.

This general equivalent is money; according to Marx, *"... only a social act can turn determined piece of merchandise into a general equivalent. That is why the social action of all the other goods differentiates a determined piece **in which they all represent their values**... its character of general equivalent turns it, by means of a social* *process, into a specifically social function of the selected piece of goods.* ***This is how it turns into money."*** *(23)*

The expression of value of a commodity when commercially exchanged is known as price. Price and money are two absolutely different elements: price is the expression of value in a determined historic and social context; money is a commodity that allows for prices to be concrete and for the exchange of existing goods and values in them. But as they do not contain human labour, **price and money are figurative expressions of value and can be used to measure values, but are not value.**

In order to represent value as near as possible, money must be supported by money material that will contain human labour, will act as general equivalent and will endorse the bills. In general, capitalism has consolidated gold as world support for money.

First of all, gold and silver coins appear acting in representation of gold and precious metals. These coins are figurative expression of the value of commodities, which allows us to buy them and measure them against each other, until the step was taken for money and bills to appear. According to Marx, *"**So values of goods are transformed into quantities of figure gold and of different magnitude...** Before gold and silver became money, gold, silver and copper already had such metal patterns in their metallic weights... ".* **(24)**

It is here that capitalism develops the contradiction **between value on the one hand and money on the other,** which together with price, is imaginary expression of value, reaching the extreme that goods have price but not value, the same as bills or unfarmed land, for example. There is also the fact that the price of money goes up or comes down with no relation at all to goods. This happens because money is a commodity that is imaginary expression of value and achieves independence from value; this allows the manipulation.

Why does the contradiction between prices and money develop on the one side and value on the other? Because money and prices, have always been manipulated throughout history by the ruling classes. We have already seen, for example, the activity of the first bankers as goldsmiths in the Middle Ages, sometimes emitting more papers that what they really had as backing in precious metals.

That is to say, bourgeoisie permanently manipulates money as goods that are used as a general equivalent expressed in coins, bills or papers. We can see that in the falsification of money or in the "great inflation of XVI century", when states accumulated gold and silver and emitted fiduciary money to finance war and looting. Another case we have seen is that of Fed manipulating money and prices through the control of dollar or the Smithsonian accords of President Nixon in 1971 in the USA the broke dollar-gold parity to manipulate the price of the dollar and push the debts of the USA down.

All these are but some examples of the mechanisms that capitalists and states carried out in order to confront and counter the crisis. But these mechanisms, far from countering the crisis, aggravate the contradiction of the value on the one hand and prices and money on the other – Crises expose the contradiction between price and money with value and this is how Karl Marx explains it: *"In the crisis, the antithesis between goods and its value figure, ex.: money, is exacerbated and becomes an **absolute contradiction...**"* (25)

Prices and money develop with the process of circulation

Price and money thrive in the sphere of circulation that engulfs a number of economic processes, part of which are: traffic of goods, money-trade, exchange of currencies and the emergence of banks. The process of circulation is the first capitalist economic process, the oldest of them all. It was built round trade and evolved autonomously in different societies and modes of production where it interwove and among which it developed the exchange.

The process of circulation allowed capital to develop much before capitalist mode of production existed. Karl Marx argued against the great bourgeois economists such as Adam Smith and David Ricardo, who thought that capital had emerged with capitalism: "The great economists such as Smith, Ricardo, etc., *because they actually regarded that the fundamental form of capital was industrial capital... **they were totally flabbergast when faced with commercial capital as an independent species.** The theses relative to the formation of value, profit, etc., derived directly from the examination of industrial capital cannot be applied directly to commercial capital. That is why in real life, they push it out to the margin and only mention it as variety of industrial capital."* (26)

As we could see in chapter V, with the Trading Nations, capital emerged many centuries before the capitalist mode of production and, as centuries went by, evolved due to the exchange between different societies: Asiatic, primitive communist tribes, city-states, etc. What kind of capital surfaced there? It was the commercial capital that, according to Marx is divided into 2 subspecies, *"...Merchant capital or trade is divided into two forms or categories: commercial capital and financial capital".* (27)

Marx calls these two types of capital: "the capital dedicated to the trading of goods" commercial capital proper and "the capital dedicated to the trading of money", financial capital. In turn, according to Marx, commercial capital – whether commercial or financial – is independent from the industrial one and cannot be should not be confused with it, for a number of reasons among them: because they have been there for a long time before capitalist industry was born.

This is the way Marx explains it, *"...nothing can be more absurd than to regard commercial capital, whether in its commercial or financial form.... as a particular kind of industrial capital... commercial capital is older than the capitalist mode of production, actually, it is historically the oldest mode existence of existence of capital ..."* **(28)**

With the emergence of Commercial Nations about the X century, the development of capital in trade became stronger and so did the process of circulation of goods and money between societies at different stages of evolution, modes of production and social formations.

As Marx pointed out, *"I have already pointed out how the money system is originally developed in general,* **by the exchange of products between diverse communal entities.** *That is why the money commerce, the commerce with money commodity, is developed primarily as from international traffic ... with whom the merchant negotiated, the owner of slaves, the feudal lord, the state (for example the despots from the east) represent the fruitier wealth towards which the merchant spreads his snares... Since there are diverse national currencies, merchants who buy in foreign countries must convert their national currency to the local currency and vice-versa... That is where the exchange business, which must be regarded as one of the natural foundations of trade, comes from."* **(29)**

Marx explains that in the process of circulation, the wealth created by labour circulated transformed in good, and that the process of circulation is developed autonomously from the societies among which it mediates with its own laws and features, *"In the circulation, the product is developed first as exchange value, goods and money... autonomous commercial patrimony, as for the dominating form of capital,* **it is the autonomization of the process of circulation with respect to the extremes** *and such extremes are constituted by the very producer who exchange.* **These extremes remain autonomous with respect to the process of circulation and so does the process with respect to them."** **(30)**

The process that develops circulation is a simple mercantile movement, characteristic of pre-capitalist societies where the "metamorphosis" of the goods takes place, i.e.: the operation by means of which commodities are transformed into money, as explained by Marx, *"The merchant's operations are nothing but the operations that must be carried out in general to **transform mercantile capital of the producer into money... must carry out the process of its transformation into money."*** (31)

In this movement of metamorphosis in the simple circulation, in which economy and production must be well oriented towards **use or utility** the producer works and obtains Merchandise **(M)**; he sells it an obtains money for it **(D);** then he invests this money in inputs and tools to produce new merchandise **(M)**. According to Marx, *"This process of circulation appears first as a simple process of mercantile circulation ... **M-D-M**... the producer sells his merchandise... transforming it into money... With this very money he buys... the goods that constitute the elements of production"* (32)

The movement of simple mercantile circulation, oriented to use is what corresponds to the activity in most backwards pre-capitalist societies on which capital acts. The activity of capital, merchants and traders on these pre-capitalist societies will begin to cause a change in the movement of circulation.

Capital takes possession over production, value and dissolves social formations

When capital begins to act on pre-capitalist societies, it begins to change the movement of the circulation. As capital penetrates peoples and nations, regardless their degree of evolution at that moment, it gathers the products that these peoples elaborate for the satisfaction of their needs and subsistence and transferring them to other peoples and nations to be sold, **it transforms them into goods.**

This is what the Trading Nations did – as we have analysed it in last chapter. During this process, the Trading Nations or other forms of commercial capital took the products of the more undeveloped societies the elaboration of which is oriented towards their use or usefulness and being progressively transformed in goods, they become products increasingly oriented to **exchange** or **value**.

This is the way Marx explains it, *"On the one hand, any development of commercial capital will work for impressing a character increasingly oriented towards exchange value... Regardless the mode of production on which production of the goods that join the circulation, be it* *based I primitive community or slave production or that of smallholders and petty bourgeois or capitalist production, **this will in no way modify the character of goods**"* (33)

Capital seeks to turn the economic production of societies into goods so that they can produce their profit. But progressive conversion of production into good means that the capital appropriates the value and therefore labour contained in these goods. Being part of a system that aims at the appropriation of value and labour developed in different societies, by means of a manoeuvre consisting in taking advantage of the difference in price from one nation to another, the capital achieves profit from the buying and selling of goods that contain human labour.

In other words, the capital obtains profit from the **appropriation of portions of value of the production of** societies between which it mediates. This movement modifies the course of the movement of circulation that now changes as for it is all about money (D) that buys a property and transforms it into merchandise (M) in order to obtain more money (D´). This centripetal movement is expressed in the formula **D- M- D'**.

By obtaining profit by the exchange of products that contain masses of value and labour, capital appropriates labour and value that societies develop. Slowly but surely it penetrates the pores of the society on which it acts and reaches a point of its evolution, the penetration of the capital and the predominance it acquires over the mode of production is such that for all practical purposes its action represents a real depredation of productive systems.

That is to say, **as the capital begins to predominate, it gradually turns into a system of looting,** by means of the circulation movement expressed in the **D-M-D´** formula with which it acts and begins to predominate over this more under developed society. This is how Marx explains it, *"Apart from exploiting the difference between the prices of production in different countries, commercial capital appropriates a predominant part... of the surplus product with which he negotiates... **Consequently, when commercial capital predominates overwhelmingly, it constitutes a system of looting everywhere...** in the same way as its development in the trading nations in the ancient times as well as more recently, it is directly linked to looting by violence, piracy, theft of slaves and subjugation in colonies ... "* (34)

As it loots on the pre-capitalist modes of production, capital gradually modifies the character of the circulation. If first the movement expressed in the formula **M-D-M** was the simple mercantile activity emerged from the mere exchange of goods, it has now predominantly turned into the movement enounced in the formula **D-M-D´**.

This is how Marx explains it: *"...this **D M** D' as a characteristic movement of commercial capital which makes it different from M D M, the trade of goods between producers themselves."* **(35)** The step from **M-D-M** to **D-M-D** is the change that allows capital to depredate these societies. First it starts dissolving and corrodes the more underdeveloped modes of production and finally squashes them militarily.

It is to the extent that the circulation process modifies the orientation of the traffic of the goods from its utility to value that capital provokes changes in the economic structure of different societies that thrive "in the extremes" of the process of circulation. These changes act contributing towards the impulse for the dissolution of these different modes of production.

This is the way Marx explains it, *"in all its parts, trade has **a more or less dissolving action on the pre-existing organisations of production**... on the communal entities among which it thrives, it will increasingly submit production to exchange value... **In this way it dissolves the ancient relations.** It makes the circulation of money accrue. It no longer just grabs hold of the surplus production but also gradually starts gnawing at the production itself making entire branches of it depend on trade."* **(36)**

Since capital contributes towards the dissolution of the modes of production on which it acts, it may be worth knowing how far capital can dissolve this mode of production and secondly, what new mode of production will surface in the future to replace the mode of production that is being dissolved. Like Marx explains *"Both questions do not depend on capital alone but on inner soundness and structure of the mode of production. And as to where this process of dissolution leads to, i.e.: what new mode of production will take the place of the old one, this does not depend on the trade but **on the character of the old mode of production itself"**.* **(37)**

That is to say that the very character of the mode of production **on which the capital acts determines the "dissolving" character of the capital,** because in short the mode of production that crops up arises out of the bowels of the previous. But the capital also thrives as from exploitation of the mode of production that acts dissolving, as Marx explains, *"Nevertheless, this dissolving effect depends very much on the nature of the producing community entity. As long as commercial capital mediates the exchange of products of non-developed communities,* *commercial profit not only appears as scam and swindle but up to a great extent it stems out of it."* **(38)**

The combination of circulation and production establishes the accumulation in a definitive manner

The dissolving action of the movement of circulation on pre-capitalist societies and modes of production is beginning to bore through these societies that they end up collapsing. The process includes the expropriation of social classes of small and large owners and end by their military annihilation, which allows for the gradual world-wide consolidation of the capitalist mode of production.

Once the capitalist mode of production is consolidated between the XVIII and XIX century, the development of industry ensures the process of production of goods for world market. It is at that historic moment that 3 economic processes are linked in an inter-related even if belonging to completely different historic epochs.

1) Firstly the joint economic processes that are part of the economic processes of circulation that we have been analysing

2) Secondly, the modern set of economic processes that affect capitalist mode of production in the centre of which there is industry as Form of Accumulation.

3) Thirdly, the combination of the uneven development of both gives place to the process of amplified world reproduction or capitalist accumulation, by now already in its definite form

Even though the amplified capitalist accumulation or reproduction has been developing since previous centuries and establishing regimes in partial or transitional form, in determined geographic regions and coexisting with diverse modes of production, due to the combination of circulation and production, it is now beginning to consolidate and establish in the definite form and to dominate all over the world.

At the same time, the already established process of amplified reproduction or accumulation is the process by which, the capitalist mode of production, like any live organism, seeks its own reproduction. Each one of these processes – even if all closely related – are different with laws and mathematical formulae that express its fundamental movements.

1) Firstly, **the circulation process with** its formulae **M-D-M** y **D-M-D** already seen above, where neither value nor surplus value are created

2) Then the **process of capitalist production,** synthesised in the formula:

$$\frac{Cc+ Cv}{P}= g$$

It consists of **constant capital (Cc)** that is: the infrastructure, machines, technology and tools, added to **Cv or variable capital.** i.e.: wages. Both are divided by the surplus value or waged that employers failed to pay variable capital **(p)** and result in **(g) profit** or gain. It is in this process where human labour is exploited, that value and surplus value are created.

The **combination of both** spawns the process of **amplified capitalist reproduction** that takes its definite form. The formula that expresses it in its totality is **D- D',** that is: money (D) seeking reproduction achieving more capital expressed in money.

This formula is the expression of the entire process of the functioning of capitalist system. In this way, the entire process of amplified capitalist reproduction has one target: that (D) should turn into (D´): the capitalist invests money and what he pretends is to obtain more capital expressed in money. This is how Marx explains it, "*D- D* : here we have a primitive point of view of the capital: money in the D-M-D is reduced to two extremes *D- D'* where *D'= D + D*, that is to say, money creates money... It is the accomplished capital that joins the processes of production and circulation and consequently at different intervals will produce a given surplus value". **(39)**

That is to say, in the capitalist mode of production processes **are integrated** that in historic times developed **in an autonomous and separate ways.** In the old days, circulation took place separately from the processes of production that existed.

Regardless the degree of development, circulation had a movement diverging from production; they did not come together and acted in a depredatory manner. But, when the capitalist production process emerge, circulation changes. Act interacting with the process of production. This is how Marx explains it, "*...in capitalist production, both things take place. The process of production is completely based* *on circulation and circulation is a mere stage, a phase of transition of production..."* **(40)**

That is how, when the capitalist mode of production implies that the processes of production and circulation occur in combines and interrelated manner. The combination of the movements of these different forms of capital elevates the dispute for the attainment of profit to a higher degree. Now capitals use circulation to go along different branches of production, in quest of what is most convenient to increase profit.

And circulation acts on production, where the most serious and fiercest battles take place for the attainment of profit. These increasingly convulsive and accelerated of capitals accelerate in turn the constitution of the average rate of profit and then the movement to the decreasing tendency of it.

The interrelation of production and circulation accelerates levelling of the rate of profit

Capitals acting in the amplified process of reproduction seek reproduction and attainment of more capital. They do so fighting each other and competing for portions of surplus value so as to ensure profit. This is how Marx explained it "... goods are not simply exchanged for money as merchandise but as product of capitals that demand a participation in the global mass of surplus value, a participation proportional to the magnitude of capitals..." **(41)**

The phenomenon that took place with industry is that when the process of expropriation of the small property and other pre-capitalist social classes, obstacles that impeded capitals from moving from one branch of production to another were eliminates and are circulating in quest of profit in different productive spheres.

And as Engels explains it: *"the great industry increasingly brings down the costs of production of the goods, eliminating unavoidably all the previous modes of production... it definitely conquers home market, puts an end to small production... eliminates the direct exchange between small producers and place the entire nation in the service of capital... ensuring the predominant place for industry... having removed part of the obstacles that have so far been opposed to the transference of capital from one branch to another"* **(42)**

The capital that expropriated the small production is now free to go from oe branch to another of production in quest of profit and rotates from the branches of a lower rate of profit to those of higher rates of profit. This movement of circulation of capitals among different branches of production tends to level the different rates of profit of the different branches of production into one rate of profit.

The joint activity of the process of circulation and of production accelerates the process of levelling the rate of profit. As Engels explained in the same article, *"...industry... levels the rates of profit of the different branches of commercial and industrial business, reducing them into a sole general rate of profit"* **(43)**

On the other hand, the commercial capital contributes to carry out the levelling the way that Marx explains it, *"When we studied it for the first time, the general rate or average rate of profit had not materialised for us to see it in its definite form... This first study was completed ...* **we exposed the participation of the commercial capital** *in this levelling,"* **(44)**

It is this constant shifting among the different branches towards the highest rate of profit what finally levels the different. In the interrelation of the industrial capital with the commercial one, the levelling of the average rate accelerates and its conformation takes less time.

In the days of Primitive Capitalist Accumulation between the X and XI centuries when the precarious regimes of capitalist accumulation were constituted mediating between the pre-capitalist societies, the Forms of Accumulation developed profit and the average rate was de outcome of a process of levelling the development of which took a longer time, produced by the commercial competition because there was no process of capitalist production.

But in the XVIII century, when the process of capitalist production surfaced and economic condition were more developed, capitals began to rotate faster shifting to different branches and sectors of production in quest of better conditions to obtain them. The result of this process is that the faster the rotation of capitals the more accelerated the levelling of the average rate of profit.

According to Marx, **"The capital achieves this levelling up to a greater or smaller degree in accordance with the more elevated of capitalist development** *in a determined national society, that is to say, the more adequate the conditions of the country in question to the capitalist mode of production."* **(45)**

The fall of the rate of profit perturbs the Process of Amplified Reproduction

Let us insist that we are analysing these movements and activity of these deep laws of economy in a schematic manner, but they actually act in a simultaneous and convulsive manner. Let us now analyse the different reasons for which in the amplified reproduction is developed in a movement that follows the trend of the fall of the rate of profit. And as this movement, it perturbs the process of the Amplified Capitalist Reproduction.

Different factors cause this trend movement. First of all, the movement of the levelling of rates of profit caused by the how the capitals that dispute the global mass of surplus value prepare the conditions for the slide-down of the rate of profit. This dispute establishes a social average profit, and this caused that, on the one hand the rate of profit is levelled and may be the same for all capitalists, regardless of magnitude of their capitals.

Secondly, when production surfaces, it makes goods cheaper and reduces the margin of profit; this also drives the rate profit to descending dynamics. As industry develops as predominating Form of Accumulation and when machines are introduced, cheaper good started surfacing due to the dwindling of the time necessary to produce them. This made that the fraction of labour and therefore value, that each one of them possesses is smaller and so goods are cheaper and cheaper with what is known as production prices.

This is the way Frederic Engels explains it: *"If manufacture managed to prevail due to the cheapening of products, the great industry does so much more for with its ever renewed revolutions of production beats the prices of goods down increasingly..."* **(46)** Even though these prices of production are the outcome of greater productivity of labour that favours the capitalist, has another aspect: simultaneously they reduce the margins of obtaining profit for the capitalists and tend lo lower the rate of profit.

But a third issue, the decisive one, joins the other two. The profit obtained by the capitalist is transformed into accumulated capital that needs to be valued, that is to say, it must now provide a greater proportion than what was obtained before so that this new accumulated capital may maintain its value. In order to obtain a proportion of profit higher than what he has been achieving so far, he must reach a higher rate of exploitation. If he cannot reach this target, the rate of profit collapses automatically. And if he does manage to do so, he will overcome the conjectural crisis but he will be incubating a new, superior one, which he will then have to value.

Since capitals are over-accumulated, possibilities of valuing imply more complicated targets for the capitalists, increasingly difficult to reach, only attainable through brutal confrontations with the exploited. If that is not reach, the rate of profit will descend once more. This need to sustain the rate of profit explains the atrocities of capitalism and the constant destruction of productive forces that is the main feature of this economic system. The prices of production, the levelling of the rate of profit and the surplus-accumulation of capital, the latter in a decisive manner tend to lower the rate of profit. But there is a fourth movement that comes together with the other three; it is caused by the commercial capital in the process of circulation.

Capitalists produce the goods but then they have to sell them in shops, which is where the process of circulation is active. But **circulation process does not produce value.** This is the way that Marx explains it: *"Commercial capital is simply the capital that circulates within the sphere of the circulation. The circulation process is a phase of the global process of reproduction... But within the process of circulation no value is produced, and consequently no surplus value is produced either. Only* **formal modifications are produced in the same mass of value.** *Actually, nothing happens except the metamorphosis of the goods, and this as such has nothing to do with creation or modification of value."* **(47)**

Commercial capital **produces no value or surplus value at all.** It only causes **"metamorphoses"** of goods, that is to say, the exchange of goods for money and vice versa. According to Marx, this commercial capital that circulates without producing any value, acts throughout time as limiting factor of the production of value, *"... inasmuch as these metamorphoses consume time of circulation,* **this time in which capital produces absolutely nothing and therefore produces no surplus value constitutes a limitation for the creation of value,** *and the surplus value will be expressed as rate of profit, precisely in the inversely proportional form of duration of time of circulation."* **(48)**

That is to say, as for Marx, **the longer the circulation time, the smaller is the general rate of profit.** That is to say, the surplus value and the rate of profit originated in the process of production are inversely proportionate to the time of circulation of commercial capital. This means that the time circulation takes acts as adjunctive time that stresses and deepens the general tendency to the fall of the rate of profit.

Acting in an interrelated manner, all those above mentioned factors cause a downward trend movement of the profit rate that Marx called Law of Decreasing Trend of Rate of Profit. When the rate of profit falls, a crisis occurs and the process of Amplified Reproduction is perturbed or rather, it is paralysed; it is halted. This **Perturbation of the**

Process of Amplified Reproduction is a permanent and chronic crisis as part of the natural process of rebellion the Law of Value enacts against private property of the means of production and is periodically expressed in crises, recessions, bankruptcies, etc.

The Law of Value rebels against private property because only labour creates value but for private property labour has value only is it generates profit. If it generates no profit, private property needs to destroy value and labour so as to restore the lost rate of profit. Value and private property clash and become absolutely contradictory. Perturbation or Amplified Reproduction Process means that the fall of the rate of profit produces withdrawal of capitals from production and interrupts the process of reproduction of capitalism.

This is how Nahuel Moreno explains it: *"...When is there a crisis? When capitals invest no more... when the dwindling of the rate of profit makes that capitals are not invested ... capitals do not join the process of material production, crisis occurs ...* **As capitals only go where there is surplus value, they go. And when they go, hollow remains... there is no more capitalist accumulation. There is no more capitalist accumulation so nothing is done***... When there is little surplus value and little profit, capitals go somewhere else and there is crisis"* **(49)**

According to Marx, *"periodical devaluation of existing capital ... perturbs the conditions within which the process of circulation and reproduction of capital takes place, and that is why it is accompanied by sudden paralyses of the process of production... the diminution of this degree of exploitation below a determined point causes* **perturbations and paralyses of the process of capitalist production, crisis and destruction of capital."* **(50)**

The role of the credit in the Perturbation of the Process of Amplified Reproduction

When capitals leave the process of production, it causes recession, crises and perturbation of the process of accumulation or amplified reproduction. When the increasing incapacity of the capitalist mode of amplified reproduction capitalist **appeal to credit in order to reanimate the process of circulation of money and revive the process of amplified reproduction.**

With the development of banks and the system of credit, the entire process of circulation is accelerated because credit accelerates the speed of the metamorphosis of goods. IN this way, credit causes the acceleration of the process of amplified capitalist reproduction, because it makes it easier for owners of money to get the capital to reproduce by means of capital interest and credit for the capital to reproduce itself.

This is the way Marx explained it, *"... credit accelerates metamorphosis of goods... acceleration by credit of the main phases of circulation... and therefore acceleration of the process of reproduction in general... the system of credit... accelerates the process of reproduction in general... accelerates the material development of capitalist production... the immanent characteristic of credit system to develop the engine of capitalist production..."* (51)

Credit accelerates the sphere of circulation and so manages for force the process of reproduction, overcoming the limits that private property had imposed. According to Marx, *"...this is due to the fact that the process of reproduction, elastic by nature, is now forced to its extreme limits ... All this does is to prove that the valuing of capital, based on the contradictory development of capitalist production it allows the development of really free development only up to a certain point and it is actually an inherent obstacle and a barrier for production, demolished at every turn by the credit system."* (52)

But development of credit results in two phenomena. On the one hand, credit accelerates the development of contradictions in the capitalist mode of production. Forcing the process of amplified reproduction "to its extreme limits" when it is jammed by private property, can only accelerate all the contradictions of capitalism. On the other hand, the credit keeps on accentuation the predominance of financial capital, which begin to accrue and turn dominating, creating this atmosphere of "commercial super-exploitation" as Marx called it, characteristic of decadent capitalism.

When financial capital becomes dominating, it repeats its historic movements, turns into a system of looting, it plunders production and accelerates all the contradictions of capitalist mode of production. This is the way Marx explains it, *"...simultaneously, credit accelerates the violent outbursts of this contradiction, the crises and consequently the elements that dissolve the old mode of production... to turn it into the purest and monstrous system of speculation and gambling..."* (53)

The emergence of banking system, the emission of debt documents, loans and securities are, according to Marx the most developed product achieved by the capitalist mode of production and a powerful lever that tend to put an end to capital itself, *"Banking system, as far as formal organisation is concerned and its centralisation, is* **the most artificial and developed product that the capitalist system of production could achieve...** *The social character of capital can only* *materialize and be achieved due to the full development of credit and banking system. On the other hand, these systems lead further than that: they deposit in the hands of industrial and commercial capitalists all the money available in society... This annuls the private character of capital and **potentially, but only potentially, the elimination of capital itself"**.* **(54)**

Why does Marx assert that credit contains the potential for the elimination of capital itself? Due to the development of banking system and the emerging of stock companies, boards replace individual capitalists. A fundamental change takes place here: **individual private property is suppressing itself, capitalists are being expropriated by these great forms of capital** that concentrate property in fewer and fewer hands.

That is to say that capital resumes its depredating and expropriating role. Only that if before it expropriated the social classes that were owners of pre-capitalist modes of production and now it begins to expropriate the very capitalists within the capitalist mode of production. In the monopolist stage of capitalism that credit helps to develop as fast as possible; and also, prepares the conditions for the expropriation of capitalism.

This is how Marx explains it: *"... the credit system... is on the one hand an immanent form of capitalist production and on the other hand it is **an engine for its evolution to a higher form, towards its last possible form...** The constitution of joint stock companies (leads to the) consequences (of) an enormous extension of the scope of production and companies that would have been impossible for isolated capitalists... the capital that by definition is based on social mode of production and presupposed a social concentration of means of production and its labour force, adopts here the form of social capital in a direct manner (capital of individuals directly associated) as opposed to private capital. Their firms, then, are presented as social firms as opposed to private firms. It is the abolition of capital as private property within the frameworks of capitalist production itself."* **(55)**

Marx and Engels managed to envisage the first Form of Accumulation of the Monopolist stage of capitalism. They perceived the tendency towards the domination of financial capital, the pre-eminence of the stock exchange and the emergence of stock companies, which they regarded as "supreme development of the capitalist mode of production. These entities are the beginning and the predecessors of the development of trusts, monopolies and multinationals.

This is the way Marx analyses it: *"... in certain spheres **monopoly** is established and the causes the intromission of state. It causes a new **financial aristocracy** to be born, a new kind of parasites in the shape of promoters, speculators and merely nominal directors. A whole system of frauds and cons by means of the promotion of the corporations, of emission **and traffic of shares; it is private production without the control of private property."** (56)

For those who have had any illusion that credit might allow a peaceful passage from capitalism to socialism, we have these words of Marx: *"Finally, there is no doubt that the **system of credit will be a powerful lever for the passage from the capitalist mode of production to the system of production based on the association of labour** However, it can only be an element in association with other great commotions of the mode of production itself. In contrast, **illusions as to the miraculous power bestowed on credit and on banks of acting towards socialism,** stem out of total ignorance of the capitalist mode of production and of the fact that system of credit is one of its forms."* (57)

Commercial and industrial capital alternate in their predominance and finally merge

We can therefore see in the historic process of accumulation that capitalism develops both types of capital: the commercial and the industrial have a dialectic relation and take turn in their predominance. In the early days of the capitalist mode of production they do so in an interrelated manner and finally in the imperialist stage, they merge. This is the trajectory that describes the relation between the oldest and the most modern forms of capital.

During the stage of primitive accumulation it is the commercial capital and its subspecies what predominates. With the consolidation of the capitalist mode of production between the XVIII and XIX centuries, general economic development of societies and the development of production caused the scope of the commercial capital to be more restricted and then began to decline. According to Marx, *"this monopoly of the intermediate capital decays and also even commerce itself **in the same proportion as economic development of the peoples,** and whose lack of development constituted the base of the existence of this capital..."* (58)

So, after a first period of the predominance of commercial capital, it recoiled in the face of the evolution of industrial capital inasmuch as it developed a world market and the capitalist mode of production was consolidated. As Marx explains: *"Let us compare, for* example: England and Holland. *The history of the decadence of Holland as a dominating trading nation* **is the history of the subordination of commercial capital to industrial capital."** (59) This trajectory ends with the merger of both types of capital and financial capital plays a fundamental role as a subspecies of commercial capital. With credit, the rate of interest applied by the lender to the capital he lends the individual capitalist accrues

That is why, as far as Marx is concerned, the rate of interest is determined by the rate of profit. This means that between the rate of profit and of interest there is a direct relation, and this is how he explained it: *"From this point of view we can say that interest is regulated by profit or rather, to be more exact, by the general rate of profit. This type of determination is valid even for the average interest. Be that as it may, it is necessary to consider that the average rate of profit is the top limit that determines the interest in a definite manner."* (60)

The rate of profit and the rate of interest are deeply interrelated because the money lender lends money and expects the capitalist to obtain profit so as to draw his own benefit from that. The same foes for the capitalist: he needs to make his profit accrue to pay the borrowed money to the money lender. This accelerates the merger between the industrial capital and the commercial capital that takes place with increasing control by the latter. The development of this movement allows fir the combination of the oldest forms of capital and the most modern ones, where the latter are finally subordinated to the oldest laws of development.

The merger of the capital of production with financial capital causes the same consequences as commercial capital produced in the modes of production previous to capitalism only that now it happens in a more convulsive and more accelerated manner. If previously commercial capital depredated on the underdeveloped modes of production, it is now increasingly it is now increasingly frequent to use credit to unlock the paralysis of Accumulation making financial capital begin depredating of productive forces much faster and dissolving the very mode of capitalist production.

Since there is a **direct relation between the rate of profit and the rate of interest,** economic development is inversely related not only to the rate If profit but also with the rate of interest and financial capital. This is the way Marx explains it, *"the amount of interest...* ***will have a direct relation with the magnitude of the rate of profit****... As we have already seen, this magnitude is inversely proportional to the development of capitalist production; we can therefore conclude that the rate of* *interest... is also directly proportional to the degree of industrial development..."* **(61)**

That is to say, the increasing domination of financial capital in the merger of these two types of capital highlights the law that Marx discovered of inverse relation between **economic development and commercial capital.** The development of commercial capital is based on non-submission to the process of production; therefore its evolution is autonomous and independent from the process of production with autonomous objectives.

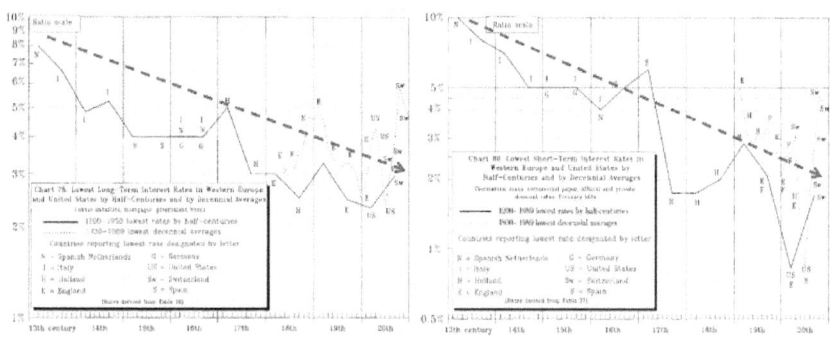

The graph shows the decreasing trend of rates of interest in capitalism since XIII century until XX century. Research made for the book "History of rates of interest" by Homer and Sylla (2005) Source: Macrofinance.

This is the way it is explained, *"Autonomous and preponderant development of capital as commercial capital is equivalent to non-submission of production to capital, i.e.: to the development of capital based on a social form of production that is alien to it and does not depend on it. Consequently,* **autonomous development of commercial capital is inversely proportional to general economic development of society."* **(62)**

The law postulated by Marx according to which there is an inversed relation between the economic development of society and the development commercial capital, in this case financial as its sub-species **becomes more evident** in the imperialist stage of capitalism the main distinctive element of which is the merger between both types of capital: the industrial and the commercial with predominance of the latter as an outcome of the trajectory traced by both types of capital.

Conclusions on the capitalist accumulation

This is how we put an end to our global and historic analysis of capitalist accumulation. First of all we saw how capitalism accumulated

The End of the Corporations

the largest ever human masses of workers and of unemployed in the megalopolis on one pole. Then we saw how masses of capital – also the largest in history – accumulated on the other pole.

We saw the distance covered by the industrial and commercial capital. Historically they act developing 3 types of movements in an interrelated manner. They are as follows:

1) During the predominance of commercial capital between the X and XVII centuries they acted divergently with the commercial capital oriented towards exchange and the production oriented to use.

2) During the predominance of industrial capital between the XVII and XX act in an interrelated manner: commercial capital is oriented towards use and industrial capital begins to move in the same direction.

3) During the imperialist stage between the XX and the XXI centuries both types of capital oriented towards use merged due to the action of rate of interest and the domination of financial capital. Usurious and financial capital and the financial one, a variant of the commercial, again prevail over capitalist economy.

When this fusion takes place, financial capital begins to deprelate the capitalist mode of production recovering its historic movement carried out over all the modes of production, only now it is much faster. ¿Why is this movement so accelerated? ¿How did commercial capital carry out its dissolving action on the modes of production?

Commercial character of capital carried out its dissolving action on pre-capitalist modes of production when capitalists developed the process of circulation in a manner autonomous from production. The movement between the spheres of production and circulation was oriented in a divergent manner with the production oriented to use and circulation to exchange.

And the dissolving action of capital over pre-capitalist modes of production was effective even if it did not establish a direct relation with production. But ever since the direct relation was established and the commercial and industrial capital merged, this changed.

Once the merging of commercial capital with industrial one began, the processes of circulation and production began to act in an interrelated and converging manner. Instead of tending one towards use and the other towards exchange, now both are oriented towards exchange. This converging movement of both spheres of capital turned the historic dissolving action of commercial capital into an even faster and more powerful movement, more effective and precise.

In this way, credit capital as part of financial capital and both of them in turn as part of commercial capital began to develop **the dissolution of capitalist mode of production.** In the imperialist stage, capital got rid of the bonds imposed on it due to the existence of social classes, owners of the previous modes of production that were expropriated by it.

It got rid of the boundaries imposed by the old modes of production that prevented it from shifting from one branch of production to another. It developed in a contradictory manner in relation to the production in which its evolution has always been inversely proportional and has now reached a complex and sophisticated expropriating machinery of the capitalist mode of production itself.

This is how Marx analysed it, *"... This result of the **supreme development** of capitalist production... is the suppression of the capitalist mode of production in its own womb, and therefore a contradiction that destroys itself and that at first sight is regarded as **a simple transitional phase towards a new form of production...**"* (63)

In the imperialist stage of capitalism, the movement of merging industrial capital with commercial one is expressed in surplus-accumulation of capital of a so far unseen magnitude. This brutal surplus accumulation is the expression of the contradiction between private property of the means of production on the one hand with the socially spawned wealth on the other. In the decadent imperialist stage, financial capital resumes its historical dissolving action that commercial capital carried out on the pre-existing modes of production.

Commercial and industrial capitals, oriented towards exchange and along this path merged into financial capital, act as a speedy expropriating machine devouring enormous masses of production. In this way they annihilate sectors of the capitalist class and accelerates concentration at so far unseen levels, as Marx explained, "jeopardise the very existence of capital." Corroded from the inside by financial capital, capitalist mode of production accelerates, expropriated in thousands of parts and with its contradictions exasperated to paroxysm by the

Multinational Corporations, is beginning to suffer from a process of dissolution.

The historic tendency of Accumulation is that capital begins to take a contradictory position with respect to capitalist mode of production. That is to say, it may begin to negate the mode of production in itself, which is, from the Marxist point of view, a negation of a negation. This is how Marx described it in Tome I, chapter 24 when he analyses the historical trend of Capitalist Accumulation.

"It is no longer the self-employed worker who is to be expropriated but the capitalist who exploits many workers. This expropriation is carried out by means of the action of the immanent laws of capitalist production, by means of concentration of capitals. Each capitalist expropriates many others. With the constant dwindling of the number of capitalist tycoons who usurp and monopolise all the advantages of this process of reversal... **the monopoly exerted by capital turns into an obstacle for the mode of production** that has been flourishing with it and under it. Concentration of the means of production, and socialization of labour have reached a point that they are no longer compatible with the capitalist outer crust. So it is made to burst. The death knell of capitalist private property can be heard. Expropriators are being expropriated. The negation of capitalist production takes place by itself, with the need of a natural process. **It is the negation of the negation...**"

The process of dissolution by financial capital suffered by capitalism is the general and historical framework that allows us to understand its crisis in the imperialist stage. It is within this framework that we shall analyse the relationship between the latter and the Accumulation and so make headway towards more precise formulations of a Marxist Theory of Crisis.

Marxist Theory of Crisis and Accumulation

A conclusion regarding the Accumulation or Amplified Reproduction is that crises of capitalism have a deep relation with it and find in the Accumulation its determining element. That is why it is necessary to assess Marxist Theory of Crisis in relation to Accumulation in order to define its laws and movements.

We know that Marx and Engels' lifetime did not suffice to work out a theory of the crisis in a systematic manner. They worked with elements in different parts of their works and never posed the crisis as a product of a sole cause because all the inner contradictions of capitalist mode of production. The tending fall of the average rate of profit sums up all the contradictions.

Even though the crisis can be explained by multiple causes, we have seen how the historic process of capitalist accumulation develops all the contradiction that later on cause the crises which turns it into their determining element. The process of Accumulation cause capitalist crisis to constitute in accordance with 2 movements that take place simultaneously and in an interrelated manner:

The first movement is that of permanent irruption of the contradictions of capitalism. This movement is expressed in bankruptcies, inflation, collapse of stock, devaluation, recession, etc. happening all the time in all the stages and phases of capitalist development.

We call this movement Quantitative Perturbation of the Process of Amplified Reproduction (P-CT). This happens when amplified reproduction or Accumulation in interrupted, is halted, is perturbed, up to the point of redoing its march. This movement takes place permanently but it does not jeopardize the survival of capitalist mode of production.

That is to say, **quantitative** perturbation is an organic movement of capitalism, chronic and permanent regardless what stage it may at that time be: in the primitive accumulation, in its apogee or in the imperialist stage. The burning and destruction of capital, even in small magnitude will help to solve it.

This first movement is closely linked to a second movement which is also the outcome of the process of Accumulation. Capitalism develops the permanent predisposition towards centralisation of capitals, and this is one of the most important laws of Accumulation.

This movement of centralisation of capitals surfaces as a need to respond to permanent outbreak of contradictions of capitalism and spawns the different Forms of Accumulation. As we noted in Chapter V, Forms of accumulation go through phases of upsurge, boom and exhaustion.

During the phase of upsurge and boom of predominant Forms of Accumulation enters a long period of economic expansion. But when we reach the phase of exhaustion of the predominant Forms of Accumulation, economy enters into a long period of stagnation.

Because there is no economic growth, or it is very weak, Amplified Reproduction is halted or paralysed for a long time as an expression of the fact that the predominant For of Accumulation has reached the limit of its development. As the Accumulation has is now suffering from an almost absolute paralysis, capitalists appeal to credit to see if they can unlock it, but as this is no ordinary crisis, credit cannot cure it or unlock the crisis of Accumulation that is suffering from an almost total paralysis .

The second movement is a perturbation that paralyses the Accumulation in an almost total movement. The solution to the crisis is not to be found in credit or in regular burning of capitals as in the P-CT, because it is caused by the depletion of the predominant form of Accumulation. Since no solution is found to the crisis, capitalist mode of production is in jeopardy and that is why we define this second movement as a **Qualitative** Perturbation of Accumulation or Amplified Reproduction (P-CL)

That is to say that it is no ordinary, regular perturbation that we have to cope with; it is not like the crises capitalism has been regularly suffering from. This is extraordinary perturbation, long-lasting one and very serious. The solution to this crisis requires of a deep process of violent annihilation of productive forces that would allow capitalism to overcome the depleted Forms of Accumulation and let it pass on to a higher Form of Accumulation.

The P-CL is of long duration and jeopardises the survival of capitalism and come together with great commotions due to the capitalism's need to destroy great masses of productive forces in order to be able to overcome it. This causes another phenomenon: the P-CL is always connected to great historic political and social events. Let us see the main P-CL suffered by capitalism since its origin.

First Qualitative Perturbation: In the XIV century, as an outcome of the first predominant Forms of Accumulation of the Trading Nations had entered into their phase of depletion. At the same time, the first Forms of Financial Accumulation, which had emerged together with them, also were depleted. As we have seen above, this P-CL caused an enormous process of destruction of productive forces, known as the Hundred Years War that permitted the consolidation of Factories as the Predominant Forms of Accumulation.

Second Qualitative Perturbation: Late XV century and early XVI, as an outcome of the predominant Forms of Accumulation, Factories were depleted, something that caused an enormous process of destruction of productive forces, the 80 years' War, the annihilation of popular insurrections that took place during XIV and XV centuries in Europe and the beginning of the expropriation and genocide of millions of peasants in Europe and the primitive communist tribes in America, Asia, Oceania and Africa. All this enormous process of destruction of productive forces was in the service of the development of Manufactures as a Predominant Form of Accumulation.

Third Qualitative Perturbation: Late XVII century and early XVIII centuries, as an outcome of the deletion of the predominant Forms of Accumulation, Manufactures, were worn out and so were the Commercial Companies related to them. This spawned an enormous process of wars and destruction of productive forces: the war of the 30 years, the Franco-Spanish, the Anglo-Dutch and the Civil War in England. The latter was actually a deep revolutionary process as an outcome of which the bourgeoisie took over. It was as an outcome of this process of productive forces that, Industry became the Predominant Form of Accumulation and the Banks and Credit became a Form of Financial Accumulation.

Fourth Qualitative Perturbation: Located in the early XIX century, when industries began to enter their phase of depletion, the Perturbation unleashed a new and violent wave of destruction of productive forces with revolutions and civil wars in which bourgeoisie eliminated the internal customs tariffs, broadened home markets, boosted national frontiers and so modern states surfaced. Hot on their heels monopolies appeared as predominant Form of Accumulation.

Fifth Qualitative Perturbation: It cropped up in the early XX century, when monopolies entered their phase of depletion. This unleashed a new and violent process of destruction of destructive forces, the First and Second World Wars, In the middle of all that, fascism surfaced and the Russian Revolution took place. Hot on the heels of all that the modern multinationals cropped up as the new predominant Form of Accumulation.

Sixth Qualitative Perturbation: It occurred in the late sixties of the XX century, when the modern multinationals entered their phase of depletion. Capitalism could cope with this Perturbation because of the violent process of destruction of destructive forces unleashed in the post-war in the underdeveloped countries including Vietnam, Korea, China, Yugoslavia, etc., and the process of restoration of capitalism that began in the seventies. All this enormous destruction of productive forces developed in the post-war allowed the Multinational Corporations to take place as the predominant Form of Accumulation.

Seventh Qualitative Perturbation: It is this current one, located in the early XXI century, When Multinational Corporations entered their phase of depletion that first became manifest with the crisis of the dot.com in the year 2000. Due to the failure of the American New Age Project that was defeated in Iraq and of the Patriot Act in the USA, there was no process of destruction of productive forces great enough to pass on to a higher Form of Accumulation. That is why the 2007 crisis broke out and the sub-prime bubble burst.

Relation between the P-CT and the P-CL

During the boom and development of predominant Forms of Accumulation, Quantitative Perturbation acts all the time. Bankruptcies, recessions, devaluations, inflation, etc. occur one after another but together with a period of economic expansion that thrives on it and is interrelated with it.

When the Forms of Accumulation enter their phase of depletion, economy enters a long period of stagnation and the movement of P-CL takes place. P.CT continues acting inside this movement and closely related to it. Both movements are linked as follows: bankruptcies, inflation, recession, and etc. act inside the P-CL but subordinate to it. The **P-CT** is subordinate to it because Accumulation was totally subordinate to it. And the movements of P-CT no nothing but aggravate the general crisis,

In short: There are two movements of the crisis of capitalism. One of them is the chronic, periodic crisis, the movement of all the contradictions synthesised in the fall of the rate of profit that becomes in a **Quantitative Perturbation** (P-CT) of the Process of the Amplified Reproduction. Another one is an ordinary crisis; it is a crisis that crops up more frequently but its duration is longer because the crisis is deeper. Its main feature is the depletion of predominant Forms of Accumulation. It is a crisis in the very heart of capitalist system, in the process of Accumulation and therefore is a Qualitative Perturbation (P-CL) of the Process of Amplified Reproduction.

The P-CL not only jeopardises the capitalist mode of production because it paralyses Accumulation. It does so also due to another reason. Talking of capitalism is actually an abstraction. Capitalist mode of production actually changes all the time and is not eternal or immutable. That is why when we talk of capitalism we talk of determined Forms of Accumulation acting at a determined and concrete historic moment.

That is to say: even if general laws of capitalism continue acting all the time and do not change, what does change are the predominant, concrete and determined capitalist enterprises that act accumulating capital at a determined time of its development. For example: when we talk of capitalism in the XVI century is to talk of Manufacture.

In the XIX century it is to talk of Industry and in the XX century it is to speak of Multinationals. Capitalism – as we have seen – is shaped in a global and complete manner round them constituting a Regime of Accumulation. But if - due to P-CL - these companies that are predominant at a determined time undergo a crisis, this crisis jeopardises not only the existence of predominant Forms of Accumulation and the entire constituted regime of Accumulation but also the concrete and determined capitalist mode of production that took shape around them.

And the threat spreads to all the corners of capitalist system leaving no totally or partially unaffected sector. This is the essential reason for which the P-CL jeopardizes the existence of capitalist mode of production.

Diagnosis of the crisis

Ultimately, Quantitative Perturbation as well as the Qualitative one are dialectically interrelated expressions of the fundamental contradiction that is there in the base of capitalism. They both express the contradiction between capital and labour, between private property and Law of Value; between the collective production and individual appropriation and all the remaining contradiction that act implacably, in all the phases and periods of the development of capitalist system.

The Law of Value acts aggravating the contradictions of capitalism, because value expressed in goods under the domination of the bourgeoisie, insofar as bourgeoisie cannot assert their domination, acts negating them through the collapse of prices of the Forms of Accumulation or the loss of the value of money which is in turn an expression of the fact that the former and the latter **have no value at all,** And so it becomes clear that capital is not the producer of value.

It becomes clear that value is only the produce of labour. Multinational corporations, capitalist states, analysts in defence of capitalism of all kinds are perplexed at the sight of such overwhelming activity of economy the deep laws of which they never understood. These characters are increasingly confined to explanations bases on deceit, periodic or secular cycles, luck, destiny, and horoscope or in short, the divine will of some superior being who determines the events.

This is what explains the **systematic and categorical failure** of all the policies of the G7 governments in quest of solution to the crisis by intervening in the market or world trade and manipulating prices.

Polices to solve the crisis by means of interventions within the scope of circulation and trade merely aggravate it even more because crisis is expressed in commerce but it is developed in the process of Accumulation that runs through the whole economic process.

Officials of capitalist governments, economists for capitalism and even some analysts considered as Marxists observe the origin of the crisis on the market, trade, the scope of circulation of goods and consumption and that leads them to mark the crisis as of overproduction, underproduction or low consumption.

These formulae are doomed to crash against reality and fail. Moreno referred to those who, from Marxist postures try to analyse crisis from the point of view of market are vulgar Marxists, *"... that is why it is called vulgar Marxism.* **We call any attempt at explaining phenomena of capitalism through market vulgar Marxism..."** (64)

With the knowledge of these movements and laws, we can now define the character and nature If the current crisis and the diagnosis of the crisis, Capitalism is going through a process of Qualitative Perturbation of the Process of Amplified Reproduction. That is to say, we are witnessing a process of depletion of the currently predominant Forms of Accumulation: the Multinational Corporations whose bankruptcy and survival through bailouts evidence that they have already entered their phase of depletion.

These forms of Accumulation are in turn the successors of the Modern Multinational of post-war and both consolidated the capitalist era in which economy is under the control of enterprises that dominate branches of production throughout the world as part of the imperialist stage of capitalism. Consequently, if we had to use a popular phrase we might define this crisis and disseminate our diagnosis saying that it was The End of the Multinationals what has caused the crisis.

Being in the middle of a P-CL, the successive injections of gigantic masses of capital to credit carried out by Central Banks through bailouts managed to revive world economy, but caused the weakest economic indicators of the last decades.

This phase has developed its potentialities to the highest pitch and has worn them out, thus opening from now on a lengthy, historic crisis that will go through depressions and short-lived recoveries. Bailouts begin a new regime or phase, in which two sets of tendencies will be developed that we analysed in Chapter II and a deep depression that will probably go on for several years.

In spite of that, world's capitalist governments' and – imperialist and semi colonial – capacity to provide answers has been effective, co-ordinated and has formally avoided the bankruptcy of Multinational Corporations. The QE and the global interventions of the states not without crises and contradictions, try to prevent the collapse.

Regardless the pace at which the situation may move. Of whether there is or is not another fall, of whether the economic assistance of the G7 that is still there, is combined with new global or partial bailouts, what we are witnessing now is the economic regime of globalisation and the beginning of a new phase or regime that has all the elements of barbarism preannouncing some of the tendencies of decomposition of capitalism.

There has been some important discussion lately regarding the meaning of the bailouts. Will they or will they not push global economy out of trouble and what consequences will they produce for the development of capitalism. We already know what effect these monstrous masses of capital will have on world economy. They will produce temporary relief. They will allow for a partial recomposition of the process of circulation, credit and money that have collapsed. But they will also further develop all the contradictions of capitalist system, the crisis and together with it the commotions, riots and social uprisings that preannounce an even greater crisis.

The End of the Corporations is a class definition of the crisis

Therefore, the analysis of the role of capital throughout history allows us to understand the role of financial capital in this last leg of the decadent capitalist mode of production and so to foresee **the possible outcomes** of its history. Agonizing and decaying capitalism threatens to drag the entire mankind to disaster and the conditions necessary for the switch from one mode of production to another. But this step is not within the scope of economy: it will be determined in the course of the forthcoming events of class struggle.

No matter how much can credit and financial capital act accelerating the dissolution of capitalism, no matter how much bailouts may place this perspective in fast and precise movement, no matter how much the acceleration of all the contradictions can rise to paroxysm, capitalism will not disappear.

Its downfall is not an economic movement even if the economic movement may place the possibility of its downfall. It is on the political grounds that the definition will occur as to whether capitalism will exist and, if it survives, how it will survive.

Perhaps analysts for capitalism will believe that The End of the Multinationals, the title borne by this piece of work, may be some kind of irony that we, the Marxists, launch in response to so many ironies received in these last 20 years. In this period we received abundant bibliography with slogans such as "The End of Marxism", "The End of Socialism", "The End of ideologies", "The End of History", "The End of Labour", etc. All of them meant to show and enshrine the final and definite triumph, of capitalism.

These authors and these texts have now been buried by reality and even if we deserve a small rematch against such a lot of bullshit pretending to be science. Conversely, The End of the Multinationals is the title of this piece of work because it is the scientific, Marxist definition of this crisis. If there is anything important about the debate underway related to the world economic situation it is precisely the making of a deep, scientific diagnosis to be able to reveal its nature.

According to Marx, scientific study of economy proves to be extremely difficult because the number of enemies opposing it, *"within the scope of political economy **free and scientific research runs into many more enemies** that in other scopes of exploration. The particular nature of the subject it deals with raises against it and against the battlefield the most ardent and passions the meanest and most hateful ones in human heart, all the furies of private interest. The High Church of England, for example, would be much more willing to forgive an attack against thirty-eight out of the thirty-nine articles of faith than against the thirty-ninth part of their income."* **(65)**

That is why our definition of the crisis will run up against many enemies. Most of the economic analysts, defenders of capitalism as well as many Marxists, highlight movements of stock market movements, the growth of the GDP, the price of currencies, of debts, inflation, etc.
But how many articles referring to the world crisis of capitalism analyse multinational corporations? How many studies are there on their situation and development? What Marxist research is there on the multinational corporations, their evolution and their role? Our readers would find looking for pieces of work posing answers a tiresome task.

And yet even the common citizen, one most far-away from the knowledge of the complex laws of economy, the humble workers, a peasant, an intellectual anybody with the minimum common sense knows that multinationals are entities that control capitalist economy.

Bourgeois economists know this well because they know the actual data. But even ignoring such data, ignoring the origin and evolution, having no data, being ignorant of the origin and evolution, not having studied economy, the humble worker who lives in capitalism can see the advertising and neon signs, when he buys the product necessary for his subsistence or when he buys his household appliances or a car, he will understand who controls economy.

The same as when the citizen of the Middle Ages saw a cross and castles in the distance or when a member of a primitive communist tribe saw the ships coming from afar as when a current citizen, even if he does not understand economy. It is most significant in the analysis of the current crisis of capitalism that there should be no deep studies on multinationals.

The "public opinion" elaborates about the most diverse explanations of the current crisis of capitalist crisis but practically nobody refers to the entities that every mortal regards as the most important of world economy.

Unfortunately, silence on the multinationals also engulfs texts and research produced by Marxists who in this way capitulate to bourgeois "public opinion". This silence on the multinationals is not aimless: to conceal the real nature of the crisis from the eyes of millions of workers, peasants and students, But it is the toiling masses, with their sound class instinct, who are telling us what the diagnosis is even if many of the thousands who, throughout the world fight and rebel may know nothing of economy.

Even the first emergence of the movements of the "outraged", be it through the "Occupy Wall Street", be it through strikes and demonstrations that spread throughout the world and with the criticism that spread among the peoples and workers against Multinational Corporations, millions point their fingers to the focus of the crisis, even if they know nothing of Marxist economy.

Therefore we must speak out loudly and make this message – that is our theoretic and political diagnosis – very clear for the masses and we must manifest what "public opinion", governments and leaders refuse to say for they need to conceal from the masses what is really happening.

We tried to give this diagnosis of ours following the Marxist method, the one that our masters, such as Nahuel Moreno, advised us to give class definitions when coping with this item: *"It will be useful for us to arrive at an agreement once and for all what does a Marxist mean when he says he will study Marxist political economy... For example, the is a tendency to get ourselves involved in formulae and economic laws as if they had a life of their own, as if the acted out of their own accord."* **(66)**

According to Moreno, formulae, laws and analyses of economic processes, even if they are fundamental, are worth nothing is they are carried out by themselves, isolated from political and social phenomena and class analyses. And just as lasses are who make history, Moreno advised us never to forget that classes also make economy.

This is the way he explained it: *"In my opinion, class character of everything is decisive ... it is the clue to everything... Marxist economists forget this most of the time; that classes make history and classes make economies. What do I mean by this? That if there is anything that is of the classes it is economy... we must not get lost and isolate ourselves from the class process when we make our economic analyses."* **(67)**

The current crisis of capitalism is the current crisis and the depletion of the multinationals. It is multinational corporations, entities that express the highest degree of accumulation achieved by capitalism, what went bankrupt and their bankruptcy expresses the depletion of globalisation.

When we talk of the End of Multinationals, we do not merely describe the agony of these Forms of Accumulation. We talk of the crisis and agony of a social class, the class of the owners of multinationals, of the tycoons and great capitalists who control world economy as such and hold property of practically all the most important means of production and exchange.

The End of the Multinationals is the mortal and definite decadence of the social class and with it, of the social, political and economic system. If they prevail and manage to overcome this crisis, history evidences that they can drag us to a new economic regime that will impose conditions of barbarism and exploitation of great brutality.

The same as in the case of the famous prognosis for the political revolution, this crisis also has alternative character: either imperialism imposes definite domination of capital, and a Form of Accumulation that will overrule the Multinational Corporation, or revolution will expropriate them. The result is up to the class struggles.

Expropriating multinationals is a measure that can only be carried out by triumphant revolutions that will install proletarian dictatorships. The best homage we can pay to our masters is to follow their advice and for that it is necessary to produce a class definition for this crisis and in this way fight against vulgar Marxism and analyses of "public opinion" that introduce prejudices and interests of the defender of the great enterprises and capitalism into the innards of the working class.

May this piece of work, that we had dubbed The End of Corporations, serve this purpose. We shall put it at the disposal of new generations of workers and fighters of whole world. They are already leading the world rebellion against capitalism. They need a diagnosis of the crisis in order to undertake the task and to put an end to the unjust system whose terminal crisis is unfolding in front of our eyes and whose forthcoming convulsions will mark its end.

Notes

(1) Karl Marx, Capital Book I Chapter XXIII

(2) UN. State of World Population 2007

(3), (4), (5), (6), (7), & (8) José Moreno Pau "La inmigración en Europa". with JanTalpe colaboration. Marxismo Vivo 15 año 2007

(9), (10), (11) & (12) Chris Harman. "Workers of the World" (Part 1) Source: International Socialism 96 Date: 6/12/2003

(13) Baldoz, Koeber y Kraft "The critical study of work: labour, technology, and global production"

(14) & (15) "Los nuevos proletarios del mundo en el cambio de siglo". Roberto Antunes Marxismo Vivo Junio/ Setiembre 2000

(16) & (17) Karl Marx, The Capital, Book I, chapter XVII, Transformation of value of lablur force en salay (our highlights)

(18), (19),(20) & (21) Nahuel Moreno. Escuela de cuadros de Economía

(22), (23) & (24) Karl Marx: Capital , Book I, Chapter 3, Money or circulation of good, (our highlights)

(25), (26) & (27) Karl Marx: Capital, Third Book, Chapter 20 Historic Considerations on Commercial Capital.

(28), (29), (30) & (31) Karl Marx: Capital, Third Book, Chapter 15; Capital dedicated to traffic of goods

(32) (33), (34), (35), (36), (37) & (38) Karl Marx: Capital, Third Book, Chapter. 20. Historic considerations on commercial capital.

(39) The Capital, Third Book, chapter. 16, Capital dedicated to traffic of goods

(40) Karl Marx: The Capital, Book 3, chapter. 20, Historic Considerations on Commercial Capital

The End of the Corporations

(41) Karl Marx: The Capital, Book 3, Chapter 9, Formation of a New Average Rate of Profit

(42) & **(43)** Frederic Engels: Supplement and Complement for Book III of The Capital

(44) & **(45)** Karl Marx, The Capital, Libro III chapter. X Levelling of the general rate of profit by competition, Our highlights

(46) Federico Engels: Supplement y Complement to Book III of the Capital

(47) & **(48)** Karl Marx: The Capital, Book III, Chapter. XVI Capital dedicated freight traffic

(49) Nahuel Moreno. Escuela de cuadros de Economía

(50) Karl Marx: The Capital, Book III

(51), **(52)**, **(53)**, **(54)**, **(55)**, **(55)**, **(56)** & **(57)** Karl Marx, El Capital, Book III Chapter XVII Role of Credit in capitalist production.

(58) & **(59)** Karl Marx: The Capital, Book III, chapter XX, Historic Considerations on Commercial Capital

(60) & **(61)** Karl Marx: The Capital, Book III, Chapter XXII, Division of profit, interest rate, "Natural" rate of interest Our highlights

(62) Karl Marx: The Capital, Book III, cap. XX, Historic Consideration on Commercial Capital

(63) y **(64)** Karl Marx, El Capital, Book III Chapter XVII Role of Credit in Capitalist Production

(65) Nahuel Moreno. Escuela de Cuadros de Economía

(66) Karl Marx, Capital, Tome I, Preface to the First German Edition

(67) & **(68)** Nahuel Moreno. Escuela de Cuadros de Economía

www.ingramcontent.com/pod-product-compliance
Lightning Source LLC
Chambersburg PA
CBHW051639170526
45167CB00001B/250